BARBARA PATTERSON is an instructor of business administration at Edmonds Community College, Lynwood, Washington. She teaches a course in professional development at the college and has also served as a consultant to businesses on professional development for office workers.
NANCY MEADOWS, a trained nurse and former director of John Robert Powers School, Seattle, Washington, is the owner and director of Face Clinique.
CAROL DREGER is an instructor of business administration at Edmonds Community College, specializing in business communications.

THE SUCCESSFUL WOMAN

*Sharpening your skills for personal
and professional development*

Barbara Patterson
Nancy Meadows
Carol Dreger

A SPECTRUM BOOK

PRENTICE-HALL, INC. Englewood Cliffs, New Jersey 07632

Library of Congress Cataloging in Publication Data

Patterson, Barbara.
    The successful woman.

    "A Spectrum Book."
    1. Vocational guidance for women.
I. Meadows, Nancy.   II. Dreger, Carol Holcomb.
III. Title.
HD6057.9.P37   1982   650.1'4'024042   82-7704
ISBN 0-13-875492-6   AACR2
ISBN 0-13-875484-5 (pbk.)

This book is available at a special discount when ordered in large quantities. Contact Prentice-Hall, Inc., General Publishing Division, Special Sales, Englewood Cliffs, N.J. 07632. Printed in the United States of America.

A SPECTRUM BOOK

10 9 8 7 6 5 4 3 2 1

ISBN 0-13-875484-5 {PBK.}
ISBN 0-13-785492-6

Editorial/production supervision by Cyndy Lyle Rymer
Manufacturing buyer Cathie Lenard
Table 7-3 on pp 104-105 adapted from an unpublished paper by Kathleen Beem, development education instructor.
Drawings in Chapter 5 by James Reddin and Kent J. Ord and Associates.

Prentice-Hall International, Inc., *London*
Prentice-Hall of Australia Pty. Limited, *Sydney*
Prentice-Hall Canada, Inc., *Toronto*
Prentice-Hall of India Private Limited, *New Delhi*
Prentice-Hall of Japan, Inc., *Tokyo*
Prentice-Hall of Southeast Asia Pte. Ltd., *Singapore*
Whitehall Books Limited, *Wellington, New Zealand*

CONTENTS

PREFACE

Most of the formal training people take concentrates on technical subject matter not directly related to personal lives and habits. Personal development skills are often acquired in a haphazard fashion. This book will help you to study yourself and develop personal skills in a formal, systematic way. In each chapter you will find specific suggestions, systems, and techniques to help you in your own development program. Although the personal skills we are concerned with here are directed toward career success (thereby contributing to your professional development), these same skills and other information given also will be useful to you in other aspects of your life.

The purpose of the book is to introduce you to many different aspects of yourself as a successful career woman. The choice of topics are those most necessary for women who have little experience in today's business world. Each topic by itself could provide enough material for a separate book, but we hope that by taking a holistic or overview approach to your personal and professional development, you will be able to identify those areas that are most valuable to you and see how many different avenues there are for growth.

The original idea for this book came from the need for a text to use in a personal development course taught by business instructor Barbara Patterson. Students enrolling in this course are typically a diverse group of women students with varying academic backgrounds and career aspirations. They have in common the need or desire to seek employment. Much of the material in the book comes from seven years of observation of these women recording their reactions to the exercises, following up on their experiences, and observing their success.

In addition, two other people cooperated in the effort to prepare material for the book. Nancy Meadows, owner and director of the Face Clinique in Seattle, Washington, provided the expertise on appearance and wardrobe (Chapter Five). Carol Dreger, a business communications instructor who has research employment correspondence extensively, provided the material on job-search correspondence (Chapter Eight). We share the belief that personal growth does not happen by chance; rather, it involves skills and techniques that can be learned and implemented, thus allowing individuals to plan and influence their own growth and development.

The book:

- provides an overview of personal and professional development that allows the individual to assess her own needs and interests
- serves as a reference and review for working women in a variety of job categories
- takes a practical approach and is easy to read and use
- assumes that women have neither a great deal of time nor a great deal of money to spend exclusively on themselves
- emphasizes career growth encompassing nonmanagement and technical careers as well as management and professional careers
- recognizes women as individuals and shows them how to adapt general information and guidelines to fit their unique needs

This book has been written out of respect and concern for the many women who are either returning to work now or who are trying to develop their career skills while fulfilling many other roles at the same time. It is a way of expressing some of the joy and satisfaction we have experienced as we have watched our students and clients use and benefit from these materials as they seek growth and awareness.

ACKNOWLEDGMENTS

Many people have been involved in the creation of this book and should receive special mention: Dave Garrison, a former college textbook representative for Prentice-Hall, helped get the project started and continued to give moral support throughout; the editors and proofreaders at Spectrum Books who took great care with the material; Kathy Beem, a reading specialist, made many thoughtful suggestions on organization, word selection, and style; Kent Ord and Jim Reddin provided the illustrations; Roy Ghazimorad, Marva Brown, and Ruth McCormick from the Edmonds Community College Counseling Center provided many useful materials for research; Bonnie Lewman, Laura Enstone, and Debbie Lytle typed manuscripts; Sharon Cavender and Velma Welling coordinated and scheduled much of the typing and duplicating. Finally, special thanks to our families who provided love, tolerance, and support.

chapter one
WHO ARE YOU?

TODAY'S WOMEN

Margaret sits in the college advisor's office, her hands shaking, her face hidden behind the quarterly schedule of classes. After twenty-five years of marriage to an engineer and caring for a home and five children—two of whom are still at home—she is beginning to feel the need to achieve in activities not related to family and homemaking. As her husband earned his master's degree and her children started on various academic courses, Margaret began to feel her lack of formal education more and more. Now forty-three years old, she has never graduated from high school and feels that the family to which she gave so much time and energy is now growing away from her. She wants to complete the high school equivalency exam and learn some job skills.

Betty Jane is the next in line to see the college counselor. She has just graduated from high school and become engaged to her steady boyfriend of the last two years. Although her head is full of future marriage plans, her parents have urged her to take a few secretarial courses "just in case she ever has to work."

Doris was referred to the college advisor by her attorney. After twenty years of marriage, she is getting a divorce and has to think seriously about supporting herself. She had taught elementary school with two years of college training and a provisional certificate many years ago, but she knows that present-day educational requirements and a current shortage in teaching positions may make it difficult to

1

return to this occupation. Besides, after raising two children and giving years of volunteer time to school activities, she now wants to work primarily with adults in a regular business environment. Her government educational grant will last for a limited time only, so she needs to make some career decisions soon.

Finally, Arlene has come to see the college advisor because her welfare counselor has sent her. Twenty-seven years old with three young children and no job skills, she has been twice married and divorced and now wants desperately to make it on her own. She is concerned about leaving her young children with a babysitter while she attends school and looks for a job.

These women come from different backgrounds and different educational experiences. Their ages, family responsibilities, and even their values and expectations from life vary. But they have this in common: they want or need to go to work and they need to develop the skills required in the present business world. These four women are typical examples of the cross-section of women entering the work force today. Some of this group of women are what many educators and social scientists have termed the "re-entry woman" or the "displaced homemaker." Actually, the re-entry woman is a "second career" person. She checked out of the labor market after graduation, marriage, or pregnancy and now wants to re-enter the work force. Very often she retains the career of homemaking and motherhood in addition to the new one of part-time or full-time employee. The displaced homemaker is a woman who planned a lifetime career as a homemaker, but now through divorce or death of her spouse finds herself forced to return to the job market through economic necessity. In addition, many young women directly out of high school and college are planning lifetime careers as well.

During the past decade thousands of women entered the U.S. work force. For many of these women, taking a job was not a short-term proposition; there was a definite commitment to a lifetime career. Is this where you are headed too?

CONSIDERATIONS FOR SEEKING A CAREER

Identifying Your Reasons

There are many reasons for a woman to enter the work force or change occupations if she is already working. You may not be aware of all of your own reasons. Before you start planning for your new career, ask yourself why you want to do this. The checklist provided in Table 1-1 may help you identify some of your reasons. There may be others you can add to the list.

Table 1-1 Reasons for Seeking a Career: A Checklist

___ You feel bored and restless staying at home.
___ You would like some economic independence.
___ You would like to be paid for your services rather than doing everything on a volunteer basis.
___ You think a career would give you self-fulfillment.
___ You need to be the main financial support of yourself and a family.
___ You are interested in several types of jobs, and you would like to find out if you can do them.
___ You would like to meet some new people.
___ You cannot meet your family's needs on your present family income.
___ You want to have your own identity—not just to be Bob's wife, or Bobbie's mother, or Bob Smith's daughter.
___ You see many things that need to be done to help our society, and you want to make a contribution.
___ Many of your friends are returning to work part-time or full-time, and you feel left out.
___ You want to contribute financially to your family.
___ You would like to have a few luxuries, such as designer clothes or expensive jewelry.
___ You feel the need to do something different with your life.
___ You would like to help build economic security for your retirement years.

How do you know that getting a job, or changing to a new one, will allow you to achieve any of the things you want? You don't. But if you don't find out, you may always wonder whether you really could have succeeded. More than ever before, new opportunities, new positions not previously available, and new resources are beckoning to the working woman. Exploring these opportunities and resources can be an exciting challenge.

Who Are Your Role Models?

When you decide to join or are forced to enter the paid work force, you may be bewildered by decisions and problem-solving situations that your past experiences and training have not prepared you to

3

handle. Many of the behaviors and beliefs you adopted while preparing for marriage and motherhood may now come into conflict with decisions about job training and career plans. How many women do you know who decided not to take courses in mathematics, physics, or other highly technical subjects in school because they thought they wouldn't need them in their later lives? How many women do you know who usually skip the business sections of the newspaper and turn, instead, to the sections dealing with recipes and household hints? Most women have avoided technical or business-related subjects because they did not observe other women doing them or in some cases were actually discouraged from doing them.

Most of us have patterned our beliefs and behaviors on parents and other influential adults around us. Consequently, many women have not been provided with a model of a working woman because their own mothers did not work outside the home. Women who did work were grouped primarily into traditional women's occupations such as elementary school teaching, nursing, or secretarial work. Now that these roles are being challenged by women seeking to enter all areas of the work force, you may face conflicts within yourself as you attempt to sort out what you should do to fulfill your responsibilities both to yourself and to your family. Even though the number of women in the work force is increasing, many women still do not have a career orientation toward their work and think of it only as a means to accomplish short-term goals such as "saving for new living-room furniture" or "helping out with the orthodontist's bills."

Who are the people who have had the greatest influence over your life so far? Which of these influential people have careers you admire? If you can identify no one you admire who has a career, you may need to deliberately look for people who fit this category and get to know them.

Playing a Role

We all play many roles in our lives—daughter, worker, student, sister, neighbor, best friend, mother, and so on. Sometimes our behavior in these roles is dictated by the expectations of other people. Often we forget that our behavior in certain roles is not always the behavior we would choose if we were absolutely free from the expectations of friends or family.

How, then, does a woman attempting to enter the work world learn to direct her life through the confusions and conflicts to the role

4

of career woman? One way to begin is to find out what your values really are.

DEVELOPING LIFE VALUES
AND CAREER VALUES

Just what are values anyway? How do we determine what our own values are? How do our role models and the roles we play influence our values?

While there may be many definitions of the term "values," for our purposes, we can define "values" to mean the beliefs and behaviors we have chosen as being right for us and which we act on repeatedly and consistently. For example, if you believe physical activity is a necessity for good health and a good life, you will probably devote quite a bit of time and energy to participation in athletic activities, practice and exercise, and emphasize sporting events instead of reading and TV watching. If, on the other hand, participation in sports is not terribly important to you but hobbies such as arts and crafts or reading are important, you may spend little time at athletic events and more time at the public library or browsing through bookstores or hobby shops in pursuit of these creative activities. One value is not better than the other; they are simply different.

As mentioned earlier, most of us learn our behavior and beliefs from parents, relatives, teachers, and other adults around us. When we are asked our opinions concerning politics, religion, work, money, family, personal tastes, and so on, we often give answers reflecting the attitudes and beliefs of the role models we have had. What happens, then, to the woman who wants to have a career outside the home but whose female role models have been housewives, mothers and volunteer workers? Confusion, conflict, and guilt are very often the result. It is important to understand, however, that you can add new values and forms of self-expression without giving up the old.

Values and Self-awareness

Before we go much further in our discussion of values and their relationship to going to work, it is important that you begin to distinguish your own values from beliefs and attitudes imposed upon you by members of your family or the society we live in. It is

5

especially important that you consider values such as economic independence, achievement needs, and desired standard of living that relate most closely to work and careers.

Discovering what really matters to you can be exciting, surprising and even challenging. So many women have devoted the major portion of their energy to the attainment of other people's goals—particularly those of spouse, parents and children—that they may lose sight of their own needs and desires.

To identify your deepest values, apply the following "tests" to those values you will later single out as yours.

1. *Have you chosen these values from several alternatives?* In other words, do you really have a choice about these particular values? Let's say that you place a high priority on a spiritual life or certain religious beliefs. Did you choose this from a variety of religious beliefs?

2. *Did you consider the consequences of choosing these values and still choose them freely?* If you want an exciting life with many adventures and liberal spending of money, and your mate wants quiet, order and a large savings account, will the consequences still let you choose these values?

3. *Do you really care about these values? Do you defend them when talking to others?* For example, if you love to read and study, would you defend this to a good friend who makes fun of "bookworms" or "pedants"?

4. *Have you acted on these values repeatedly and consistently?* If you say you want to be a good musician but find very little time to practice, do you really value this?

In a moment you will be trying a brief values clarification exercise. Before you do, however, think about the "tests" given above and some other important guidelines: (1) Do not try to assess whether your values are right or wrong; (2) Do not, at this time, compare them to what others may list as values; and (3) Do not try to list values people you most care about would want you to list (unless you unqualifiedly believe them also).

Now try the values clarification exercise in Table 1-2. This exercise contains a list of life values. Pretend you have $100 to spend in "purchasing" (choosing) your most important values. No value on this chart may be purchased for less than $10 and you must spend at least $25 on your number one value. Think carefully about your past actions as well as what appeals to you right now. Take your time and spend and re-spend your money until you feel comfortable with the results.

Table 1-2 Ranking Some Life Values

____ A comfortable life (prosperity, nice home, etc.)
____ An exciting life (stimulating activities, varied opportunities)
____ Family security (being with and taking care of loved ones)
____ Personal freedom (being able to do what you want, when you want)
____ Economic independence (the need to depend only on yourself for money)
____ Financial recognition (wealth, great financial success)
____ Contentedness (freedom from inner conflict)
____ Self-respect (self-esteem)
____ Status (prestigious title, public recognition)
____ Pleasure (enjoyment, amusements, leisure)
____ Mature love (sexual and personal intimacy)
____ An intellectual life (pursuit of scholarly research)
____ A sense of accomplishment (making a lasting contribution)
____ A powerful life (controlling events, making things happen)
____ A spiritual life (subscribing to a cause, believing in a force greater than yourself)
____ A creative life (pursuing an artistic talent such as music, writing, art, etc.)

---

1. What value did you pay the highest price for?
2. Were there any values you would want to pay the same amount for? What are they?
3. What values did you *not* purchase?

Look at those items on the chart you have spent the most for. If you were to apply the tests and guidelines mentioned previously, would these still emerge as values for you? If you listed "economic independence" as a major value, have you taken advantage of the opportunities to achieve it or is it a value you think you would like to have in the future? It is very important for you to differentiate between *what is* and *what you think you would like to have.*

Another consideration. Will the values you have given the highest ranking help you to a successful career or will they present conflicts that you must carefully work out? Be honest. If family security is of the utmost importance to you, acknowledge it. If pleasure is extremely important, recognize this. Then you will be better prepared to deal with the conflicts that may arise when your need for pleasure or family security gets in the way of career values such as achievement and economic independence.

Career Values

Although many life values may relate directly to a career, others do not. If you are contemplating a new career, you do need to take a closer look at career values. Let us assume for the moment that having a fulfilling career is important to you. Within the larger concept of a career, there are values relating to work that may give you guidance in your choice of jobs. Acting on those values will help you to be contented and successful. For example, if "creating" and "expressing yourself" are important to you, you may want to choose a work environment that will allow that. If having close interpersonal relationships is something you value, that may be important in your career choice as well. To find out what career values are important to you, try the ranking exercise in Table 1-3. Combined with your life values, an awareness of your work values will help you plan your career.

Working out Value Conflicts

If, after completing the values exercises, you find that some of your values seem to conflict with others, don't worry. It is possible to work out conflicts. You may choose one value above another or you may decide you want the best of both worlds and try to work out opportunities for both. As you read further in the book, you will find some suggestions for goal setting and time management that will help your value conflicts become more manageable. Conflicts with the values of other people who are important to you will be discussed elsewhere as well. For right now, however, concentrate on yourself—what you believe, think, feel, want, and can do.

Also try to remember that *values* are not the same as *opinions* and it is important that you distinguish between them. A value is a strongly held belief of your choice on which you base your behavior;

Table 1-3 Ranking Career Values

Rank each work value according to its importance to you. Put a 1 on the line in front of the work value which you think is most important. Put a 2 in front of the one that is second in importance. Continue ranking until you have ranked all the values you consider important.

_____ Adventure—Doing exciting things; being in new or uncertain situations; engaging in competition.

_____ Artistic Expression—Producing something pleasing to the physical senses.

_____ Creativity—Beginning a new idea or product.

_____ Monetary Rewards—Receiving high pay for what you do.

_____ Independence—Being able to plan your own work activities; being free to change procedures.

_____ Intellectual Stimulation—Solving complex questions; applying ideas and knowledge to problems.

_____ Leadership—Influencing others in their work; making decisions.

_____ Orderliness—Following set procedures; doing well-ordered routines.

_____ Physical Performance—Being able to do difficult physical tasks that require timing and coordination.

_____ Productivity—Making a product or doing work which results in something usable.

_____ Recognition—Being known to many people; receiving respect from others; having a title or status.

_____ Social Service—Working for the benefit of others and society.

_____ Variety—Being involved in many different activities or problems.

_____ Responsibility—Having other people depend on you.

_____ Nice Environment—Being able to work in an attractive, comfortable setting.

_____ Interpersonal Relationships—Being able to work with people you like.

_____ Growth Potential—Being able to advance to other positions.

_____ Security—Having a stable job with no worry about layoffs.

_____ Privacy and Anonymity—Being able to work on one's own—not always with or surrounded by a group of people.

an opinion is a personal attitude about a specific subject. For example, you may have the opinion that your daughter should not be dating the boy she is presently dating. You value, however, a good relationship with your daughter. Ideally, you will not let your specific opinion keep you from acting on the more important value. Value conflicts frequently crop up when loyalty to family or friends comes up against loyalty to your employer or to authority figures. Sorting through your feelings carefully and deciding what is really most important will help you resolve your conflicts with yourself and others.

Values clarification is important. It is a skill that you can practice over and over until it becomes a way of thinking. This can help you to make decisions which are important for you, your family and your career.

Changing Values

Even though we have stated that values are beliefs we act upon consistently, don't be surprised if you find yourself making values changes. It is healthy for people to grow and expand their awareness and capabilities. Frequently, this means giving up or giving lower priority to values that were very meaningful five or ten years ago and selecting new ones. Of course, you probably won't be changing your mind every day, but some kinds of changes are simply part of being a vital, fully developed person. Also, you may find a need to develop new values if your circumstances will not allow you to live comfortably with the old. For example, many women have found that divorce or widowhood may require a change in emphasis on certain life values.

IDENTIFYING YOUR TALENTS, INTERESTS, AND PERSONAL STRENGTHS

Many women are not aware of their major strengths and interests. Talents and interests, like values, are important self-awareness tools for career preparation. You may have been taught to be modest and humble, or have become so self-critical that you really don't believe you can do anything very well. If that is so, put those feelings aside for the moment and imagine that you have been given the opportunity to boast about how wonderful you are. What would you boast about? (It's not fair to boast about your children, pets, boyfriend or spouse—you must boast about *you*.) Do you have at least three or four "boasting" items?

If boasting about yourself does not feel comfortable, try this exercise instead: Examine your past for five incidents you recall with tremendous pleasure and pride. These may be momentous experiences such as the birth of a child or more ordinary things such as learning to ride a bicycle at an early age, or cooking a gourmet dish, or having a poem published in the literary magazine. Once you have chosen the five incidents, examine them for the personal qualities or talents you displayed in each. You may begin to see a pattern of repeated personal strengths.

Now that you have completed the personal-qualities exercise, can you really say you have nothing to boast about?

How Well do You Know Yourself?

Do you ever feel that you know friends or members of your family better than they know themselves? It is true that sometimes other people are more aware of our strengths and weaknesses than we are. Listen to people when they give you positive feedback and compliments. Don't always discount it as flattery. They may see some things about you that you do not see.

As a teacher, I know that many students discount my telling them, "You're doing well. You have definite potential. You can learn this." It's self-defeating to discount praise; learn to believe the good things you hear about yourself.

One way to learn to believe the good things you hear about yourself would be to imagine for a moment that you can step outside yourself and observe your own actions. Pretend you are one of your friends whom a potential employer has called for a job reference. Talk out loud, as if you were really giving the reference, and tell this potential employer about your "friend's" skills (both personal and technical), working habits (handling details, meeting deadlines, working without close supervision, and so on), relationships with others, and functions she can perform well.

How did that sound to you? Were you completely candid? Did you play down any strengths? Now write down the items that you determined were your "friend's" strengths and keep the list for future reference. At a later date, play the same game and see if your imaginary friend observes any new strengths.

WHERE DO YOU GO FROM HERE?

If, at this point, you are asking yourself whether determining values, talents and interests is worthwhile or you still feel confused about what really are your values and talents, let me give you some assurance. It takes time to develop honest self-awareness, but we all must start somewhere if we really want to develop ourselves personally and professionally.

Women have so frequently been told that they "don't know what they really want" or "they should want what is best for their families," that it is not surprising that you may feel uncertain. But as you start to examine your needs, wants, and aspirations and as you start to measure them against what you actually do and say, you will begin to put your life together in such a way that you can achieve almost anything you really want.

Why is the self-discovery process so important? Why can't you simply be given the "secrets of success" or the "ten commandments" for career planning? Primarily, because you are unique and many rules and guidelines that work for some people may not work in the same way for you, or must be especially adapted to your individuality.

Another, more practical reason why you need to undertake this self-discovery process now is that you may be starting your career planning later than many other people in the job market if you are a re-entry woman or displaced homemaker. You may not have time to serve a long apprenticeship or a number of apprenticeships to determine your career goals. You must know as quickly as possible where you are headed and how you want to get there.

Finally, if you are entering the job market at a time in your life when you are undergoing a traumatic personal situation such as divorce or widowhood, or your children leaving home, you need the tools to help you work through the problems and the conflicts you are facing.

As you deal with the challenges, you will find that it's really a very exciting time to be a woman. There are opportunities for self-fulfillment and achievement in the work world for women. Let's start now to cover some important topics to help a very important person—you.

chapter two
PLANNING
YOUR FUTURE

"Men Plan Their Careers; Women Do Not"

Pick up any recent book or magazine article concerned with working women and you will frequently read that men plan their careers and women do not. At first glance this appears to be true, but what may actually have happened is that many women have chosen to be mothers and homemakers and these choices by themselves can be full-time careers. But, you say, men choose to be husbands and fathers and they still plan their careers. That is also true, but our society has not required husbands and fathers to spend as much time or energy on these aspects of their lives as it has asked women to spend being homemakers and mothers. Traditional values have placed a great emphasis on the "breadwinning" aspects of men's lives and the "care and nurturing of home and family" aspects of women's lives. Even though traditional roles are changing, you must realistically consider home and family responsibilities when choosing career goals. The values related to families and the roles of mother and wife continue to have a definite effect on how much time and how much flexibility a woman can give to career plans. Before you get discouraged, however, keep in mind that many women have successfully combined a number of roles with the role of career woman, and many women now consciously choose to emphasize success in a career as a top priority value. You may also want a combination of values—career, family, and personal values. Remember the life values that you established in Chapter One as you plan your future and set your career goals.

GOALS AS POWERFUL TOOLS

Goals can prove to be a powerful force in your life. Commitment to an idea or goal can provide the courage to take calculated risks that may lead to accomplishments and self-fulfillment. A goal may stimulate your excitement and energy and allow you to take productive action. Further, goals are a vitally important tool for you if you seriously want to succeed in a career.

It is not enough just to have goals, however; you must also have some kind of realistic plan developed for achieving them. This takes time, thought, organization, commitment, and personal accountability. Sometimes it means giving up activities you do now. Sometimes it means readjusting your thinking. Sometimes it means coming into conflict with another person's goals and values. How often have you made New Year's resolutions only to have them lapse into nothing by February? When that happens, how much time, energy, and commitment have you actually put into those resolutions?

For some people the thought of setting goals and planning implies restraints or rigidity—being "locked in." If you are a "free spirit" who dislikes following a prearranged schedule, think of goals as benchmarks, not absolutes. Planning does not have to be compulsive or inflexible. Planning and goal setting can actually be a freeing experience. You gain control over how you shape your life according to your needs and values; you are not just an agent for the plans of others. For some people, developing more spontaneity is a worthy goal.

Goals You Can Live With

Many people fail to attain their goals because they make them so general or vague they can't be sure when they have achieved those goals. For example, you may say, "I just want a happy life." What does "happy" mean? How do you know if you have achieved "happiness?" Sometimes people make their goals so difficult to attain they cannot help but fail in their attempts. A classic example of the "impossible" goal is the kind set by many dieters. They invariably wish to lose a large amount of weight in a short time period. Of course that goal is seldom achieved—at least not without drastic consequences!

Make your goals measurable. It's not enough to say you want a "fulfilling career." Define "fulfilling career." How will you know when you have achieved it? When you have a title after your name? When you have a large income? When you see specific results from your work?

As a first step, take a blank piece of paper. List a few goals you would like to accomplish in your lifetime—the things you would like to be able to look back on when you are seventy-five. Make the goals specific, such as earning a college degree, purchasing a vacation home, building a stock market portfolio on an initial $5,000 investment, mastery of ice skating, conversational ability in French, and so on. Now list your professional goals, specific things like a salary of a certain amount, election to a specific office in a professional society, or a particular job title—not generalities such as "a promotion" or "success and prestige." Now list your personal or family goals, such as being able to afford a weekly cleaning person, a month's vacation in Europe, or providing piano lessons for the children. Again, don't list ideas such as being a good mother, a good lover or a good friend, or any other idea difficult to define. Do these goals fit with the values you have defined in Chapter One?

Skills and Talents

To further make your goals realistic and attainable, think about what skills and talents you possess. Do your goals make use of these skills and talents or will you have to develop new ones in order to achieve the goals? Sometimes the goal itself involves the learning of new skills; that may be very good. Just remember, though, that new skills are built, in part, from previously learned skills, and if you attempt something that is too far removed from the skills you have, you may be in for a frustrating time. Let me explain further. If one of your lifetime career goals is to be an engineer, you must think about what mathematics skills you possess. If you have little math background, you may have to set and complete a series of intermediate goals before achieving your main goal.

Many women fail to recognize the skills they have because they are usually not paid to perform them. A skill is merely the ability to do something well, efficiently, and easily. Organizing a babysitting pool or riding a bicycle involves the use of skills. Consider what it takes to operate a calculator for a minute. It involves manual dexterity, hand-eye coordination, concentration, and the ability to recognize arithmetic errors such as misplaced decimal points, etc. The skills you have now may well transfer to areas in which you have no experience. In Chapter Seven you will have a chance to identify your skills more completely and discover many career areas where they may be used. But for now, make a list of those skills you can identify now (for example, writing well, organizing detail, or playing a musical instrument).

GUIDELINES FOR GOAL SETTING

In order to establish goals that will be meaningful and useful to you, it will be helpful if you follow some guidelines while attempting to set your goals:

1. Is the goal *measurable*? Will you have a specific way of knowing whether or not you have actually achieved or not achieved your goal? If, for example, you have established a goal to plan and purchase an attractive, comfortable career wardrobe, will you know when that goal is completed? How many suits? How many shirts and sweaters? And so on. With fuzzy or unclear goals, much energy is wasted on confusion and anxiety. By clarifying your goals you can liberate some of that energy for more productive achievement. With better focus, you can work smarter instead of harder.

2. Is the goal *achievable*? Given your values, skills, time, energy, and financial circumstances, is this goal realistic for you? Using the example of the career wardrobe mentioned above, is your goal to own designer clothes when your budget can only tolerate well-made ready-to-wear suits?

3. Is the goal *motivating* to you? Do you believe you can reach your goals? If you do not really believe that you can accomplish what you have said you will accomplish, you will have a very difficult time achieving the goal. For most people, this kind of non-achievement leads to an attitude of defeat, indifference, or extreme self-criticism. You must believe that you really can accomplish the goal. Applying our wardrobe example here, do you feel that finally achieving the career wardrobe you want will give you pleasure?

4. Is the goal *meaningful*? Is it something you really want? Does it fit with your values? The goal must be important enough to you that you are willing to give up something else you like, or even suffer some discomfort, in order to accomplish it. Again using the wardrobe example, are you willing to give up something else you like that costs money to save for an investment wardrobe?

Now that you have done a "reality check" on your possible goals, consider one more idea: Don't be so realistic that you set your sights too low! Sometimes you have to stretch your imagination and abilities a little beyond what you realistically think you can accomplish. You may surprise yourself!

Fantasy May Help

Before you start writing down your "realistic goals," take a little time out to go on a quick fantasy trip. Imagine you can do or be anything you want no matter how outrageous. What would that be?

When you have finished with your fantasy, take your mind backward in time and think about some goals you may have had earlier in your life that you have abandoned. Could they be dusted off and revitalized? Do you still have some need to fulfill the desires of your youth?

Both fantasy and history may be important keys to determining what your goals really should be.

Investigate, Enhance, and Act

Very often a goal requires a person to change a particular behavior or successfully complete a specific act—specific action goals. It is also possible, however, to set goals that merely require *investigation* of a specific idea or to set goals that *enhance* a skill or behavior you may already be doing. Investigative and enhancement goals can be just as important as action goals. They may, in fact, lead to action goals. For example, if you set a goal which requires you to find out what specific skills are required to be an executive secretary, that may lead to the action goal of getting that type of job. Or, if you determine that enhancing your writing skills is something you should do, you are setting a goal that will help you improve a skill you already have and lead you to an action goal of using that skill in a specific way.

Now that you have some guidelines for setting goals, you should begin to define your goals. Think back for a minute to the quick list of lifetime goals you jotted down as you read the first part of this chapter. Also, think about your fantasy goals and your abandoned goals. Keeping these items in mind, now fill out the exercise provided in Figure 2-1 to determine your goals.

First, fill in the center section, taking the personal values and work values you determined in Chapter One. These values, combined with your other characteristics, should be central to your goals.

Second, fill in the outer boxes with the talents and skills, personal strengths, areas to improve and activities and interests you determined from other exercises.

Third, consider some possible obstacles which may hinder you in achieving your goals.

Fourth, once you have determined your goals, figure out what activities will help you, the goal achievement date, and the immediate obstacles to be faced.

Finally, considering all of the above elements, define some workable, challenging personal and professional goals that you wish to accomplish in your lifetime. (This same chart can also be used for short- or long-term goals.)

ACHIEVING YOUR GOALS

Successfully achieving goals means accepting the fact that you are responsible for just about everything that happens to you. If you are not meeting the goals you have set for yourself, ask yourself the following questions:

1. *Am I doing all of the things that are required of me to meet the goal?* First of all, reconsider some of your successful past experiences you listed in the exercises in Chapter One. What were the activities that allowed you to achieve those successes? Are you skipping some of the steps or changing the process you used in previous achievements? Or are you simply not acknowledging some of the necessary steps? Do you need more information? For example, if one of your past achievements was cooking a gourmet dinner and now you are trying

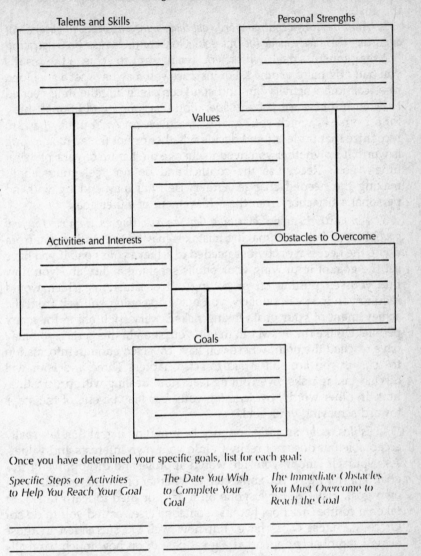

Figure 2-1 Goals Chart

Talents and Skills

Personal Strengths

Values

Activities and Interests

Obstacles to Overcome

Goals

Once you have determined your specific goals, list for each goal:

Specific Steps or Activities to Help You Reach Your Goal

The Date You Wish to Complete Your Goal

The Immediate Obstacles You Must Overcome to Reach the Goal

to capitalize on that success by setting up a small catering business, are you counting on your cooking abilities to see you through when, in fact, you may need to concentrate more on your bookkeeping and organization skills? Perhaps you need to pursue more training, or, at the very least, investigate further the kinds of action required to meet the goal.

2. *Am I meeting a contradictory goal that's more important to me and not admitting that I have made the trade-off?* Goal conflicts may be frustrating but they must be dealt with if you really want to achieve the results you had originally planned. For instance you may have set a goal for a physical fitness activity but find you keep cancelling the time needed to achieve it because you are spending that time in additional study for a course in which your goal is to achieve an A. You may have to recognize that trade-off and decide whether or not the extra studying is worth it or whether you need to change the nature of your physical fitness goal. Recognize the conflict and do not feel guilty about making the needed change. Otherwise, you may end up with no personal satisfaction from the achievement of either goal.

3. *Am I actively doing something that is preventing me from meeting my goal?* Fear of failure or making mistakes may be preventing you from doing the necessary activities needed to achieve your goal. If you have set the goal of improving your public speaking ability and you now find yourself putting off or getting out of situations which would require you to speak publicly, you may be keeping yourself from the achievement of your goal. Taking risks is very frightening for many people. Unlike the answer to the first question in this series, you may have reached the point where you have collected enough information to act, yet you are still afraid to act! Chapters Three and Four will discuss taking risks, overcoming fears, and dealing with procrastination. In other words, overcoming your fear may be one of the steps toward achieving your goal.

4. *Is this really my goal?* You may be pursuing a goal that is socially acceptable but does not really fit into your own interests and values. Ask yourself who in your life would approve and disapprove of this goal. This may give you some clue to whether or not this is really your own goal. Have you ever gone on a diet, or tried to learn to ski, or taken a course in school because someone else wanted you to do so? Of course most of us have, but how well we succeeded in those activities probably depended a great deal upon how much we really wanted to do that activity. Unless the goal is a high priority in your life, you will probably not devote enough attention or effort to really succeed at it.

5. *Who can help me achieve this goal?* Often the people we want to be the most supportive of our goals are not. That doesn't mean you

should abandon your goal. There may be others who can help you. Sometimes the people closest to you have selfish motives for not wanting you to achieve certain goals. Find someone who can encourage and help you rather than listening to people who would hinder you.

6. *Do I have a system to reinforce or reward myself along the way to completing my goal?* A planned reward system can be a terrific motivator for completing goals. Just be sure that your reward is not in conflict with your goal. Many a dieter has been ruined by a conflicting reward system! But do find a pleasurable way to pat yourself on the back.

Finally, in your pursuit of success, you may be concentrating too much on the results. A small victory is better than no victory at all. Even if the results you achieve are not quite what you had in mind when you started, they may still be worthwhile results. You may have underestimated the amount of time that it will take to fully complete your goal or the goal may require more skill than you currently have. Reassess what has happened. There may still be hope for your goal.

Changing Goals

Although I have introduced the concept of goal setting early in the book, you may want to work through the exercises again after you read the entire book. Goal setting is a process which can be practiced at all levels of career development. Additional knowledge and experience may bring many modifications and changes.

MOVING FROM GOALS TO DIRECTIONS

Now that you have worked through the process of setting and attaining specific goals, you need to develop an awareness of what can happen when those goals are achieved. Quite frankly, one of the most exhilarating aspects of goal setting is working towards the goal! Just because you reach a goal does not mean you will live "happily ever after." The sense of achievement from reaching a goal can tarnish very easily if it is not renewed in some way.

Life is an ever-changing, dynamic, and often complicated process. Goals, on the other hand, are usually specific, fixed and unchanging. Goals should not be ends in themselves. Rather, they should lead you *somewhere*. Setting goals can help move you in the *direction* you want your life to take. It is the direction, and process of moving in that direction, that enables you to live a purposeful, fulfilling life. We have only to look at women who have set goals—"getting married" or "having three children" —not directions—to see that goals by themselves are not fulfilling unless there is continual growth and movement. Children grow up and leave; a spouse may die. The goal that was once so important is now gone. In fact, getting a job may be a goal, but once you have gotten that job, you must move on to something else. You must then set different goals in order to keep the job. So use your goals as stepping-stones to the direction you want to take in your life. Be flexible enough to change them if the situation warrants. Allow yourself to fail at some of them. Reward yourself for achieving some of them. But do use goal-setting skills to help you chart your course through life's complications. And, above all, give great care and thought to your career goals. The work you choose to do will determine, to a great degree, how you live. Your career should be a matter of choice, not chance.

chapter three
FINDING THE TIME
TO DO
WHAT YOU WANT

The lament of most people today is "If I just had more time I could. . ." or "If I could just get this place organized, everything would be okay." For the woman who wants to change her life and set off in new directions, the problems of "finding time," "getting started," and "getting organized" become very critical. It's not enough just to define values, goals and plans; you must also find the time to carry them out. While time may seem to be your enemy—particularly if your need to go to work is an urgent one—time can also work for you if you allow it to. Let us concentrate now on finding the time to do those things you said you wanted to do in Chapters One and Two.

GETTING STARTED

It may be helpful, first of all, to think about what *time* is and what it is not. Dictionary definitions will probably not be very helpful. Perhaps more to the point would be Benjamin Franklin's saying, "Time is the stuff of which life is made." Time cannot be reversed; time cannot be replaced. You simply must make do with what you have.

Given the perspective that the essence of time is life itself, we really must concentrate on the quality and the effectiveness of the time we have. You can delay getting started on the goals you have in mind. You can spend even more time worrying about the time you have spent delaying getting started. You can spend time worrying about mistakes you have made in the past in the way you have used your time, but STOP right there. *If you gain nothing else from this chapter, learn to stop feeling guilty about the way you have used your time in the past.* Learn from your mistakes, but don't agonize over them. You cannot replace the lost time, but you can keep from losing more time worrying about it.

Getting started can be extremely difficult because we can all think of so many supposedly valid excuses. For example, I had a tremendously difficult time getting started on this chapter. I kept making up little delays such as telling myself "I really need to read more background material before I can begin writing" and "I'll wait until after Winter Quarter is finished so I'll have more time" and "I really need to rearrange my daughter's closet" and "Maybe I should write the chapter on personality first." The truth of the matter is that writing is disciplined, hard work requiring concentration, organization, and some inspiration. The manuscript deadline was months away so the tension was not severe. But the guilt feelings were real and I knew very well that delaying writing this chapter would put me in a bind later on, destroy my plan, and possibly delay the publication of the book. I simply had to come to grips with why I was not "getting started." A recognition of the habits of procrastination, a certain element of fear, a wish to avoid more work in an already busy schedule were the real reasons. Once I recognized and acknowledged these elements of delay, I was able to start putting words on paper. Bit by bit, I divided the task into workable parts and charged ahead, not caring, initially, whether or not the results were very good.

Let's break down my experience and see how it applies to you.

1. *Having the knowledge to begin.* First of all, I told myself that I didn't know enough to proceed with my work. I had to get more information. That was really only partially true. I knew enough to start. I continued to learn as I went along.

2. *Waiting for the right time.* Waiting for the end of Winter Quarter was not really a valid excuse. The time is never *right*. We are always busy—even during vacations!

3. *Taking care of trivia first.* Rearranging my young daughter's wardrobe was certainly not an emergency or a matter of any great priority or value to me—or to her for that matter—but it filled in a

piece of time that I could have used working on this chapter and therefore made me more anxious about the delay.

4. *Being frightened of the whole project.* The thought of writing a book frightens me tremendously. The thought of writing a chapter frightens me quite a bit. The thought of writing two pages doesn't scare me quite so much. Breaking a big goal or plan into its smaller, more manageable elements does help. And I did have the time in the midst of a busy teaching schedule to write a little bit at a time.

5. *Indecision.* Trying to decide which topic to research and write about first is often a tremendous delaying action. In the long run, it really wasn't going to make a difference which chapter was written first, so delaying that decision had little validity. Indecision is a tremendous time-waster.

Rewarding Yourself

Perhaps it will help you get started if you think of rewards instead of punishment. Punishing yourself for wasting time is not as effective as rewarding yourself for the times of success. If you start a project and have to quit in the middle of it, congratulate yourself for having started the task, instead of punishing yourself for not finishing it.

If you have problems getting started, you are probably dealing with a long-established habit and must work on modifying your behavior. One important principle of behavior modification is that *any behavior that is followed by something pleasant tends to be reinforced and is more likely to happen again.* Try to find pleasant ways of reinforcing the times you use time wisely, start a task without procrastination, turn down an unimportant but time-consuming request, or stay with a priority item instead of getting side-tracked to something else. The reward can be something small as long as it has pleasant connotations. You don't have to spend money for your "rewards."

YOUR TIME HABITS

Before you can make plans and develop new time habits, it is a good idea to look at the way you are using time right now. Draw two large circles on a piece of paper. Imagine that these circles represent pies which have been cut into twenty-four pieces (or 24 hours). In the first pie, divide the pieces into what you would consider an "ideal" use of your time in a day. In the second pie, divide the pieces the way you think you really do spend time. Pick a day between Monday and Friday as an example—not a weekend day. What does this exercise reveal to you about the way you spend your time? Is this satisfactory to you or do you want to make a few changes?

Now try an even more precise measurement of how you are spending a "normal" day. Keeping a Time Record Sheet such as the one in Figure 3-1 for two or three days should help you see just where your time really goes. You may be saying to yourself at this point that you *know* where your time goes and it is not necessary to keep a record to prove it. I assure you, however, none of us is as self-aware as we may think and this particular exercise will help a great deal when

Figure 3-1 Time Record Sheet

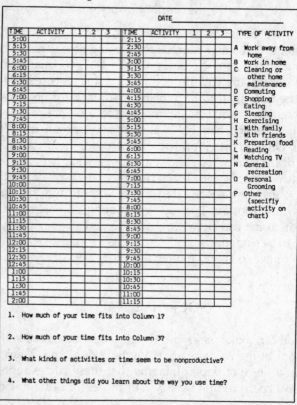

you get to the sections on planning and scheduling (trade-offs and eliminations). Here are the basic instructions:

1. Enter the date on the appropriate line.
2. Put in the space provided the Legend Letter which states what kind of activity was being performed at that time.
3. At the end of the day, look back over the columns and check Column 1, 2, or 3.(On some items you may check more than one column.)
    Column 1—Another person had control of your time during this period or task.
    Column 2—This time you feel good about.
    Column 3—This time you do not feel good about.

A careful look at your daily charts for a few days (or better still, a week) should give you a pretty good idea of how you are spending your time. After you have done that, go back and look at your IDEAL pie again. Where are the differences between what you are doing now and what you would like to be doing?

TOOLS FOR PLANNING AND SCHEDULING

The lifetime goals that you developed in Chapter Two should serve as the first tool for planning and scheduling your time. The second useful tool picks up where the lifetime goals leave off—specific activities that can help you achieve your goals. It is important to remember that you cannot *do* a goal. You can only *do* activities that lead to goals. When you plan well on both long-term and short-term goals and activities you will find them all fitting together like the pieces of a jigsaw puzzle. They should make up a *whole* picture—the picture of your life.

The Daily "To Do" List

If you felt overwhelmed before you started dealing with new goals and activities, you are probably feeling doubly overwhelmed now that you are thinking of adding new activities to your schedule. The third tool of scheduling your time requires that you put your long-term and short-term goals aside for the moment and ask yourself: *What do I have to do today?* Here's where the third tool, the To Do list, enters the picture.

Obviously you have to find time for essential tasks such as eating and sleeping. And we all have to give a sizable proportion of the day to the kinds of routine tasks that make up much of daily living. In fact, for many of us so much time is taken up on the essential and routine tasks of living, we don't get around to doing the special things we want to do.

First of all, let's define what we mean by essential tasks and routine tasks. *Essential* tasks include such items as eating, sleeping, dressing, grooming, commuting, and being on the job. There may be variables, but basically, these are the minimums necessary for normal functioning. *Routine* tasks include such items as reading the newspaper, opening the mail, writing checks for payment of the bills, and so on. They are much like essential tasks in that they occur often and most people feel the need to perform them. How many routine tasks you have will depend a great deal on family obligations, social obligations, civic obligations, etc. They may also include such items as exercise time.

Pick a Priority for Now

Initially, when you select the activities for today that will help you toward achievement of your lifetime goals, make them as short and feasible as possible. Begin with the easiest task in the activity. That will give you a priority for the day. Once you begin to understand how setting priorities helps you achieve your goals and manage your time, you will find that you can set your priorities naturally and routinely with little effort. Let's consider how this can work by going back again to my example of writing this chapter. As I broke down my goal into its various tasks and activities, making an outline emerged as a short, feasible task which should have a high priority. Also, it is much easier for me to make outlines than it is to write paragraphs and sentences, so this was a logical place to begin. Once that priority task was completed (even knowing that it might be modified), I felt that I had achieved part of my goal and I was positively on my way to the completion of the total activity. I then was able to go on to lesser priorities for the day, but I felt good for accomplishing the tasks I *most* wanted to achieve.

If you have kept your time record carefully, you probably observed that much of your time is used for life essentials and routine tasks. If you recorded your activities especially carefully, you may also have noticed that chunks of time were claimed by interruptions and crises. Unexpected interruptions and crises are not only annoying, they can be tremendously time-consuming. They take on an urgency that gives them a top-priority rating, thus knocking out other planned priorities. Perhaps one of the best ways to think about handling interruptions and crises is to compare them with cheating on a diet. If you are really trying to reach a desired weight goal, you try not to let lapses and indiscretions keep you from going back on the diet. You forgive yourself for those lapses and begin again. Take the same attitude with crises and interruptions; consider them a short "cheat" from your time plan and then go right back to it.

In addition to the essential activities, routine tasks, interruptions and crises, you may also find that much of your time is consumed by previous commitments. Some of these commitments may not give you the same pleasure or sense of fulfillment now that they did when you made the commitment. I am not suggesting that you shirk responsibilities, but perhaps you do need to see if some of these commitments can be eliminated, or at least modified. If a previous commitment is still important, however, you must find a way to fit it into your schedule and give it a priority rating.

Many women have taken on commitments to tasks or activities they don't want to do because of guilt or the inability to say no to other people. We will explore these ideas more later, but you might begin now to think about whether this applies to some of the activities you are currently doing.

Quite frankly, whether you can find the time for pursuit of personal and lifetime goals in spite of essential activities, routine tasks, interruptions, crises, and previous commitments will depend a great deal on how important it is to you to find the time. But in order to find that time, *you must plan it*. There simply is no other way!

FIGURING OUT PRIORITIES

Let's go back now to one of our major time-planning tools mentioned earlier—the To Do list. Even if you are not a list maker by nature, this is one tool that every person wishing to plan time should use. Some people choose to use a designed form which they keep in an easily accessible, visible place. Others may use desk or pocket calendars, appointment books, or other convenient items. It is important to date and keep the list, at least for a week or two, in order to give some continuity to your plan.

In order to help you set priorities each day, let's look at the categories and talk about what should and should not go on the list. Are you going to write down everything you do? Or are you only going to list special items that might not get done otherwise? To begin with, it is probably better to over-plan than to under-plan. As you become more used to planning and organizing you may begin to drop some of the more routine items. But until you have your time planned the way you want it, you probably should be as complete as possible.

Use the following categories to help you assess and evaluate how you are spending your time now:

1. *Important and Urgent.* These are the tasks that *must* be done immediately, or at least very soon. They may include such items as paying your electric bill before the power company shuts off the lights, turning in a research paper if you want a grade for the term, etc. Procrastination is no longer possible without some negative consequences. Activities in this category may be essential, routine, or special goals. This category, however, is seldom where the time management problems exist.

2. *Important But Not Urgent.* It is this category of activities where effective individuals are distinguished from merely efficient individuals. Activities in this category are usually those that will contribute to lifetime goals. Items such as exercise programs designed for a lifetime of physical fitness, educational courses that upgrade your professional skills, drawing up a will or a long-term financial plan are all examples of important but not urgent activities.

3. *Urgent But Not Important.* In this category are many routine tasks and activities imposed on us by other people. Examples of items in this category are such things as errands and shopping trips. This is the category that frequently requires the most time and probably could be changed in some way. It depends a great deal on what the consequences are when we say no to activities in this category.

4. *Busy Work.* Activities in this category are usually neither urgent nor important but they may give a feeling of accomplishment (unless

30

they are being done primarily to avoid important but not urgent activities). Items here may include such things as straightening up closets, putting pictures in photograph albums, and so on. For many people, busy work can be relaxing and stress-reducing. If too much of your time is being spent in this category, to the exclusion of other important tasks however, it may just be procrastination.

5. *Personal Time.* The last category included on the To Do list is Personal Time. This is "alone" time or "meditating and dreaming" time. Most people need at least some of this kind of time every day to get in touch with themselves and put the day's activities in perspective. This kind of activity can come in a variety of ways, depending upon your preference, but you should have it somewhere on your To Do list and allow yourself to have it guilt free!

The Evolving List

Although it is a good idea to set aside some time every day to make your To Do list (most people prefer early morning or the evening before), the chances are good that you will add to and subtract from the list throughout the day. Also, it is a good idea to review your completed, or partially completed list, before you make the next day's list. You probably won't complete everything on your list every day. What is important is that you have set some priorities for the activities you want to accomplish.

One other thing to remember about the To Do list is its limitations. Because it is a daily plan, not a long-term plan, it is easy to forget to include activities that contribute to lifetime goals. Always try to include at least one or two activities that contribute to the goals you set up in Chapter Two.

ORGANIZING YOUR WORK ENVIRONMENT

Effectiveness versus Efficiency

You probably know many people who have spotless houses, spotless offices, and a place for everything! These same people may also plan down to the smallest detail, cover all their bases, and generally appear to be super-organized and highly efficient. In fact, you may be one of these people, or, at least, wish you were one of these people. Before we go any further in our discussion of "getting organized," it is important for you to understand one very important concept: *Efficiency and effectiveness are not the same thing.* Just because someone *looks* organized does not necessarily mean that that person is using time effectively. In fact, this type of person may be more interested in being organized than in accomplishing anything! The whole point of "getting organized" is to help you with time, not create more tasks to add to your To Do list! How often have you sat down to write a letter, only to end up cleaning the desk drawers instead? Don't let "getting organized" be the end result. Use organization to achieve effectiveness. Efficiency means finding the best way of performing a task. Effectiveness simply means making the best use of your time so you can accomplish what you want and need to do. The *effective* person is the successful person!

Clutter

There is no absolute requirement that your work environment be totally neat in order to work effectively. However, clutter can be diversionary and keep you from concentrating on the task at hand. Also, the ability to quickly put your hands on the tools or objects you need for your activities is helpful in using your time well, so however you arrange your work environment, you should keep those items in mind.

A Personal Place

Regardless of your circumstances—whether you are working in an outside job, going to school, or working at home—you need a place where you can make your plans, store necessary work materials and take care of the paper handling that is an important part of daily life. For some people, this "place" may be an office or a special room; for others, a kitchen nook or even a closet may serve the purpose. Wherever your "place" is and however lavish it may be, it should be yours alone and it should be comfortable and convenient for you.

Establishing your own place to conduct your thoughts and business may require some compromise with other members of your household, but establishing a comfortable working space should become a priority. Even children need a place of their own where they can store their "stuff" without a great deal of interruption. Many women have been reluctant to seek this even though they allow other members of the household to have it. A personal place is not a luxury for a person who wants to be organized and use time well—it is a necessity.

Choosing Your Place

The first consideration for selecting a working space should be your comfort, likes and dislikes. If you choose a space simply because it is practical, you will probably use it very seldom. For example, if you have set up a study desk in the back bedroom with the idea that quiet and privacy seem right and practical, and then find yourself studying in the family room with the television on or in the living room next to the fireplace, you may need to assess what your likes and comforts really are. Here is where an understanding of yourself is important, so do the exercise in Figure 3-2 and see if that will help you find an acceptable location for a personal place for you.

Figure 3-2 Choosing Your Personal Place

Instructions:	Possible Sites				
1. In the boxes to the right, list five possible sites in your living quarters where it would be possible to have a personal work space.					
2. Now answer the questions below, rating each possible site with 4 for excellent; 3 - good; 2 - fair; 1 - poor; 0 - completely inadequate.					
1. Is there enough space for a desk or at least a small table?					
2. Is there a convenient electrical outlet?					
3. Is there any storage space available?					
4. Is the area warm enough or cool enough to suit you?					
5. Is this area used for any other household functions? (If so, could any of these functions be shifted to another place?)					
6. Is the area structurally sound?					
7. Is this area in a busy traffic pattern?					
8. Do you like the look and feel of this area?					
9. Can you reach an agreement with other members of your household that this area would be your personal place?					
10. Can you convert this space to your personal place with a minimum of hassle and expense?					

Which of your possible sites received the highest number of four's and three's?

33

Once you have chosen a place, arrange it so that you have adequate working space, supplies and storage. That way you may cut down on the time it takes to run somewhere else to get your needed materials.

Using Your Personal Place

Once you have found a place that is comfortable for you to think, plan and do your work in, you need to organize and use it. Time can slip away from you in getting started on a task if your work area is not organized. Although the work habits of individuals will vary considerably, here are some general principles to keep in mind when organizing your personal work place:

- Your work area should be cleared of all work except the specific task you are working on. This increases your concentration on that task.
- Your place should be organized so that you do not spend time looking for necessary supplies such as pens, paper, envelopes, etc.
- If you work in a room that has other people also doing activities, face a wall or partition so that you will not be distracted.
- Use lighting that is more concentrated than normal over-head lighting. Desk lamps or other kinds of task lighting are helpful in reducing fatigue as well as saving on electricity.

Enjoy your own personal work place. In addition to saving time, it can also become an enjoyable place for creative thinking, dreaming and personal time.

SPECIFIC WAYS TO FIND MORE TIME

Previously we have been talking about finding time by better planning and organization. In reality, most women must actually give up, or at least lessen, many of their regular activities in order to find more time.

Asking for Help

While many time management consultants and authorities suggest delegating tasks to others as a way of freeing time to do the things we want and need to do, most women know that they are more likely to be the people *delegated to* than the ones who get to do the delegating. Asking others to help, however, may be necessary from time to time. If there is no one to assist you, then you must look for trade-offs to make, tasks to eliminate, and other ways to combine tasks and save time.

Asking for help is one of the trickier aspects of time management because it involves the time of another person as well as your own. It also means that you may have to follow up to see that the task has been accomplished. Learning to ask for assistance, however, may save you invaluable time and hassle. One of the biggest time traps of all is the "If-I-want-it-done-right-I'll-have-to-do-it-myself" syndrome.

The Trade-Off

A trade-off occurs when you exchange one kind of activity for another. Most of us are involved in trade-offs all the time. Those that we consciously and willingly choose, however, give us more control over our time than trade-offs made without planning. Let me give you an example. If I set a goal that includes taking courses at a local college and these courses are offered on an evening that I have previously used to do volunteer work for a charity, I will have to examine which has higher priority and "trade off" one activity for the other. Many women have found that returning to school or work means that they "trade off" an always-clean house or gourmet meals or coffee with the neighbors. You must examine your values and your long-term goals to give you some feeling about what to trade off. Looking back at the time record you are keeping, consider what items you could "trade off" for a period of time in order to accommodate your new activities and fulfill your goals.

Eliminating Tasks

Most of us have had the experience of performing tasks that are probably unnecessary because they gave us a lot of temporary satisfaction. We could see the results right away without a great deal of fuss or bother. Many of the unnecessary tasks we perform are easy, habitual and familiar and include such activities as tidying up desks, drawers and closets, recopying written work to make it neater, and so on. Many of these tasks are also terrific time-wasters if you are trying to find time for new plans and activities. Perhaps these tasks could be eliminated altogether.

Eliminating tasks is different from trading off tasks so it is probably important to understand the difference right away. When you trade off a task, it is assumed that whatever you traded off is still something that you like or need to do and it has been temporarily replaced by something else. Eliminating tasks, however, means looking at the kinds of activities you are doing now that would be better left undone and deciding to eliminate them. For example, if you are spending your time looking through magazines to find recipes you won't have time to try (particularly when you have already clipped a stack you haven't yet used), you may well be wasting your time. With eliminations and trade-offs, you need to look at the consequences. If the consequences are something you can live with, go ahead and try to eliminate this activity. You probably will not miss it.

The best way to accomplish the elimination of unimportant tasks is to use the wastebasket and to learn to say no. Sometimes you simply have to let go of a task and try not to worry about it anymore.

Giving up Perfection

During my years of teaching, I have watched many students do assignments over and over again trying to obtain a perfect paper. Sometimes so much time is spent trying to get that perfect paper that they forget other aspects of the course work. The final grade, then, is not "perfect" but, instead, shows the sum result of a number of tasks and activities that comprised the whole course. The point is simply this: If you want to make effective use of your time you may not be able to do everything to perfection. Furthermore, the world will not come to an end if you don't. I am not suggesting that you *not* try to do what you do well; I am suggesting that many activities are simply not worth spending the amount of time that is required to produce the "perfect" job when it may not make any difference anyway.

There are some tasks for which it is important to do your best work. For example, you will want your job application letter and resumé to contain no errors! But re-copying class notes because your originals are not neat is probably a waste of time. Think carefully about what level of quality is required for the kinds of activities you are doing.

Combining Activities or Time Sharing

Often you can plan two or more activities to coincide so that several objectives can be accomplished at the same time. Breakfast meetings, reading the newspaper on the bus or train, exercising with a friend, are kinds of activities that can be combined with little damage. This may be an especially good way to keep personal and family relationships going while accomplishing other goals, too.

Also, setting aside very specific and planned times for talking to and being with family members and friends will allow you to maintain those relationships while making the other person feel special. It is not enough just to plan your career goal activities; you must also plan your personal time or it will simply slip away from you, making those you care for feel rejected and estranged.

Finding Your Best Time

All of us have times when we have more energy and are more alert than other times. We've heard often that some people are morning people, some are night people, and so on. Chances are, most of your best work and accomplishments happen in a relatively small portion of your day. Think of this time as "prime time" and try to use that time for the tasks that require the most energy, alertness, and creativity.

In another chapter of this book we will discuss increasing energy and vitality, but it is important for you to begin to think about your energy cycles as of now. You want to make the best use of your best time!

SOLVING TIME CONFLICTS
AND ACCOMMODATING OTHER PEOPLE

Up to this point, we have talked primarily about how you use time as if every hour each day were yours to command. The truth is, however, that most of us spend a great deal of time in commitments to other people. After all, you knew when you accepted a job or signed up for a class or got married that you were giving up some freedom to decide how to spend your time in exchange for other important things—money, love, security, knowledge, and so on. Some demands by others simply have to be accepted. None of us is totally independent. We do have responsibilities and commitments to others. Knowing that, however, does not mean that you always allow other people and commitments to use up all of your time.

Sometimes the way you choose to use your time will make other people unhappy. Sometimes they will not understand your choices. This, then, brings about conflicts and, for many women, guilt, sacrifice, and martyrdom.

How then can you solve some of the conflicts that arise when you are making your own time plans and decisions? Let's consider the following ways:

- Learning to say no
- Learning to compromise
- Learning to give up guilt and feelings of martyrdom

Learning to Say No

Some women have a great deal of trouble saying no. They have spent so much of their lives trying to please others and taking orders, that they find it difficult to say no for fear of hurting someone else. But having the ability to say no is one of the most important skills a person should learn if she wishes control over her own time and life. In your eagerness to have everyone like you, you may find yourself with no time to do the things you want to do. People who cannot say no frequently end up having other people take advantage of them or, worse yet, spending a great deal of time with built-up resentments and antagonism toward others. Also, "maybe" is *not* a good substitute for "no"; you will only mislead people. Finally, it is really very inconsiderate *not* to say no if you really do not have the time or the energy to perform what is being asked of you.

Learning to Compromise

When you are trying for a cooperative effort with someone, look at his or her priorities and then look at your own priorities. Those priorities that are different will call for a reassessment of the situation and, perhaps, some persuasion on your part. For example, if your room-mate feels you should spend all day each Saturday cleaning the apartment and running necessary household errands and you would like Saturday to do recreational activities, you may be able to compromise by spending half a day on Saturday and a few hours some evening during the week to accomplish the normal Saturday tasks.

If you make a special effort to be considerate of other people's time, they will usually do the same for you.

Learning to Give Up
Guilt and Martyrdom

Today's working woman must constantly cope with conflicts in her values, goals and time use. This frequently produces guilt—the kind of guilt that comes from the belief that you must live up to someone else's expectations. You may be able to get out of the guilt trap by reminding people that you will do the best you can, but that is all you can do.

Many people use making others feel guilty as a way of avoiding their own responsibilities. Try to recognize when this is happening to you. Maybe the neighbor you have been driving to the grocery store is now angry at you for not wanting to do that any more. Maybe your husband or boyfriend becomes indignant when you suggest he could take care of his own laundry. Try to understand their feelings without feeling guilty!

It may help if you talk about your guilt feelings with the people who are close to you. This will not only lighten your load; you may discover that your friends and family don't expect you to do all the things you thought they did. When you voice your concerns, you are allowing others to actively support your decisions.

Some Final Thoughts on Time

The habits of a lifetime cannot be changed in a few days, but don't let that stop you from trying. Learning to manage your time well is an important key to your personal and professional development. Learn to focus on the things that really count. It may seem to you that you do not have enough time, but you have all the time there is. As you develop your personal philosophy of time, enjoy it. Time is life.

chapter four
DEVELOPING A PROFESSIONAL ATTITUDE

A Real Pro

You probably have heard the expression "she's a real pro" or "he's a true professional." Most people have a sense of what that means. If asked to define the term "professional," however, you might find many different answers. Sometimes the term professional is applied to specific job categories such as those in medicine, law, or education where an individual performs a service based on specialized knowledge and skills. In this chapter, however, the term "professional" will refer to attitudes and behaviors. Professionalism and success on the job are sometimes considered to be the same thing. Certainly, developing a "professional" attitude can help you succeed.

Success in a career is based on more than just self-awareness, goals, skills, and time management. Success is also based on how you look, how you talk, and how you act, in other words, your professional demeanor. In this chapter we will concentrate on the "how you talk and how you act" part of the success composite.

RELATING PROFESSIONAL ATTITUDES TO SUCCESS

A professional attitude has many aspects; some of these you may find you have already developed because of your experiences so far. A professional attitude means:

1. *Having a commitment to the work.* This means accepting responsibility, believing that the job you are doing is important, supporting the objectives of the organization you work for, meeting deadlines and completing assignments, and maintaining high standards for yourself.

2. *Being able to work with others.* This means being able to take directions, viewing yourself as a member of the team, maintaining a sense of humor, handling disappointments, taking criticism, and setting aside personal problems at work.

3. *Making good judgments.* This means being objective and sensible, evaluating your own work realistically, knowing when to assert your rights and when to be silent, and judging co-workers by their competence rather than by personality.

Thinking of Yourself as a Success

In the musical comedy "How to Succeed in Business Without Really Trying" a young window-washer rises through the ranks to become chairman of the board by some rather bizarre schemes and a great deal of luck. While that kind of plot may make enjoyable entertainment, most authorities on achieving success consider "trying" or "working at it" to be an essential element of success. Nevertheless, the young window-washer did have one character trait that will also be important for you—he could imagine himself successful. In order to develop a professional manner and confident attitude, you must be able to see yourself as capable of success. Developing a professional attitude includes seeing yourself as a capable, effective worker.

To actually define *success* is difficult. For some people success means being president of the company; for others, it may mean doing your job well, regardless of what that job is. Whatever your definition of success, you need to believe you are able to fulfill your own definition.

Are Women Afraid of Success?

As more and more women enter the world of business, politics, and other areas of life previously dominated by men, researchers have begun to explore how women feel about success. The traditional definitions of career success have been based on money, titles, power, and authority. Furthermore, our culture says that competition, independence, competence, and success are male goals. Researchers have also noted that for women to achieve this kind of success, they have had to be more shrewd, determined, and directed than their male counterparts. They have also frequently had to make difficult choices about marriage and children. Many women simply have not opted for this type of success because they feel it makes them appear unfeminine. Some women feel they have to choose between being a woman and being a success. It may appear that women are afraid of success—at least, career success in the traditional sense—but that does not mean women cannot be successful or shouldn't try. While there may be some evidence to support the statement that women are afraid of success, it is important to overcome this. You not only have the right to succeed, you probably have just as good a chance as anyone.

BECOMING A DECISIVE PERSON

Part of your personality and character development for career success includes examining the way you make decisions and assessing your willingness to take risks. The two frequently go hand in hand. For most of us, making decisions is a fairly commonplace activity. But some people have confidence in their decision-making skills, while others will go to great lengths to avoid making even the most trivial decisions. Many people are really not aware of the choices they could make and some feel better letting others make the decisions for them. Even if you don't make a decision, however, you have made a choice. So whether you make a decision yourself, allow someone else to make a decision for you, or simply avoid making a decision altogether, *something will happen*. Of the choices just listed, making the decision yourself gives you the most freedom and control over your own life. There are some skills involved in learning to make decisions that can help you become a more decisive person. If you are not comfortable with your decision-making ability, you should concentrate on learning these skills.

Acquiring skills in making decisions is especially needed by many women. Frequently, society and various life experiences have kept women from decision-making roles, so they are often not aware of the choices open to them.

You have learned specific steps in the previous chapters for determining your values, goals, and the use of your time. So you have

42

already completed some of the steps in decision-making. Now let's go on to some new steps in the decision-making process.

Selecting from Alternatives

A decision is an act that requires choosing or selecting among several possible alternatives. Sometimes the alternatives are very clear-cut and you have no difficulty making the decision. But frequently all of the alternatives have both a good side and a bad side. It is when decisions have this kind of complexity that many people avoid making them. But consider this: you are unique and if someone else makes the decision for you, the outcome may suit that person but not you. Two individuals facing a similar decision may not want the same outcome. Think over decisions you have made in the past. What is a good decision you have made? Why was it good? What was a poor decision you have made? Why do you consider it to have been a poor decision? How often have you avoided making any decision at all?

Writing out some of the components of the decision-making process may help you. The chart in Figure 4-1 will assist you in doing this. This may give you a clearer picture of the decision-making process.

Figure 4-1 A Decision-Making Exercise

1. Write down an important decision you need to make soon: _____
   _____
2. What resources are available to help you? _____
   _____
3. Why is this decision important? _____
4. List the actions (or alternatives) you can take related to this decision. Then list the pros and the cons of each possible action:

   Action 1 _____ Action 2 _____ Action 3 _____

PRO	CON	PRO	CON	PRO	CON
___	___	___	___	___	___
___	___	___	___	___	___
___	___	___	___	___	___
___	___	___	___	___	___
___	___	___	___	___	___
___	___	___	___	___	___

5. What is your final decision? _____
   _____

Should you trust your head or your heart in making decisions? Actually, you need to use both. Sometimes the most reasonable, well-thought-out decision is one that depresses you and you really don't "feel" like carrying it out. You may not have made a good decision if you have not used your feelings to help guide you also. On the other hand, decisions based only on feelings of the moment can be impulsive and disastrous.

The following guidelines should be of help as you think about your own decisions and decision-making processes:

1. Obtain as much information as possible about the good and bad sides of any choice you will make, in other words, the pros and cons. Weigh each alternative carefully and rationally. If the most reasonable choice makes you uncomfortable or unhappy, take your feelings into consideration. What seems reasonable the first time may not be something you can live with.

2. If you are tempted to make an impulsive decision, spend more time thinking about it. If you still decide to go with your feelings and disregard what seems the most reasonable, you should at least be able to anticipate some of the consequences.

3. Realize that most decisions you make are not set for eternity. Usually you can change or modify a decision if it is not working for you. Consider how your changed plan will affect others but do not let that unduly influence you.

4. Even the best plans do not always turn out as you might expect. Include the possibility of some failures in all decisions. Many would conclude that it is better to have failed than never to have tried!

5. If you simply cannot decide, talk things over with someone you trust. Maybe he or she can help clarify your thinking and help you sort out what you really want to do.

6. Prepare yourself for any negative consequences that may come from the decision. That way you will probably be able to cope with it more effectively.

Using these guidelines plus the chart in Figure 4-1, practice your decision-making skills. By doing this, you are building a behavior pattern that will help you with career success. Most people like to work with others who are not afraid to make decisions. Working with an indecisive person can be extremely frustrating. Also, making *good* decisions often benefits others besides you.

Here are a few more thoughts to consider when you are involved in the decision-making process:

- Being decisive does *not* mean you must make decisions instantaneously without any consideration or caution.
- Changing your mind is permissible. Sometimes new information gives you a new perspective.
- Taking the advice of an authority figure does not relieve you of responsibility for your own decisions.
- Decision-making can be a challenging and risky venture.

Decisions force us to commit ourselves. Also, decisions are interconnected. For example, going to college may reflect a decision you made in the ninth grade when you decided to take a college preparatory curriculum. Or the secretarial job you are seeking may relate to a decision to take a typing course many years ago. We become what our decisions allow us to become.

Taking Risks

People who let others make decisions, or make only the most cautious decisions (those with a pretty certain outcome), are usually people who fear failure and demand perfection of themselves. It may surprise you, but some of the most successful people are those who have also experienced the most failures! What is significant, however, is not that a failure occurred but what the person learned from that failure. I am not suggesting that you should blithely blot out or deny the mistakes, setbacks and failures that occur from decisions but, rather, that you learn to accept them, analyze what went wrong, and learn from them so you can improve the next time. Most successful people have learned that mistakes and failures can provide some of the best growth experiences a person can have even though they may not be enjoyable or comfortable.

Knowing that successful people make mistakes does not make it easy to suddenly begin making more risky decisions. You may have to acquire this ability gradually—with practice. Learning not to let setbacks destroy your confidence can be a major breakthrough in your personality development.

When you are about to make a risky decision, tell yourself the following things:

- I am making this decision on the best information available to me right now.
- It is not possible to please everyone.
- If this turns out to be a bad decision, I will not waste time fretting about it to the point where I cannot make other decisions or, perhaps, correct this one.

We live in an imperfect world and if we try to be perfect, we will probably end up frustrated and unhappy. No one likes to make mistakes but everybody does make them. The characteristic that distinguishes the successful person from the unsuccessful one is how he or she handles the mistakes.

ASSERTING YOURSELF

One of the things that is probably apparent to you after practicing the decision-making process is that this process may cause you to confront other people and you may have to assert yourself in order to take risks and make decisions. If you are bothered by the term *assertiveness*, let's take a few minutes to see what this really means.

Many people confuse the words *assertive* and *aggressive*. For our purpose in this book, we will draw a very definite distinction between assertiveness and aggressiveness. *Assertiveness* involves making your own choices and defending yourself appropriately. *Aggressiveness*, on the other hand, is the type of behavior that minimizes other people or violates their rights while you are standing up for yours. The purpose of aggressive behavior is to humiliate others or "put them down." We will assume that *assertive* behavior is usually the most appropriate behavior.

Nonassertiveness or passivity, on the other hand, is a behavior that allows others to choose for you instead of your being actively involved in the decisions of your life. Interestingly, many nonassertive people become aggressive when finally moved to take action. Most of us have known at least one person who appeared on the surface to be easygoing but became quite violent either in words or action when finally provoked.

Asserting yourself in the work area affects not only your earning capacity but your attitude toward yourself and other people you work with. An assertive woman feels comfortable about expressing her feelings, reacts in a positive manner, expresses her feelings without violating the rights of others, and possesses self-respect. Do these characteristics describe you?

What Happens if You Are Not Assertive?

Nonassertiveness can take a number of forms, but here are some examples for you to think about:

- Excessive procrastinating and daydreaming as a way of avoiding action or commitments. (This should not be confused with choosing to daydream or waiting for additional information before taking action.)
- Griping about the awful employment situation or the bad working conditions without suggesting or doing anything constructive.
- Not being able to say no, thus taking on every request made of you to the point where you cannot accomplish the things you need to get done.
- Not being able to say yes to something because your family or friends may not approve.

To be assertive in your career, there are a number of personality characteristics you need to learn. We have already discussed procrastination in Chapter Three, so let's concentrate on some of the other aspects of nonassertiveness:

- Overcoming passive, dependent behavior to become action-oriented.
- Learning to say what you need to say—regardless of whether that be a "yes" or "no" in a given situation.

From Passive to Powerful

Passive people are often powerless people; powerless people usually remain powerless by their passive behavior. What does this really mean and how does it apply to you? Quite frankly, it first of all means accepting responsibility for your own life—your own decisions, mistakes, achievements, and tragedies. It means getting out of the habit of self-pity and resentment and developing a more constructive attitude toward behaviors and events. For example, if you have received a low grade on a test, instead of spending time resenting the instructor who gave you the grade or the student in the class who got the top grade, turn to something that will get you into a more positive frame of mind by doing something you enjoy. After you have worked through the resentment you may be able to go back and look at why you did not do well and make plans for a better performance the next time. Maybe you can even work up the courage to discuss the problem with the instructor and thus resolve the problems or clear up any misinformation you had.

Decisions about how you exercise your rights, just like the decisions we discussed earlier, should be based on your own feelings and the possible consequences of action. You may deliberately choose not to exercise a right to which you feel entitled in order to avoid hurting another person. The important thing to remember, however, is that you *make a choice* about exercising your right; you do not engage in the nonassertive behavior out of fear or resentment.

When to Say Yes and When to Say No

Much has been written in recent years about people learning to say no when confronted with something they really don't want to do. The flip side of that is equally important, however—saying yes when presented with something you want to do but are afraid to.

Obviously, you have to be careful about telling your employer you don't want to perform a task that may be part of your job description, but there are many occasions, both at work and home, when people ask you to do things that are not your responsibility. For example, how often do you do personal errands, such as buying birthday gifts or picking up items at the store, for other people? If you truly enjoy doing that and you have time, fine, but if resentment is what you feel about such tasks now that you are busier than ever, saying no is definitely in order. It isn't easy to change the habits of a lifetime (yours and those of the people who expect you to do for them, too) but here are two pointers that may help:

1. Remember that you have the right to consider your own needs and to change your behavior or life situation.
2. Start your answer with the word *no* and keep your answer firm, brief, and clear.

In order to feel comfortable with your new skills, practice. Think of several unreasonable requests that have been made to you recently. Now think of how you can say no directly and honestly. You may wish to tell the person you are saying no to that you understand how important the activity is to him or her. Practice will make it easier. While you are busy saying no, there is one very important thing to remember: *Don't say no when you want to say yes.*

Learning to say yes, interestingly enough, has many of the same components as learning to say no. If you are offered a job which includes some out-of-town travel and you are afraid your family won't like it, remember that you have the right to accept challenges and make your decision based on evaluating their needs and your needs. If you want to do it, figure out appropriate arrangements for your family responsibilities and say yes.

Many times great opportunities come along at what may seem to be inopportune times, but if you postpone or delay the decision or say no, the great opportunity may not come again. Being able to "grab the brass ring" when it is offered is an important part of career success.

LEARNING TO PLAY ON THE TEAM

More people have been fired from jobs for not getting along with their co-workers than have been fired for lack of technical skills! There is no question about the necessity of getting along with your employer and co-workers if you hope to have a successful career—the question comes in how to do it. How do you achieve your own rights and fulfillment and still accommodate others? In every workplace there are at least two or more people, and two people make a group. Group behavior is important because whatever you do affects the way someone else in your group feels. When your actions make another person feel more positive toward you, you have contributed and that person usually does a more effective job.

Does this mean that we should always behave in ways that make others feel good or give them exactly what they want? Not really. Most of the difficulties people have in groups are caused by lack of confidence or lack of genuine feelings and communication, such as we have just discussed.

Communicating Effectively

Because each of us as an individual is slightly different from everyone else, communication gaps can occur. All of us have our own set of biases, misperceptions, and prejudices that color our view of "reality." Add to that the limited number of people most of us are exposed to and it is possible to see why communication can be difficult. Look at yourself. How have your nationality, religion, family financial background, and the geographic area where you grew up affected your outlook? You may have to work with people whose backgrounds are much different from your own. You may need to modify many of your original perceptions to communicate effectively with others. Some of the following suggestions should be helpful as you think about developing pleasant working relationships with people:

1. Be sensitive to individual differences. Try to imagine what it would really be like to see a situation as someone else would.
2. Try to approach people when they are not tired, irritated, or preoccupied with something else.
3. Work on developing a genuine interest in other people.
4. Learn how to negotiate and reach compromises with your group. Many business decisions are made collectively.

Many women have not had the opportunity to play team sports or participate in other types of competitive team events. Those who have, however, can tell you that this is a good experience for learning to play on the team in the business world. Some of the important lessons to be learned are these:

- Teamwork takes preparation and practice.
- If you are knocked down, you have to get up and try again.
- You belong to something bigger than yourself.
- A team needs a leader and followers.
- Some team members are better than others, but you need the whole team in order to play.

Handling Criticism

Criticism is negative, destructive, and hurtful. Right? Is that statement true all of the time? When your work is criticized, how do you react?

Do you have hurt feelings and then go on to blame yourself? Or do you say to yourself, "Who is the criticizer? How important is he or she?" Even if the criticizer is important, can you accept that sometimes you win and sometimes you lose?

Most employers want their employees to succeed, even though it may not seem that way when you're being reprimanded for doing something nobody bothered to tell you was the one thing to avoid at all costs. Criticism simply says that you've done something somebody either doesn't approve of or thinks can be done better.

Learning to handle criticism is a vital part of learning to get along with others. Some people fear criticism so much that they avoid challenges, decisions, a different job, or any situation where they might encounter it. If you are a person who has some difficulty coping with criticism—and most of us do—here is something for you to think about: *Criticism doesn't mean that something is wrong with you!* Instead of feeling hurt and defensive, ask yourself the following questions:

1. Have I really been criticized?
2. Consider the source of the criticism. Is there a particular motive behind this particular criticism?
3. Did I understand exactly what was said?
4. Is the criticism specific, or is it couched in terms like "no good" or "you can do it better"?
5. Is the criticism a personal attack on me?

Some criticism is justified and you need to be able to accept it as such and use it for your own improvement. Frequently a supervisor is required to criticize your work in order to improve the overall performance of the unit he or she is supervising. How you handle the criticism and what you do with it in the future will be far more important than the reason for the original criticism in most instances. Employers do not expect you to be perfect. They do expect you to learn from your mistakes, however. Criticism from other employees who do not directly supervise you should be considered in the same way. You may be receiving valuable information, but sometimes you may not. Try to separate the justified criticism from unjustified or put-down kinds of criticism and deal with criticism assertively. Also remember that people who know how well they are doing are more likely to succeed than those who are kept in the dark!

There are many paths to success. If you were to interview a number of successful people, each would probably have a different idea of what the steps to success are. Reasons for failure may be just as diverse. There are, however, some identifiable reasons why some people *do not succeed* in their careers that you should be aware of. Besides the obvious ones such as frequent absenteeism, disloyalty, lack of competence, and unwillingness to accept responsibility, there are some other career realities you should be aware of that are much more subtle. These include attitudes about what the organization you work for "owes" to you. Adopting these attitudes colors your behavior and can be quite destructive to you. Let's consider some examples:

1. *An employer should meet my needs for fulfillment and not keep me in a boring job.* While it might be very nice if all companies could help define and achieve life values and career goals for individuals, most companies are much better at meeting the needs of the company than meeting the needs of individual employees. In other words, most of the responsibility for finding and keeping a "fulfilling" job will rest squarely on your shoulders.

2. *If I perform well on my current job I can be assured of continued employment in the company.* Wrong again. Most organizations have difficulty planning their own long-range survival, let alone the individual future of each employee. Even though some jobs are considerably more secure than others, in the end, you are responsible for your own survival.

3. *I can succeed on the job and perform well if I know what the company expects of me.* For most of our lives, we have been taught to try to conform to whatever the system (that is, society, organization, country, and so on) wants. But most organizations are not living, thinking beings. The skills and competencies your company expects from you will depend on such varied things as the economy, changes in laws, the unknown outcome of mergers or business reorganizations, and so on. You will need to be flexible. You will probably need to like to do many different kinds of things.

4. *The company should always be fair. Justice should prevail.* Our culture promises justice; our legal system promises justice. But you do not have to look very far to see that lack of justice is a common state of the world. That doesn't mean you should not try to help get rid of

injustice; you just need to realize that injustice in the workplace is fairly commonplace and you do not want to be psychologically defeated by it. Being upset because others get away with breaking the rules, complaining that others make too much money for what they do, or insisting that because someone else did something to you, you must now "get even" with them is a great energy drain. The simple fact is that no amount of griping or trying to get even will bring about any positive self-changes in you.

Successful careers seldom happen by chance. People who really get what they want in a career do so because they define clear objectives, develop plans and schedules for achieving these objectives, and, above all, develop a professional attitude and accept personal responsibility for their plans, decisions, and relationships. They also change or improve their plans when they are not getting desired results, and they persevere, even in the face of setbacks and failures, until their goals are achieved. They do not wait for things to happen to them—they take charge.

chapter five
CREATING
A PROFESSIONAL
APPEARANCE

Your appearance distinguishes you from everyone else. An attractive and appropriate appearance is important for career success because such an appearance projects a confident and businesslike attitude. That, in turn, enhances the image of the organization you work for.

In this chapter we will talk about some skills of personal presentation—those skills that help you to look your best. A professional-looking appearance is your way of packaging yourself. It is a reflection of your self-image and indicates how you wish to be seen by others. Even though there may be some constraints, it is entirely possible to adapt your own style and uniqueness to the style of your company.

TRANSMITTING A PROFESSIONAL IMAGE

What Do Others See?

Every day we transmit to others and receive from others countless images, impressions, facts and feelings. They are positive or negative but rarely neutral. This information determines how we react to everything and everyone we encounter. No matter how you have physically assembled the package you call "you," an image of what you like is being transmitted for the entire world to see. You are projecting your character. This physical exterior may present greater insight into who you are and how you feel about yourself than the credentials which appear on your resumé. Do you inspire trust and confidence, or do you come across as timid and unsure? Do you look organized or do you look disorganized?

Think for a moment of the effect other peoples' appearances have on you. Would you feel secure in entrusting your banker with your money if she wore a tattered blouse and faded blue jeans to work? What if your dentist had teeth missing? What if your surgeon had dirty fingernails? These are wordless messages which you've evaluated as negative. It is clear that we attach specific meanings to specific looks. Our interpretation of these meanings determines how positively or negatively we relate to others—and, of course, how others relate to us.

In Chapter Four we talked about developing a professional attitude; in this chapter we will include appearance in that attitude. This attitude forms your self-image which, in turn, enhances your opportunities for career success. Stated simply, your self-image is your view of yourself—the way you feel about yourself.

We must also consider the kind of appearance necessary for success in business. Even though you may find it distasteful that so much importance is attached to appearance, you cannot ignore this reality. Your business associates will judge you by the clothes you wear, the way you shake hands, your hairstyle and makeup in addition to your job performance and attitude. Since organizations also "transmit images," the way you complement this image can be very important.

Your Impression of You

When the person hiring comes down to the final decision between two people with equal qualifications, the more attractive one will often get the job. Everyone has the ability to project an attractive attitude and image. But first *you have to like and to feel good about yourself and the way you look.* You can always tell the people who feel good about themselves—they smile more. They carry themselves erectly. They project vitality and energy.

Above all, learn to accept yourself. Part of a positive self-image also comes from accepting things you can't change (or really don't want to change). We do not get a choice about our age, sex, race, inherited physical characteristics, and so on. If any of these operate as negatives in your self-image you can learn to accept them and keep them in proper perspective. Do not let them get in the way of things you want to change. Also, do not let them overshadow your assets. Everybody has some things they like and some they don't like about themselves.

The Standards of Attractiveness in the Business World

There are many varieties of "attractiveness." The kind of attractiveness that may allow you to win a beauty contest will not necessarily win you a job. It will be helpful to you to have an awareness about what people in your career field find attractive.

What is considered attractive in a business setting also depends upon the type of business. You would probably not find exactly the same standards applied in a health club as you would in a banking institution. *Appropriateness* is probably the number one component of attractiveness in a business setting. An appropriate appearance says to others in that business that you understand what they are trying to do and you emulate it. This may include everything from the clothes you wear to the speech patterns you use. For example, businesses such as banks, law firms, and insurance companies tend to be conservative. You will find that most successful employees in these institutions wear classic clothing, trim hairstyles, and conservative makeup. They try to look competent, trustworthy and solid. They are usually not flamboyant or "sexy." Other types of businesses may be more casual, with corduroy jackets, pants, plaid shirts, or very style-conscious, with designer clothing or a more avant-garde appearance depending on the service they offer or the clientele they serve. The importance of "appropriateness" is that it allows you to fit in so that your appearance does not detract from the business at hand.

The second major component of attractiveness for a business setting is an *updated* appearance. This does not mean that you buy a new wardrobe or completely redo your hairstyle every year. This simply means that you continue to add "current" touches to your appearance, so that others see you as someone who is flexible and keeps up with what is going on in the world.

The third and final component of attractiveness we will discuss here is *confidence*. Confidence comes from feeling good about yourself and your talents, feeling clean, healthy and fit, wearing clothing and makeup that fit *you* well, and exhibiting an aura of both serenity and energy. People regard you as attractive when they enjoy your company and think of you as an asset in any situation.

Body Language

Part of the image you project to others comes from physical reactions—in other words, nonverbal behavior or "body language." These physical reactions may be voluntary or involuntary, but either way they may result in your being seen as alert and attentive or as despairing and helpless. For example, such actions as casting your eyes down, slumping your shoulders, wringing your hands, or shrugging your shoulders may convey the impression that you are desperate or despairing. Looking people straight in the eye, standing or sitting in an erect but comfortable posture may, on the other hand, create an image of alertness or attentiveness. We may have no real idea of what our body language is saying about us, and yet it is a tremendously important part of transmitting an image.

What are you saying about yourself in the way in which you stand, sit, or speak? The easiest way to observe yourself is in front of a body-length mirror. Observe how you walk, how you stand, how you sit. Do you seem confident or tentative? What do you like? What would you like to change?

A mirror, however, only gives you two dimensions. Other people rarely look at us straight on as one does when facing a mirror. So just using a mirror may not give you a total impression to work with. For these reasons, using a videotape may be the most effective method of observing your body language, to see what's right and what's wrong. I should caution you that first sight of yourself on videotape can be a shock. Seeing your body and hearing yourself speak can be like looking at a stranger. But, after your initial nervousness and discomfort, seeing yourself on videotape will be more helpful than looking in the mirror because you will see yourself much more objectively.

In addition to observing your nonverbal behavior, taping will also allow you to work on how you speak and the pitch of your voice. A high pitch is very distracting and unbusinesslike. The more emotional you become, the higher the pitch, which, ultimately, takes away from whatever you're saying. Also, talking too rapidly or too slowly or pausing often to insert phrases such as "you know" or "well" may also be distracting and may lead to a negative impression. Your facial expressions are also very important. Others judge what they think your mood is from these outward expressions.

CREATING A PROFESSIONAL FACE

The Importance of Skin Care

When you look in a mirror, a large part of how pleasing the reflection is depends on how healthy your skin is. Many problems are based on a lack of understanding of the skin and the variety of conditions that can affect it. Your complexion is influenced by many factors. Foremost is genetics; acne, broken capillaries, or pigmentation are inherited tendencies just like blue eyes or red hair. Besides genes, climate plays a role in how your skin looks. Exposure to cold weather, or spending long periods in the sun are two examples of how climate affects your skin. The quality of your life will also affect your skin. Are you relaxed or under prolonged stress? Each condition makes its mark on the kind of face you show the world.

In order to do justice to the make-up suggestions that follow, you need to seriously consider what your skin is like. Many skin problems can be easily corrected by the proper care routines suggested by a skin care specialist. And many severe skin problems can be corrected by processes suggested by a dermatologist or other specialist. Improving one's skin is not just a concern of career women either. Many skin care specialists can attest to the increased interest by men in taking care of their skin because they know it makes a difference in their overall business image.

Makeup and the Business World

In less sophisticated times only actresses and "ladies of the night" used makeup—and they were not considered "ladies." We are more liberal today. Makeup, however, must be used very discriminately—particularly in a business situation. You want to make your face its most attractive in the most inconspicuous way.

By enhancing your features with neutral colors you can present an attractive face. The idea is to look as "natural" as possible. You want your makeup to fit into your overall professional image—to blend in with and enhance your good features and your wardrobe. You do not want it to stand out on its own. The key word for business makeup is *subtle*.

You are seeking an overall effect. You are not trying to make one part of your face stand out (as it would, for example, if you wore bright lipstick with no eye makeup or darkly lined eyes with no lip color). You will also be trying to complement your clothing to achieve a "total" look.

Common Makeup Mistakes

Almost anyone can recognize a glaringly bad makeup job, but many people still make minor mistakes which can keep them from looking their best. The following examples are among the most common errors in cosmetic application.

1. Too much blush that is not applied correctly. (Some women apply "little red apples"—round circles which are never blended—on their cheeks. Or they draw wide strips which look like magic marker stripes.)
2. Too much mascara, which causes eyelashes to become stuck together.
3. Lipstick which is either too pale or too dark, or wearing bright lipstick with no other makeup, causing the lips to stand out.
4. Eyeshadow that is not carefully blended.
5. Makeup foundation that is not the same shade as the rest of the skin, specifically the neck. The result is an obvious line of demarcation between what is made up and what isn't.
6. Poor job of blending. Blending is the most important aspect of makeup, including professional makeup. It should be impossible to tell where one makeup ends and the next begins.
7. Eyebrows that are plucked too thinly or penciled too darkly. The brows are a frame for the eyes and should not distract from them. Rather, they should accent them.
8. A face that is too powdered or too shiny.
9. Undereye shading cream that is too light. The result is a "raccoon effect."

Understanding and Enhancing Skin Tones

Is your skin "cool," "warm," or "neutral"? The answer depends on your undertones—the subdued shades which determine your *skin type* and, ultimately, the makeup shades which will help you look your best. Undertones are so subtle that they are not easily picked up by the untrained eye. However, several factors will help you figure out yours.

The easiest way to identify skin type is whether you burn or tan when you sunbathe. If a person burns, and cannot be in the sun more than fifteen or twenty minutes at a time, she probably has cool skin with blue undertones. A woman who doesn't burn will, most likely, have yellow undertones. If you first burn, then tan, chances are yours is a neutral skin with equal amounts of yellow and blue undertones. The other factors determining skin types are hair and eye color. Like your skin, warm makeup colors have yellow undertones and cool makeup colors have blue undertones.

With these subtle shading possibilities in mind, remember: *you can't make a flat statement that a certain color is not for you.* You can come up with many different shades of the same color with proper blending. Perhaps you can't wear bright red, but you might look very nice in a salmon shade. If you are not sure what colors are really good for you, you may wish to seek professional advice on selecting colors to fit your personality or your business image.

Makeup and Money

Money is, obviously, an important consideration in buying cosmetics. In this time of escalating prices, the price of cosmetics is a concern for most of us. Are expensive cosmetics better and safer than less costly preparations? Will you look better with a high-priced cosmetic item? That answer to these questions is an emphatic *no*!

The ingredients for a lipstick, foundation, cheek color, eye shadow, mascara are fundamentally the same regardless of the brand. What *does* change is the packaging, the advertising, the fragrances, and sometimes, the color, but the products are still, basically, the same.

The Only Tools and Supplies
You Will Ever Need

Every artist has tools to create something beautiful. A list follows of the tools you need to become the artist of your own face. But, first, an important note: make sure that you apply your makeup in the best possible lighting—strips of light placed on each side of the dressing room or bathroom mirror. Lighting placed in this manner distributes even light exposure to the face and eliminates the shadows that come from overhead lighting or a light above the mirror. If you can't illuminate your mirror this way, use natural daylight as an alternative. To do this, place the mirror about six feet from the window. Face the window and place the mirror in front of you.

Here's what you need:

1. *Cotton swabs* (also called Q-Tips): Excellent for blending and removing any smudges.
2. *Magnifying mirror:* This enables you to examine your blending closely.
3. *Eyelash curler:* This device is still one of the best ways to "open up" the eyes. There are some rules, however, for it to be its most effective:
   *never curl lashes that are mascaraed
   *curl as close to the base of your lashes as you can
4. *Large powder brush:* For applying both cheek color and face powder.
5. *Eyeshadow sponges:* To apply powder eyeshadow.
6. *Lipbrush:* Use for applying a thin, even coating of lipstick.
7. *Fine eyeliner brush:* Use of this is the most effective way to apply undereye concealer. You cover only the dark areas using a brush, whereas a finger covers too broad an area.
8. *Eyebrow brush:* Brushing brows up helps "lift" the face.
9. *Pencil sharpeners:* A sharp point on makeup pencils allows for subtle and accurate application of color.
10. *Makeup sponges:* Use these for a smooth, thin application of foundation.

Selecting and Applying Makeup

In Figure 5-1 you will see examples of an approach to applying makeup. This is called a "paint by number" approach because the numbers indicate the order in which the makeup should be applied and also correspond to the enumerated list explained in the text. Once you have placed the color in the proper place, blend carefully with a sponge (or a cotton swab around the eye area) so there are no sharp edges. Blending is tremendously important to achieve a really professionally done effect.

The following list of cosmetics are those you will need for creating your "professional face." They are available at drug and department stores throughout the country.

1. *Makeup foundation:* This smooths out skin tone and makes the complexion seem more perfect. It also acts as the base for other makeup. The most effective way to apply base is to dot it on (see

Figure 5-1a Paint-by-Number for Caucasian Face

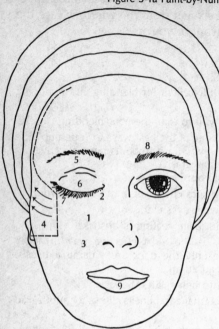

Example of Painting by Number

1. Foundation (eyelids too)
2. Undereye Cover (press-pat on)
3. Baby Powder Over Entire Face (eyelids too)
4. Cheek Color
5. Cheek Color as Highlighter
6. Charcoal Shadow
7. Curl and Mascara
8. Brush Brows Up
9. Lip Color

Figure 5-1b Paint-by-Number for Black Face

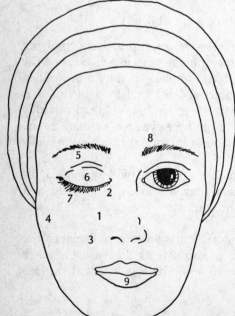

Example of Paint-by-Number for Black S'

1. Foundation (eyelids too)
2. Translucent Powder (eyelids too)
3. Red-Umber Cheek Color
4. Cheek Color as Highlighter
5. Navy Blue Shadow
6. Soft Black or Charcoal Shadow
7. Black Pencil
8. Mascara
9. Red-Umber Lip Color

Figure 5-2) and apply in downward directions with your sponge. The color you need is determined by matching the foundation shade to your neck. The best tones are the true beiges. Generally, it is not a good idea to choose a foundation shade darker than your skin tone.

Figure 5-2 Applying Make-up Foundation

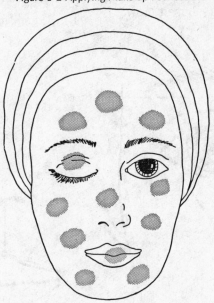

2. *Undereye concealers:* Apply with a fine eyeliner brush to the correct area, then blend with a press-pat motion. Apply on top of foundation only in the darkened area—do not apply over entire undereye area. This will help conceal dark shadows and repair a "tired look."

3. *Face powder:* This is used to "set" foundation and absorb skin oils. Using a large cosmetic brush, lightly dust on translucent or baby powder.

4. *Cheek color:* Also called "blush," this gives your face contour and color. See Figure 5-1 for correct placement.

5. *Eye shadow:* This is used to contour the eye and make it more expressive. Generally, subtle browns and grays are best for your business appearance. See Figure 5-1 for an example of the proper placement.

6. *Mascara:* This is used to deepen eyelash color. Use sparingly and carefully to avoid a smudged or thick look. Use the tip of the brush to color the lower lashes. Generally, brown mascara is softest and best for a subtle effect.

7. *Eyebrow pencils:* These are rarely needed but may be used to fill in sparse brows. Figure 5-3 will give you an example of how to determine a well-shaped brow.

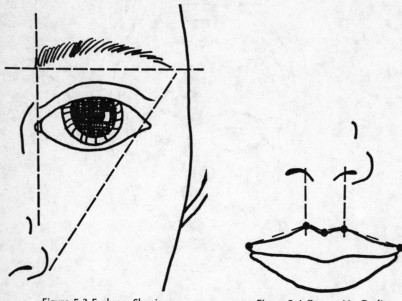

Figure 5-3 Eyebrow Shaping   Figure 5-4 Correct Lip Outline

8. *Lipstick and lip gloss:* An almost universally accepted cosmetic, lip color helps you look healthy and vital. Moderation is the key word here. You do not want your lips too bright or too pale. Also, you want to achieve a reasonable contrast with your skin and eye color. The more contrast there is, the more obvious the lip color is. See Figure 5-4 for correct lip outline.

Special Considerations for the Asian Face

The information given thus far in the makeup section is directly applicable to the Asian face. Asians do have, however, one unique facial characteristic: the shape of the eye and eyelid area. This is referred to as the ideally shaped almond eye. Because Asian eyes are usually small, there is a tendency to outline the eye (usually in black) in an attempt to give it prominence and make it appear larger. The result, however, is the opposite, and may give the face an overall harsh appearance.

Special Considerations for Black Skin

In recent years, cosmetic companies have been starting to offer makeup especially for black skin. Before the advent of these specialized cosmetics, black women were forced to make do with products which were not made for their skin color and resulted in an uncomplimentary gray, ashy look.

Black women have different pigment displacement in their skin; hence, the makeup colors used should be different from those designed for lighter skins. Foundation tones should be as close as possible to facial skin color. Slightly darker tones are better than lighter ones. Tinted face powders are also available for black skins. The best shades for eye makeup are dark browns, charcoal grays and navy blues. Pastel colors do not work well. Good cheek colors are plum, bronze, and amber. Red lip color with burgundy or brown shades creates a natural, attractive color and works better than pinks or oranges.

Nail Care

Most working women's hands are on display much of the time. As insignificant as your fingernails may seem to you, split, chipped, and poorly groomed nails can undermine your total appearance. If caring for your nails is a problem for you, consider having a professional manicure on a regular basis. This is a relatively inexpensive treatment and it may inspire you to take better care of your hands on your own.

Whether or not you wear colored lacquer will depend on your style and where you work. Generally, clear polish is less trouble and is always appropriate.

Eyeglasses and Makeup

Eyewear, like everything else you wear, should be chosen with care and with the help of a fashion-knowledgeable expert. The style you choose must complement your face—giving it the right contour, providing emphasis or de-emphasis of your features. The colors of the frame and the tint of the lenses should achieve the same purpose. If lenses are tinted, select a light tint in a gray or brown, never a pink, lavender, or other high-fashion color as these are usually not appropriate for business.

When applying makeup, there is not a different set of rules for eyeglass wearers than there is for those who wear contact lenses or do not wear glasses at all. However, it is important for the woman who wears glasses to concentrate a bit more on her bottom eye area because this part of her face tends to become obscured.

Some Final Considerations About Makeup

The time you spend practicing makeup techniques will pay off in several ways: you will become more adept at applying it well and you will learn to do it quickly. Don't be afraid to try new makeup techniques; if you don't, you may be depriving yourself of the most attractive face you can have.

Taking professional makeup instruction may also be a worthwhile career investment. There is one important warning to consider when seeking professional makeup instruction: You will probably be more satisfied with the results if you get help from someone whose principal purpose is instruction, not cosmetics sales. Many women have come away from the experience of having a cosmetics salesperson show them how to apply makeup feeling like a clown. If you cannot find a professional makeup consultant, you may be better off asking advice from someone you know who does a good job of makeup application and can point you in the right direction. You need to feel comfortable in your makeup and not as though you are wearing a mask.

YOUR HAIR STYLE FOR BUSINESS

When you're working, you need a simple, no-fuss hairstyle that is neat and easy to maintain. Here, the rule of thumb is *moderation;* not too long; not too short. It should be *functional* for doing business. If your day starts with making breakfasts and lunches and getting the kids off to school while you're trying to prepare *yourself* for work, the last thing you need is a complicated hairstyle which requires a lot of fuss. Also, a style that's too exotic will look ludicrous in a business situation.

Please understand, however, that with all this talk of "simple," "easy," and "basic," I'm not recommending pixie styles for every working woman in America. First of all, hair must be proportioned to the body. Hair is an accessory and should provide an attractive frame for your face.

If you color your hair, you should again keep in mind the word "natural." Even if your hair is not your natural color, it should look natural. I firmly believe any coloring should be done by an expert. Although this process in a salon is not inexpensive, a good job is well worth the money. (Another important point is that the products used on your hair by professionals are generally milder than those on the market.) Coloring is not like experimenting with an eyeshadow that doesn't work and can be easily washed off in seconds. Even a bad haircut can be lived with until it grows out, but a bad coloring job is different. A trusted hair technician can actually save you money while protecting your hair and your image.

Your hairstyle should adapt to your lifestyle, time demands, appearance, and local climate while complementing your overall professional appearance.

PUTTING TOGETHER A CAREER WARDROBE

Putting together a wardrobe for work can be a major investment in both time and money. Clothing not only reflects your personality and attitudes, but also can contribute to or detract from a professional appearance. Wearing the *correct* clothes can be important to your career success. Although a good work wardrobe is a necessity for both men and women, there are some problems in this area that are unique to women. A pattern of appropriate dress for men at work has evolved over a longer period of time and is more established in tradition. There is an old saying that "men dress for business and women dress for pleasure." This old stereotype of women dies hard.

The ideas presented here are not the "final word" on dressing for business, but they will help you plan a wardrobe that fits you and your career. The emphasis is on traditional business dress, but we will consider some issues of individual style and taste as well.

Expressing Your Individuality

Many people want the clothes they wear to express their individual personalities and personal philosophies. When this individual philosophy goes against the image an organization wants to project, real conflicts may arise. (There are even court cases to prove just how serious some of these conflicts can be!) Some people may simply not know (or care) what is acceptable in a given organization, and may impede their career progress because of it.

Before we go any further in the discussion of appropriate business dress, examine your feelings about dress as a point of individual preference and expression. Then consider these feelings in relation to your career choices. If you despise wearing traditional suits, do not pick a conservative organization or a position where this type of image is expected. Find an organization where your mode of dress will be accepted.

Another important consideration: some highly successful people break all of the rules of traditional business dress. There are always exceptions to every rule, but you should understand the risks you assume if you choose to be an "exception" to your organization's image or traditional standards when you are starting out. You run the risks of being considered naive, uncaring, bizarre, or just plain rebellious. You may undermine your authority and credibility and convey the impression that you are not really serious about business. Dressing for business usually means dressing conservatively. But you need not fear the "cookie-cutter" syndrome; we are not talking about "uniform" dressing.

Dress Differences Among Organizations

Although basic business dress will fit well in most organizations, there are some differences in what is appropriate based upon the type of organization, its location, and the position you hold in the organization. If you work in an organization where persons in the same job category as you wear designer jeans and boots, you may seem out of place if you show up in a tailored navy wool suit with a white blouse. Compromises may be necessary.

The type of business also makes some difference in what is acceptable dress. Financial institutions, insurance companies, private law firms, and some high-technology manufacturing firms usually project a conservative image. Organizations involved in retail sales will often want you to dress to fit whatever image they are trying to convey to their customers. Organizations such as newspapers, colleges, and government agencies may be very casual or extremely conservative depending on a number of factors. The point is: *Pay attention to the overall image of the organization or the job category you are seeking.*

Some organizations have dress codes; some do not. Even the organizations that do not have written dress codes have some unwritten standards. Violating the dress code may not get you fired, but it may impede your progress in the organization. It is a good idea to find out about dress codes before you go to work.

Dressing for an Interview

Extra care is needed in dressing for an interview because this may be your only chance to convince the interviewer that you are *the* one for this job.

It is always best to check out the company dress policy *before* the interview. This can easily be accomplished by spending some time (discreetly) in the lobby of that company's building around lunch hour or just after five o'clock. If you're lucky enough to know someone who already works for the firm, ask her what the women in different job categories (including management) wear. You want to impress the interviewer with your capability not only to handle the position for which you're being interviewed, but more responsible positions as well. Granted, you must also have the necessary education, skills, and personal and intellectual capabilities, but if you show up in loafers, skirt and sweater (even though they may be appropriate for the job you are applying for), the interviewer may not see these qualities in you.

Generally speaking, for most jobs, the skirted suit and blouse, or a dress and jacket, will work the best. If you are being interviewed for a management or professional position, wear a skirted suit and blouse. You are always safe in a navy or gray suit and a white blouse if you are at all unsure. This is a good time to carry an attaché (without a handbag).

For technical, clerical, or other nonmanagement positions, consider carrying a leather portfolio (again, with no handbag). There is not enough room in a portfolio for a clutch, but you can pack lipstick, comb, and wallet in your portfolio. The interviewer is much more impressed by a clean, unwrinkled resumé pulled from a portfolio than by a folded-up resumé pulled from a crowded handbag.

The Professional Wardrobe

The type of wardrobe discussed here will fit most business organizations. Whatever your age, basic clothing needs are applicable to most career women: the same primary outfit works equally well on a 20-year old and a 50-year old. Of course, the outfit will look entirely different because figures, faces, and attitudes vary, but *a traditional career wardrobe is almost universal*. The main consideration is to tailor the clothing to the figure type.

Here are some general guidelines for your professional wardrobe:

1. *Comfortable and well-fitting*. When clothes fit well, you don't have to think about them during the day. Improper fit creates a negative impression and makes the wearer look (and act) uncomfortable.

2. *Inconspicuous and noncompetitive*. Dressing inconspicuously means your clothing does not shout "I'm here!" When you enter a room, others should immediately become aware of *you;* not your clothing. In your mind, compare two individuals: a woman wearing a neutral-colored skirt and jacket and another woman in a brightly-colored, large floral print dress. Which outfit do you think you would remember? *That* is the whole point. It's not the clothing you want remembered—it is *you* and what you have to say which, in essence, is what you have to offer to your business.

3. *Chic*. Dressing for business does not mean foresaking chicness. Being "chic" is defined as "dressing smartly, even fashionably, but quietly." Your personal style *never* detracts from you and the business at hand.

4. *Appropriate for the situation and job*. When you're preparing to dress in the morning, ask yourself these questions:
   "What are my activities today?"
   "Whom will I be seeing?"
   "How do I want others to respond to me?"
   "What do I want to achieve?"

Once you have answered the above questions, dress accordingly. It will affect how people react to you and, most importantly, how you feel about yourself.

Starting your professional wardrobe doesn't require an enormous amount of money. You don't necessarily need such finery as cashmeres, the finest grade silks or the best melton wools. Even if your bank account can't accommodate that much now, you owe it to yourself to buy clothes that are made from the best fibers and fabrics you can afford as you assemble your planned wardrobe over a period of time.

If all you can afford right now is one suit—a skirt and matching jacket—*wear it every day*. That's preferable to dressing in a "polyester special" from the neighborhood bargain store. And it's not as terrible as it might sound. A secretary in Paris will buy an Yves St. Laurent designer suit which may have cost her two months' salary. Yet, she will wear it every day (keeping it drycleaned, of course) and she always looks "right." Settling for more clothes of lower quality will be more expensive in the long run.

Accessories such as scarves and belts will add immeasurably to your look. Lesser items like plain or small-patterned blouses, or a sweater for under the jacket can be purchased for relatively little money. So, although you are still wearing the same skirt and jacket, you can give them several very different looks.

Building a wardrobe and discovering what works best for you is a continuing educational process. It doesn't happen overnight. Furthermore, you will continue to add, cut back, and change according to changes in your career, so this plan should always be built in to your financial plans.

Building a professional wardrobe requires a plan, a method, similar to planning a meal. Just as you wouldn't go to the supermarket and purchase all the ingredients for your menu before checking what you already have on hand, you don't go clothes shopping before examining your needs and cross-checking what you already have. Your kitchen is probably better organized than your clothes closet. Usually, the kitchen is systematically divided into compartments: spices in one area (sometimes, even alphabetized); pots and pans, dishes, silverware, glassware, and so on all in specific areas. Such planning rarely extends to the clothes closet, and yet, it is just as important. Your plan should begin with a look at what you have now.

First, seperate winter clothes from summer clothes (depending on where you live; some areas have more distinct climate changes than others). Next, separate your garments into sections: coats, jackets, dresses, blouses, skirts, sweaters, pants, shoes, and boots.

Compartmentalizing accomplishes two goals:

1. *It isolates clothing bought as sets.* You see immediately how much more clothing versatility you have. For instance, you may have purchased a three-piece navy-blue suit (skirt, vest and jacket). Separating these items shows you that the navy jacket makes another outfit with your beige skirt; the navy skirt works well with a tweed blazer; and so on. When you mix and match, your clothes become much more interesting to you—and far more cost efficient.

2. *It illustrates gaps in your wardrobe.* You see your clothing strengths and weaknesses and what pieces you need to purchase. If you have many blouses, but few skirts, blouses will not be on your "need" list.

Your next step, the hardest one, is removing garments you never wear (no matter how good they are). Clothes you no longer wear have no relationship to the rest of your workable, professional wardrobe and, in fact, confuse your wardrobe plan. Give the garment away to a group or individual who can use it.

You have now reorganized your closet, separated winter clothes from summer clothes, and discarded useless items. How many different outfits can you make from your existing wardrobe?

Now, you begin to appreciate *color coordinating*. A rainbow of colors will not allow you to mix and match outfits as successfully as several neutral colors which work in harmony with each other. Neutral colors such as beige, brown, navy, black, white, and cream are the most practical. Also, solid colors work better than patterns for versatility. It is very difficult to mix patterns, but you may have some patterned clothes that combine well with many solids. Tweeds, however, can be combined easily with solids. For instance, a dark brown and beige tweed jacket works beautifully with a cream, beige, or dark brown skirt, or as a jacket to a tailored dress in any of these solid colors. Remember, you can add color by using small-print blouses or scarves.

If you feel you must have color, consider the deep greens or burgundies as your "neutral" color. Always bear in mind, however, that much of the research done on professional dressing has shown that the neutral colors give the best impression.

The following two lists give examples of a basic working wardrobe for both winter and summer.

Basic Winter Working Wardrobe

Wool coat—Chesterfield or wrap

Raincoat—Trench or Duster (may have removable lining)

1 matched suit—single- or two-button jacket and eased skirt

1 jacket—tweed

1 skirt

3 blouses—1 man-tailored, 2 silk or silk-like, 1 print; bow or drawstring neck

1 jewel-neck sweater

1 silk or silk-like dress

1 pair of trousers (if job permits)

2 pairs of medium-heel pumps

2 handbags (1 envelope, 1 shoulder)

1 wool or wool-blend dress

Basic Summer Working Wardrobe

1 winter raincoat (with lining removed)

1 linen-like suit

1 linen-like jacket (different color)

1 skirt

3 blouses

1 pair of trousers (if job permits)

1 2-piece cotton knit dress

2 pairs of pumps (plain and spectator)

2 handbags (1 envelope, 1 shoulder)

The Classic Look

A professional wardrobe is a classic wardrobe. In this context, "classic" means "clothes that are almost dateless and seasonless." A classic style is never out of fashion and, depending on the climate in which you live, it can be worn year-round. For instance, a light wool gabardine in a moderate climate knows no season. In climates whose temperatures do change radically, the fabrics change, but the style of these classics does not.

By contrast, contemporary clothes are those that are the pacesetters of fashion. They represent the "latest thing" in the fashion world. This type of dressing is expensive because the styles are in season for such a short time, then fade away to be replaced by a new, trendsetting look. More importantly, this type of fashion is generally not suitable for most professional wardrobes.

A way to achieve wardrobe versatility is through *fashion multiplication*. It means you can take one outfit, perhaps a skirt or jacket, and "multiply" it many times more into different outfits. This can really only be done with classic clothes. They allow you to look great with fewer clothes. Each season, as you have the money, you can add more pieces, thereby multiplying your wardrobe that many more times and also updating your look at the same time.

Fabrics are also an important consideration in a classic wardrobe. The very best fabrics are made from natural fibers: wool, cotton, or silk. Since they are also the most expensive fabrics, care must be taken in their upkeep. However, they last longer, fit the body better, and help to present your best image. Next on the list are the polyester blends. These combinations—in various percentages—of man-made and natural fibers are less expensive than 100 percent natural fabrics and can also look very good. The bottom rung of fabrics is stretch polyester which I do not recommend under any circumstances. In the long run, it costs you a great deal of money because it doesn't last, doesn't fit well, and gives the wearer a poor image. A good, well-constructed garment, made from fine fabrics, can generally be worn from three to five years—an excellent investment in your business future.

Accessories

Accessories are multi-purpose, multi-dimensional accents to your wardrobe. Some accessories, like handbags, shoes, and nylons, are necessities. Others, like scarves and jewelry, add zest and allow you to change your classic clothes so they don't always look the same. Careful use of accessories will multiply the number of different looks you can achieve with your basic clothing.

Using accessories will help you create an individual sense of style and add to your total look. At the same time, keep in mind that your accessories should not upstage you. Although accessories may be a relatively inexpensive part of your wardrobe and you may be inclined to purchase quite a few, be careful about the accessories you choose to put together. *Few* and *simple* are good words to remember with accessories. You do not want to create a "cluttered" look. The same rule of quality that applies to your clothing also applies to accessories: buy less and buy the best. This is particularly true of jewelry.

Shopping Considerations

Contrary to popular myth, not all women love to shop. For many, it is a tiresome and frustrating task. The following guidelines can make your clothes shopping trips more productive and less costly:

1. *Make a list.* You already know what you presently have in your wardrobe. Make a list of what you need to fill in gaps. Don't wander aimlessly from store to store. A list helps remove the temptation to make emotional buys you don't really need.

2. *Scout ahead.* Before actually spending any money, take some time to scout the various stores and boutiques to see what they have. You'll save time in the long run because you'll know *exactly* what is where. If you see an item that might be workable in your wardrobe, have the store hold it for a day or two. This gives you time at home to check if it's really a good buy for you and, if you are unsure, to think it over.

3. *Match fabrics and shades.* Snip color samples from a seam or hem of your garments, put them into a credit card holder wallet and carry them with you when you shop so you can easily mix and blend clothing you are buying with clothing you already own. You never realize how many shades of one color there are until you have brought home a navy blouse you were *sure* would exactly match a navy skirt at home, only to find it several shades off. With a sample, you can immediately see if the colors work together. Also, if you can, check the colors in *daylight* because store lighting can be deceiving.

4. *Check other departments.* If you are small, you can buy many garments such as jackets, skirts, and shirts in the teen departments. Many of the name clothing designers also style for the younger set, so you can have top quality fabric and construction for far less money than if you purchase in the women's department.

5. *Watch for sales.* Shop sales whenever you can. Be sure to follow your plan carefully when shopping sales or you may end up with bargains that don't work out well.

6. *Shop when you feel good and have adequate time.* You need to exercise good judgment when making expensive purchases. If you are hurried or overly tired, you are more likely to make mistakes. Also, shopping alone will allow you to operate on your schedule, not someone else's.

7. *Identify some reliable sales clerks.* Finding clerks you can trust to remember your preferences and call you when something comes in can be extremely helpful. They may also help you find creative ways to complete your wardrobe plan.

8. *Get a good fit.* Be sure that a garment fits you well. If a lot of alterations—aside from shortening cuffs or hems—are necessary, the cost of the garment rises considerably. Even if you sew to save alteration costs, too much altering may destroy the lines of the clothing so that it never looks right or fits properly.

9. *Returns are okay.* Finally, if after all your careful planning, you find you have made a mistake, do not be timid about returning the item. This is an accepted practice in most of the larger stores, so long as you do it right away, you have your sales slip, and the garment is not damaged in any way. Sales items, however, cannot be returned. Also, many smaller boutiques do not offer refunds, so be sure to check each store's policy on returns.

Some people truly enjoy the challenge of putting together a good looking wardrobe, but some do not. If you are in the latter category and your career choice requires a very professional appearance, it may be worth your time and money to seek help from a wardrobe consultant. Some large stores provide this service for the career woman or you may seek out a person who gives detailed, individual service (including analyzing your wardrobe and doing your shopping). You may make up the fee in time and money saved as well as a more attractive wardrobe. Look upon your working wardrobe as a business investment.

To Sum Up

Learning to create an attractive appearance is a career skill just like other career skills you've learned. Like other skills, it takes both knowledge and practice. This chapter has provided you with an overview of some of the major considerations of a professional appearance. If you need special help, this is an area where more detailed information and services are readily available. You will need to adapt it to your particular needs, however, since much of the advice is not aimed at a business-world image. There is no question that looking good helps you feel good. This, in turn, enhances your self-confidence and your performance.

chapter six

MANAGING
YOUR MONEY

How much time do you spend thinking about money? Where will your next money come from? What is more important to you than money? What *is* money? Money, in and of itself, is worthless, but the pursuit of money is one of the major reasons for wanting a career. And even though we may know deep down inside us that money is not a measure of our self-worth, it is a common standard by which we may be measured. How well you manage what you have is part of your personal effectiveness.

Money is a difficult and complex subject. In this chapter we will consider some very basic ideas about money and money management. For those with already well-developed money skills, the exercises and ideas may be only a review; for others, these concepts may be new and may represent the most terrifying skill of all to be mastered.

BASIC CONCEPTS OF MONEY
MANAGEMENT

Money Management Is Highly Individual

Money management is a skill in which you put some basic concepts to work but also deal with many exceptions and complications. There are no simple directions for everybody and every situation. There are, however, some general guidelines and concepts that you can tailor to your personal situation.

"I can't even keep my checkbook balanced!" is the lament of many. "How can I possibly learn to manage money?" Before you rationalize away the need for this skill with that excuse, it is important for you to understand that money management is *not* just a matter of bookkeeping. Some record-keeping is necessary but it is really only a part of good money management. Also, money management is *not* just learning to balance your spending with what you have coming in; it requires consideration of your values, circumstances, relationships, and aspirations.

Our attitudes about money are determined by many outside influences including the attitudes of parents, teachers, and others of significance, as well as by our religious beliefs and norms. These attitudes about money influence the way we behave and our emotional relationships with others. Personal finances are a sensitive, private topic for most people.

Money and Values

In order to develop money management skills, you must go back to your values, goals, and priorities. The decisions you make about money will only be comfortable only if they reflect your own value system. The fact that you have chosen, or are in the process of choosing, a career indicates something about your value system. So how are you going to spend the money you earn? How will your family want you to spend the money you earn? Value and value conflicts—we never escape them.

Try the exercise in Table 6-1 as a way of helping to determine some of your money values. Whether you recognize a pattern of repeated behaviors (values) or not, this does give you a picture of yourself as a spender. Then compare this with what you said were your life and career values in Chapter One. Once you recognize and affirm your values, you may better understand some of your financial decisions. This will also help you when you set financial goals and priorities. These decisions and goals will be far more comfortable for you if they are compatible with your values. Please remember: One person's "luxury" is another person's "necessity." The way people parcel out their money is totally individual and highly fascinating. There is not necessarily a right or wrong way to handle money—there are many different ways and many different solutions to solving money problems. Quite frankly, money management is a skill that may require your most *creative* thinking, not your most rigid.

Table 6-1 How You Spend Your Money

Instructions: Think about your expenditures for a three-month period of time. (Use cancelled checks, other records as a guide). After basic food, housing, transportation, and medical expenses, what were the main areas of expenditures? (Put in rank order.)

____ Self-improvement (hairdressers, lessons, health clubs, etc.)
____ Entertainment (movies, eating out, watching sports events, etc.)
____ Charitable or religious causes
____ Political causes
____ Clothing
____ Recreation, sports (health club membership, boats, sports equipment, etc.)
____ Furniture, artwork, other household items
____ Service to others (gifts, church, charitable contributions, etc.)
____ Education, books, magazines, newspapers
____ Family/home services (cleaning, gardening services)
____ Hobbies
____ Travel (including weekend trips, longer vacations, etc.)
____ Community causes and volunteer organizations
____ Savings or other financial investments (property, bonds, insurance, etc.)
____ Other (name)

---

1. How does your expenditure pattern fit in with the life and career values you identified earlier?
2. Which areas appear to have conflicts?

Consider what you want your life to be. Any financial plans you develop should be directed toward achieving the goals unique to you and your lifestyle. Your plan will then reflect your values, tastes, and needs within the confines of your resources.

Some Grim Statistics

In Chapter Twelve we will discuss some of the inequities for women in the labor force—some of these include pay and fringe benefits. You should be aware of some of the statistics developed by the U. S. Government Department of Labor as you begin to develop your personal financial management skills. First of all, women earn overall about 60 percent of what men earn. Yet statistics also show that the average female worker is as well-educated as the average male worker. Also, labor statistics show that a majority of women work because of financial need.

Women make up almost three-quarters of those persons living at poverty level. According to government statistics, in 1979, 42 of 100 families maintained only by a mother had incomes below the poverty level, compared to 15 out of 100 families maintained by the father only. Not having adequate money for necessities may make the entire area of financial management a totally frustrating one even though these skills are needed desperately by people at low income levels. Among the lowest income levels are divorced women with children and widowed and unmarried women over sixty-five. The ability to budget, deal with debt and credit, and set financial goals and priorities is especially important for these groups.

Seeking Professional Help

How laws affect you financially can be a highly complicated area which we will not explore in this book. But it is an area you will need some knowledge about or you may run into difficulties in financial management. As a general rule, if you have a legal question or problem, it is best to seek legal counsel. If you have no money, some free or low-cost legal aid may be provided in some areas. If you can afford a private lawyer, but do not have one at this time, try to find a friend or acquaintance who can refer you to one. The choice of a lawyer, like that of any professional, is not a simple matter. There is a lot you can learn only after you are actually in the relationship.

In addition to legal help, you may also need the help of an accountant or other kind of financial advisor. Although we are often reluctant to pay for advice, it is frequently less costly to seek help from an expert than to ask a friend or well-meaning amateur. You may need to check with your local or state Society of Certified Public Accountants or Certified Financial Planners.

When seeking any kind of professional advice, you may have to interview several people before finding the right one. One final piece of advice: personal feelings are important. Don't deal with someone who makes you uneasy, no matter how technically competent he or she may be. When selecting any or all of the professional advisors, base your confidence rating on:

1. References you can check out personally.
2. Your sense of the advisor's commitment to, concern with, and understanding of your particular needs and interests.
3. Your feelings of trust and confidence about the advisor.

Economic Independence

Economic independence and having control over one's money are reasons many women are now choosing careers outside the home. Economic independence is a worthy goal regardless of whether you are married or not. In fact, most of what we are discussing in this chapter concerns economic independence. Being economically independent does not necessarily mean that you yourself furnish all of the money for your household, although that can be the case. It may also mean having the ability to support yourself when necessary and having some control over money and property decisions that affect you. Many of the greatest value conflicts about money have come about in households where the husband works and the wife does not. Women who are in situations where they are totally dependent on someone else for financial support often lack interest in or knowledge about financial management, property rights, investments, and other aspects of financial management. The person providing the support may even have insisted upon control and secrecy in these matters. But even if you are not the major provider of financial support, you still need economic independence.

Once a woman recognizes that the responsibility for her financial affairs is really hers, she is on the way to learning good money management skills. Once she accepts this responsibility she will become more informed about laws and business practices, will be able to demand better legal and financial counsel, and will be able to plan ahead.

Wanting money is an acceptable attitude. Learning to accept reality and make the most of what you have is also an acceptable attitude. Money is a way to make the world work for us; money also gives us the power to change things. It is okay to *prosper*. The total amount of money you have is not the significant item—the attitude you have about it is.

DEVELOPING FINANCIAL PLANS

As a working woman you may now be juggling your financial resources in ways that are new to you. As a career woman you may not have the time to provide services to your family in the way you did when your work was primarily in the home. You may now want to buy the services, skills, and time of others to help you manage your home. You will need to develop a plan that is simple, flexible and workable.

You will need a plan that (1) tells you how to figure your net worth, (2) shows you where your income comes from and how much there is, (3) provides for basic needs, (4) provides for meeting financial goals, (5) provides for dealing with debts and savings, and (6) helps you acquire good money management habits.

Let's look at some of the steps for doing that.

Figuring Your Net Worth

One way to begin a financial plan is to figure out your *net worth*. Put simply, your net worth is the sum of all assets minus all liabilities—or what you would have if you sold everything and paid back all debts today. So a first step in estimating your net worth is to draw up a list of all of your assets and assign a reasonable current market value to each. Then make a list of all your liabilities (Figure 6-1).

Figure 6-1 Take an Inventory of Your Net Worth

Assets		Liabilities	
House (Market Value)	_____	House Mortgage Balance	_____
Auto (Market Value)	_____	Loan on Car	_____
Recreational Vehicles	_____	Loan on life insurance	_____
Savings Bonds	_____	Other loans	_____
Stocks & Bonds (Market Value)	_____	Other installment debts	_____
Real Estate other than home or ... other large assets	_____	Medical and dental	_____
Interest in business or profession	_____	Taxes owed	_____
Cash value of life insurance	_____	Current bills	_____
Cash value of pension plan .... (Amount you could withdraw now)	_____	Other _____	_____
Jewelry, Art Objects	_____	TOTAL	_____
Furniture and Appliances	_____		
Other _____	_____		
TOTAL	_____		

Total Assets .... _____
Minus total liabilities .... _____
Net Worth .... _____

A net worth statement is important for estate and retirement planning as well as for overall financial strategy. It will tell you whether you are building wealth or falling behind. It will also help you assess which assets perform best and which debts have climbed too high. You need this kind of information to manage your personal finances better.

Let's look at some specific items in figuring net worth:

1. *Putting a value on real estate and other property.* When it comes to putting a value on homes, cars, boats, and so on, it is the *market* value, not the replacement value, that counts. How much would somebody pay you for this item? That's what it's worth. Also, clothing and other personal effects are usually not included in the assets portion of your net worth statement.

2. *Looking at liabilities.* On the liability side, there's the mortgage balance on your home, outstanding balances on credit cards and charge accounts, gas bills, personal loans, loans against insurance policies, back taxes due, and so on. These may be easier to be precise about than assets, but they are frequently even more difficult to control than assets!

If you are assuming that because you are married, you don't have a "net worth," guess again. This is where you need to be familiar with your state's laws. You may share in the ownership of many things (including debts) and you may also have some of your own separate property.

Net worth statements should be updated at least once a year. Both assets and debts change. The update is an opportunity to review your finances, make changes, and add items you might have missed.

BUDGETING YOUR INCOME

Putting Budgeting into Perspective

For most of us the word "budgeting" is not one that makes our hearts leap with joy. In fact, for most people it brings about feelings of dread. Of course, there are those people who get a tremendous kick out of keeping detailed, precise financial records. But, frankly, this approach doesn't work very well for most of us. You are much more likely to follow a spending plan if you establish general categories, monitor them on a regular (but not necessarily daily or weekly) basis and allow yourself some changes and some failures.

But I do believe that you *should* follow a spending plan. Doing so will bring about some peace of mind and acceptance of the standard of living you can afford. If you can do this, you will have learned a great deal about accepting yourself.

Setting Up Goals

The best way to stay on track with a budget is to have some clearly defined financial goals in mind. Use your net worth statement to help you define annual financial goals and long-term goals. Establish some short-term goals and then set up your budget. Combined, your short-term and long-term goals will help you act out your values and give you an overall sense of money management. Let's begin the budget process by looking at your sources of income.

Looking at Your Paycheck

One of the major sources of income for most people is their paycheck. It is important that you understand the concept of *take-home pay* and also the assets and liabilities created by your deductions. *Take-home pay* is simply the amount of money you have left after deductions have been subtracted from your gross pay. Let's consider some of these deductions.

1. *Federal income tax.* Employers have certain IRS (Internal Revenue Service) regulations they must follow regarding money deducted from a paycheck for tax purposes, so you do not have total freedom to decide how much Federal income tax will be withheld. There are some variables, however, and you may want to get more detailed information from your payroll office on how to determine the number of exemptions to claim on your W-4 Form (Employee's Withholding Allowance Certificate).

2. *Social Security.* The benefits you receive from Social Security can be substantial (and to many people the amount deducted looks that way too!). Social Security tax rates change frequently, so you should be aware of this as you look at your paycheck to see if there are any errors. However, Social Security benefits provide a foundation for life insurance and retirement programs, so they have real significance in your financial plans for both the present and the future. Just briefly,

the benefits you are paying for with Social Security deductions are (a) retirement income, (b) disability income, (c) survivors' benefits, and (d) medical insurance protection beginning at age sixty-five.

For a detailed explanation of your Social Security benefits, contact the nearest Social Security office, where you can get informational booklets and answers to specific questions.

3. *Group insurance plans (life, health, disability, etc.).* Many employers provide some type of life and health insurance for their employees. In cases where the employee shares the costs of these programs, there may be some paycheck deductions relating to these programs. Most of these insurance policies are only in effect when you are in the employ of a particular firm. Should you quit working, you will no longer have the protection of these particular benefits.

4. *Retirement, pension plans.* Specific facts about your employer's pension or retirement programs must be obtained from your company. These plans are either contributory (you share the cost with your employer) or noncontributory (the employer pays the entire cost). If you are sharing the cost, you are usually entitled to take your share with you if you leave prior to retirement. If the company pays the full cost, you may not be entitled to any benefits until you are "vested" (that is, have been a member of a plan for a specified number of years).

It is a good idea to look at the provisions of the plan where you work. This could be worth a great deal to you someday and should be considered as you make future financial plans.

5. *Miscellaneous deductions.* In addition to the previously described deductions, there may be additional deductions for a variety of different programs. Typical of miscellaneous deductions are union dues, automatic savings plans, parking fees, charitable contributions, and so on. It is important that you understand what is being deducted—both the proper amount and where the deduction goes.

For women who haven't performed paid work previously or have not worked for a long time, the first paycheck with all of its deductions may be a real shock. In your mind you may have been thinking $1,000 a month only to have the actual take-home pay turn out to be $650. Like it or not, it's the $650 you need to work with for your budget, not the $1,000. If you are to be realistic about money management, there is one rule you must follow: *Be as honest as you can possibly be with yourself.* Don't exaggerate the facts and don't guess.

Developing Your Budget

A budget is an aid to help you spend your money wisely, meet your obligations, and reach your financial goals. Most people know approximately what they have to spend after taxes, but as we said before, approximations aren't good enough. Natural optimism often tends to inflate our notions of how much cash is really available.

Income: In Figures 6-2 and 6-3 you will find worksheets which will help you determine your net spendable income for a year—both "real" and planned. After you have figured your income, you are ready to go on to determining your fixed expenses.

Expenses: To determine expenses, go through your bills and checks for last year and see how much you spent for rent, clothing, repairs, entertainment. Put down everything you can itemize and then lump the rest together under a category entitled "unexplained expenses." Then divide the expenses you can identify into two categories: fixed expenses (those expenses which cannot be easily changed) and variable expenses (those expenses you have a little more control over).

The point of all of this, of course, is to have a little more income than expenses. This then allows you some money for investments, or other special purchases that fulfill some long-range goals. It also helps to figure a regular savings deposit as a regular fixed expense. This will help take care of emergencies, and if there's any left beyond that, you can apply it to your investment money.

Once you have figured your expenditures for the previous year, do the worksheet in Figure 6-3 which will be your budget projections. Your budget projections should be good estimates. This will be the plan you will try to follow.

A word of caution. Your first budget may not work out very well. If it doesn't, start over. Revise your limits. You may also want other family members to share in designing the plan so they can help make it work.

Considering General or "Unexplained Expenses"

It will be a great help to you if you have good records of general day-to-day living expenses. It is often in this area that the budgeting process breaks down. For example, if on Saturday you spent $30 at the

Figure 6-2 Budget Work Sheet (based on previous year)

Figure for the year; then divide by 12 for monthly budget.

	Annually	Monthly
I. Income		
Your earnings for the year	$	$
Other income (e.g. spouse's earnings, Interest and dividends, rents, royalties, etc.)		
TOTAL INCOME		
*Deduct state, federal and local income taxes		
*Deduct Social Security		
*Deduct other payroll deductions		
NET SPENDABLE INCOME	$	$

II. Expenses		
A. Fixed expenses		
Savings deposit	$	$
Mortgage/rent		
Utilities (heat, lights, phone, garbage, etc.)		
Insurance (auto, homeowners, health*, etc.)		
Loan Repayments		
Installment payments		
Child care/household help		
Dues		
Other		
B. Variable Expenses		
Food		
Clothing		
Medical		
Gasoline		
Entertainment		
Church/charities		
Vacations		
Gifts		
Books/magazines		
"General spending money" (unexplained)		
Other		
TOTAL EXPENSES	$	$

*Do not deduct if part of payroll deductions above.

DIFFERENCE BETWEEN INCOME & EXPENSES (if expenses are greater put number in parentheses)

Figure 6-3 Budget Plan (based on projections)

Figure for the year; then divide by 12 for monthly budget.

	Annually	Monthly
I. Income		
Your earnings for the year	$	$
Other income (e.g. spouse's earnings, Interest and dividends, rents, royalties, etc.)		
TOTAL INCOME		
*Deduct state, federal and local income taxes		
*Deduct Social Security		
*Deduct other payroll deductions		
NET SPENDABLE INCOME	$	$

II. Expenses		
A. Fixed expenses		
Savings deposit	$	$
Mortgage/rent		
Utilities (heat, lights, phone, garbage, etc.)		
Insurance (auto, homeowners, health*, etc.)		
Loan Repayments		
Installment payments		
Child care/household help		
Dues		
Other		
B. Variable Expenses		
Food		
Clothing		
Medical		
Gasoline		
Entertainment		
Church/charities		
Vacations		
Gifts		
Books/magazines		
"General spending money" (unexplained)		
Other		
TOTAL EXPENSES	$	$

*Do not deduct if part of payroll deductions above.

DIFFERENCE BETWEEN INCOME & EXPENSES (if expenses are greater put number in parentheses) hairdresser, then bought an $8 bottle of wine and a $25 gift for your mother, try to keep those expenditures separate so you can list them in the appropriate categories instead of lumping everything under "unexplained expenses." The more accurate you are in these records now, the more accurate you will be in planning your budget. After awhile you will get a better feel for how you are spending your money and this will give you some good information for making changes.

Also, it is really important that you be honest with yourself about your needs and habits. You can come up with a budget that looks very good on paper, but if it does not fit you and your family, it will not work. Remember, again, money management is a highly individual thing. There is no one right way or wrong way to spend your money.

Career Expenses

If you have not yet accepted a paid position, it is very important that you consider the costs of going to work when you look at your overall budget. Figure 6-4 shows you a worksheet you can use just for career expenses. It is often easy to overestimate the additional "net income" when another member of the family goes to work. The expenses go up also. However, it is important to remember that the second income may contribute more than just a little additional cash. Eating out more, buying more clothes, or obtaining household help may also serve as a pleasurable way to spend your money.

CONTROLLING YOUR BUDGET

Considering Problem Areas

Controlling wants versus needs is the constant budget battle. If you are having some problems with your expenses consistently rising faster than your income, you may need to look for ways to combat this. The American Bankers Association has set down ten questions that serve as signals to spot financial problems:

1. Do you use credit to buy many of the things you bought last year with cash?
2. Have you taken out loans to consolidate your debts or asked for extensions on existing loans to reduce monthly payments?
3. Does your checking balance get lower each month?

Figure 6-4 Financial Worksheet for Career Expenses

Expenses	At Present	If Employed
1. Wardrobe	$	$
2. Transportation		
3. Child care		
4. Personal grooming (i.e. laundry and cleaning, haircuts, etc.)		
5. Lunches (and family eating out)		
6. Convenience foods (family prepared - breakfast and dinner)		
7. Household help		
8. Social obligations (parties, office collections)		
9. Dues (professional organizations, including union dues)		
10. Witholding Income tax Social Security		
11. Other		
TOTAL MONTHLY	$	$

Above criteria should assist you in developing a bare bones budget and determine what salary structure you will need from your work.

4. You used to pay most bills in full each month, but now do you pay only the minimum amount due on charge accounts?
5. Although it rarely happened in the past, do you now receive frequent late notices from creditors?
6. Lately does the withdrawal column of your savings account have more and larger entries than in the past?
7. Are the chances of paying what you owe on your life insurance remote?
8. Do you depend on extra income to get you through the month?
9. Do you use your checking account reserve fund to pay regular monthly bills?
10. Are you juggling your rent or mortgage money to pay other creditors?

If you find yourself answering "yes" to any of these questions, your financial plan may have some trouble spots. Correcting some of these trouble spots will help you get back on track.

In addition to the ten questions used to spot spending problems, here is a checklist of early-warning signals which should help identify a mismanagement of income:

- Sudden difficulty in meeting your regular payments.
- Abuse of credit cards.
- Withholding information of a financial nature from your creditors.
- Lack of a regular savings program.
- Constantly adding to your debt level instead of a "peak and valley" credit pattern.
- No idea of the cost of living.

So where do you begin in the battle for control of your budget? Certainly some kind of system for controlling cash flow is needed. You probably need a minimum of two banking accounts: a checking account and a savings account. For families with more complicated spending patterns you may want more accounts than these (for example, household checking account, personal checking account, personal savings account). Even though you may be "sharing" income and expenses with another person or your spouse, I believe strongly that a woman should have her own personal checking account. Even if the amount you keep there is not large, there is a measure of economic independence derived from having some money that is completely under your control. There are many different kinds of institutions offering savings and checking accounts and other financial services. Shop for the institution that pays you the best return. It is also helpful to have that account be easily accessible. The primary criteria to consider when deciding on a financial institution are fees, convenience, and service.

Who Handles the Budget

Each family situation is different when it comes to handling money. But the main point is this: there should be at least one person whose responsibility it is to keep track of the income and the bills and prepare the budget sheets. This person does not necessarily have the sole say about how the money is spent, however. It is often a good idea in a situation where more than one person is contributing income and/or spending the money to trade off every now and then so all parties *know how* to take care of this matter. This is one of the necessary life skills to know if you wish to be economically independent

What To Do if You Just Cannot Stick to a Budget

If you have tremendous difficulty organizing to budget, your spending is compulsive, or there are other reasons why you just cannot stick to a budget, do yourself this favor: See if you can get into a plan in which a portion of your income is automatically deducted for savings. Starting such a program requires very little effort on your part and at least gives you some degree of financial comfort.

OBTAINING AND USING CREDIT

Credit—or the right to incur debt and defer payment for merchandise or services—has come to play a major role in our society. Credit comes in a variety of packages and at a full range of prices. Most people try to use credit with caution, knowing full well that it costs money to use credit. For many people, credit is almost a "necessity" and debt is not necessarily considered a curse. The key word when talking about credit is *manageable debt*. Manageable debt, secured for the right reason and responsibly handled, is an acceptable operating procedure.

Legal Considerations for Women

Now that the door to equal credit consideration for women is legally open, many more women are using credit as a part of their overall financial management plans. Because most credit bureaus have not carried credit histories in the names of both husbands and wives, many married women do not have a credit history in their own names. This fact can create a hardship if a married woman without a credit history becomes divorced or widowed. If you are a married woman, you may need to check this and establish your own credit history. This is another important aspect of economic independence.

What Happens When You Apply for Credit?

Imagine that you have just applied for a loan or a credit card. What criteria will the lending institution use to determine whether or not you deserve to receive credit? Some of the answers may surprise you.

Sometimes the credit assessment is done by a person assigned to that task; sometimes the assessment is done by a computer. Regardless of which way you are assessed, each system is based on the creditor's experience with previous customers. The criteria are based on characteristics that clearly distinguish between customers who paid as agreed and those who did not, and assign point values to specific attributes. For instance, one kind of assessment may consider the fact that you have a telephone in your house and a year-old car to be more important than your overall income and credit history. Most creditors keep their scoring criteria secret. This secrecy and the fact that scoring systems differ according to area and lender make it impossible to know precisely how you will be scored when you apply for credit. Most systems do attempt to measure three major areas, however:

1. character—your sense of responsibility and trustworthiness
2. capacity—your ability to repay the loan
3. capital—your assets to serve as collateral

What If You Are Turned Down?

If your credit application is rejected, don't give up. If you can find out why you have been turned down, that knowledge might help you get the decision reversed. Creditors must give you specific reasons and you may find that you simply made a mistake when filling out the application. One of the most common reasons for denial of credit is an incomplete application.

Knowing Your Limits

There is no simple way to determine just what your debt limits should be. Knowing how much you can afford depends a great deal on your own personal assessment. If you are experiencing some of the warning signals discussed earlier, you may need to revise your limits for yourself.

What should you do when you get in over your head? You will need help, but not just any help! Debt counseling can be a tricky business. Also realize that this is a problem for many people, not just for you. Almost everyone feels at least some emotional stress due to the pressures of inflation and recession or financial emergencies.

Probably one of the first and most helpful things to do is to find someone who can talk to you about the financial stress. This may be a professional or it may simply be a private person whom you trust in these kinds of matters. Finding some kind of support is important.

If you need to find a credit counseling service, check with your bank or credit union. If you do not find help here, write to the National Foundation for Consumer Credit, 1819 H Street NW, Washington, D.C. Other possibilities for resources may include the personnel department where you work, your union or your church.

Some Final Thoughts About Money

Although we have covered a number of aspects of personal financial management in this chapter, this is really just the beginning. There are many other areas of financial management you may want to investigate as you become increasingly sophisticated in your use of money: life insurance programs, investments, income shelters, tax shelters, and retirement plans are all areas to be considered. You may benefit by enrolling in a course in personal finance or personal investment. The possibilities are endless.

Financial considerations are a part of any good career plan and can give you greater flexibility when making career decisions. Whatever your circumstances, the opportunity to enjoy personal financial success starts within yourself and your ability to manage your financial assets the same way you manage other aspects of your career success.

chapter seven
MATCHING YOUR SKILLS TO THE JOB MARKET

Will an Employer Want What You Want?

Many women who have had successful experiences working for church or community volunteer groups will say when asked about their skills and work experiences: "I can't *do* anything, really. I don't know anything. Yes, I've done volunteer work, but that's not *real* work. I came back to school to brush up my typing so I could at least be qualified for some kind of job." Many women are simply not prepared to honestly evaluate what experiences, education and skills they may have that an employer would want. An honest appraisal of your skills and the job market are now necessary if you want your career plans to work successfully.

Up to this point you have been concentrating primarily on your private world—what you value, how you act, how you want to spend your time. This, of course, is the start of your professional development. Now you need to look at the realities of the work force in your community and at your own skills to see what career possibilities exist. The ideal match occurs when an employer needs what you enjoy doing well. Sometimes this is a simple process, but sometimes it is not.

YOUR JOB AND YOUR LIFESTYLE

Because you have certain natural aptitudes and a distinct personality of your own, you should choose a job and an organizational environment where these will be an asset. Otherwise, you may find the time spent on the job frustrating and depressing. For example, if you have trained to be an executive secretary and you are making a choice between taking a job in a social welfare office where you will be required to work primarily with "people" problems or a job in a manufacturing plant where your ability to work with data and machines is foremost, you need to examine what your personality and natural aptitudes tell you about the job. It is important to find a job that agrees with what you are as a person.

Equally important is finding a job that fits with your lifestyle and family relationships. The *American Heritage Dictionary* defines *lifestyle* as "an internally consistent way of life or style of living that reflects the attitudes and values of an individual or culture." Let's consider some specific aspects of lifestyle that can affect, and be affected by, your choice of job:

Work schedule. Being able to adjust your work schedule to your personal needs is a very big advantage. In fact, some people have been willing to accept lower pay in order to have a flexible working schedule. Generally speaking, the more your work interrelates with others you work with, the less flexible your hours are. Independent work usually has more flexible hours. Weigh this item carefully as it relates to your overall lifestyle.

Travel. Travel requirements can vary greatly depending on the industry, the organization, or the stage of career you are in. Most people have no problems accommodating three or four planned trips a year. In fact, this can make a nice break from the normal work routine and help keep you and your job stimulating.

Unscheduled travel or trips of long duration do have a definite effect on your lifestyle. Some people enjoy it and want it; others do not. Significant amounts of overnight travel do have an effect on your personal relationships. I have observed, however, that many women tend to be more concerned about travel and family relationships than is sometimes necessary. Quite likely, your family could get along without you for brief, planned periods of time.

Social and civic obligations. Some jobs may require that you represent your employer at civic events and organizations. Sometimes you may be expected to entertain socially. Be aware of an employer's policy on these matters so there is no misunderstanding after you take the job.

Seasonal or special work pressures. Each individual reacts differently to pressure. We will deal with overall job stress in a later chapter, but for our purpose here, think of this kind of work pressure as related to a busy season or special project. If you work for a retail sales organization, Christmas is an especially busy time. If you work for a school, there may be extraordinary pressures at the beginning or ending of a term. You alone can determine what kinds of pressures you can withstand, or, possibly, thrive on.

Bringing work home. Some jobs require occasional or frequent work at home. Again, see how this relates to your needs. Some people are willing to accept more rigid work schedules and assignments in order to avoid bringing their work into their personal lives. Others are able to mix work and personal lives in a self-fulfilling way.

Vacation time. The main things to consider about vacations are how much vacation time you will get, when you can take it, and whether you can take more time off without pay if you wish to. For example, if you like vacations in March and April, you should think twice before taking a job in an accounting office with a heavy tax practice; if you like to have Christmas vacation, working for a department store may not fit in well with your vacation plans. If you want to be able to take an extended trip some time, you need to find out if your organization can accommodate that, too.

Sometimes more flexible vacation times are available as you gain more longevity in an organization. Look at vacation time as affecting your lifestyle over the long term.

Personalities at work. Although there are many kinds of personalities in every field, you may want to decide what overall interests and common traits appeal to you among such individual groups as bankers, lawyers, engineers, artists, teachers, etc. Because you will spend a large portion of your time with them, you want to feel comfortable with those in your career field.

One final idea to remember about your career and your lifestyle—your career is part of your lifestyle and some of the personal parts of your lifestyle will have to adjust to the demands of your career. Again, you need to understand the trade-offs and compromises just as you did with goal setting and time management. Having your cake and eating it too may require a smaller piece of cake!

CHARACTERISTICS OF THE JOB MARKET

What Would You Really Like to Do?

A job that is ideal for one person may be a source of misery for another. You have already discovered through identifying your values and goals that you are a unique individual. Before you force yourself to confront the hard reality of "What can I do?" and "What's available right now?", let's do an exercise designed to help you determine some of the characteristics of your "ideal" job. Look at Figure 7-1 and follow the directions given there.

Figure 7-1 Characteristics of Your Ideal Job

Below is a list of characteristics you might look for in a job. Check the category that rates the characteristic for its importance to you.

Characteristic	Extremely Important	Quite Important	Moderately Important	Somewhat Important	Not Important
Always Busy					
Challenging					
Detailed					
Demanding					
Exciting					
Financially Rewarding					
Fun					
Physically Active					
Precise					
Prestigious					
People-Oriented					
Quiet					
Routine					
Secure, Stable					
Stimulating					
Unpressured					
Varied					
Verbal					

1. How does this compare to the career values you established in Chapter One?

2. Name some jobs you think would fit your ideal characteristics.

If you still haven't decided precisely what you want to do, don't worry about it. You may actually be in a better position because of your flexibility. Also, sometimes it is worth trying several things to really find out what you *do* and *do not* like to do.

98

Analyzing Career Economics

As long as you work and live in the United States or Canada you will be selling your services in the labor market. No matter what you have to sell, you must find somebody willing to buy it.

One of the basic economic principles that applies to careers is that of supply and demand. Also important is an understanding of how the economic decisions of our political leaders affect the labor market. For example, in the late 1950s and 1960s there was a shortage of schoolteachers. Many people entered this occupation at that time, and large numbers of college students willing to enter teaching received government loans and grants. Now there are many more persons trained to teach than there are teaching positions to be filled, and that career field is much more difficult to enter. On the other hand, the 1980s is a time of intense demand for highly skilled, executive level secretaries. Both of these fields have been affected by the laws of supply and demand and the economic decisions of political leaders.

Also, it is possible for some jobs to become totally obsolete with changing technology and the changing needs of society. It is always a good idea to have an overall awareness of national economic and labor trends.

Increasing Your Employability

In order to make enlightened career decisions, you need to find out as much as possible about career fields and specific jobs you may be interested in. The public library, many school libraries and counseling centers have copies of the *Occupational Outlook Handbook*. This book, published by the U.S. government, describes thousands of specific jobs along with information about salaries, skills and education needed; customary benefits; and anticipated demand for workers. The reference librarian or counselor can give you extra help with this invaluable book, if you need it. Talking to prospective employers, career counselors, teachers and other professionals trained in career development areas can be very helpful. This will give you ideas about what skills and training are especially desirable to employers. When an employer considers hiring you, the decision will be based primarily upon your training and your ability to handle the job.

It is easy to have mistaken notions about what people actually do on a job. Movies, TV shows, books and other media often depict certain careers in a very stereotyped way, and usually fail to show what kinds of skills are really needed. For example, lawyers are often shown in court, with little emphasis on the hours of research and writing necessary for that court appearance. Secretaries are frequently depicted as bubble-headed flirts who spend their time talking on the phone, filing their fingernails or reading novels, not as hardworking professionals who must be skilled at taking care of detail, preparing documents, making systems work, and organizing tasks. It may be worthwhile for you to interview someone who holds the kind of job you are interested in to find out what he or she really does and what kinds of skills and training are needed. In fact, before you are finished trying to match your skills to a job, you will need to identify what skills and training are needed.

Consider what type of organization the job is in, what activities and skills are involved, necessary educational background, and the various physical and psychological demands that are made on the employee. In addition, weigh the effect the job and its salary would have on your lifestyle and values.

Table 7-1 Observation of a Job's Activities and Environment

Title or position _____
Place of employment _____ Location _____

1. What type of organization is this job in?
2. What activities are a part of this job?
3. What kinds of skills did the person (or persons) who holds the job have?
4. What kind of tools or equipment are used?
5. What are the physical demands of the job?
6. What are the psychological demands of the job?
7. What are the working conditions (physical environment) like?
8. What kind of education is needed for this job?
9. What pressures or demands are made?
10. What are the chances for (a) travel, (b) advancement, (c) on-the-job training, and (d) educational benefits?
11. What is the salary range for this position?
12. How would this type of job affect your current lifestyle? Future lifestyle?
13. How would this job contribute to or affect your values?

PERSONAL SKILLS YOU CAN
OFFER AN EMPLOYER

In Chapter One you did an exercise that allowed you to identify some of your personal strengths. Undoubtedly, each of these personal strengths will be useful in your career. However, certain characteristics seem to be essential to almost all kinds of work—a sense of responsibility, efficiency, flexibility, cooperativeness, objectivity—in other words, many of the attributes of a professional attitude described in Chapter Four. In order to define more specifically what personal skills you have now and which ones you need to work on, try the exercise in Figure 7-2.

If you have answered honestly and most of your answers were "very well" or "well" in the *HOW WELL* categories and "almost always" or "frequently" in the *HOW OFTEN* categories, you have many valuable personal skills to give an employer. Those statements which you checked "not very well" and "only occasionally" or "never" are the personal skills you may want to work on in the future. Also, if you feel comfortable doing so, ask someone whose judgment you trust to rate you in the Personal Skills exercise. This feedback can also give you a more complete picture of your personal skills.

FUNCTIONAL SKILLS YOU CAN
OFFER AN EMPLOYER

Besides personal skills, there are many functional skills you already have that you can use in many jobs or fields that interest you. Sometimes these are also referred to as "transferable" skills because you can transfer them from one job situation to another. In Figure 7-3 there is an exercise that will help you identify your functional, transferable skills. These, combined with your personal skills, give you a picture of what you can do for an employer. Before you do that exercise, however, stop for a minute and think about some general functional skills—verbal skills and mathematical skills. Your potential effectiveness in a career may depend a great deal on how well you write, speak, and work with numbers. Give these skills special consideration when you evaluate your functional skills. If you have weaknesses here, you should make some special efforts to improve them. These skills are vital for success in most careers.

Figure 7-2 Personal Career Skills

After you read each statement, rate yourself for both how well and how often you have performed these.

	HOW WELL HAVE I DONE THIS				HOW OFTEN HAVE I DONE THIS			
	Very Well	Well	Fair	Not Very Well	Almost Always	Frequently	Occasionally	Never

Responsibility

1. I have taken full responsibility for the handling of some financial matter.

2. I have completed assigned tasks within the deadlines required.

3. I have completed jobs as promised even when it was inconvenient for me to do so.

4. I have seen projects through to the end even when I was bored or frustrated with them.

Efficiency

1. I have established systems to handle daily tasks.

2. I have kept my appointments punctually.

3. I have organized other people's efforts successfully.

Flexibility

1. I have been able to change my social schedule and accommodate unexpected guests or change of plans.

2. I have changed direction on a project when a better direction was suggested.

3. I have reconsidered my opinion about something when a good argument or information was given.

4. I have been able to leave some tasks half done when a more important one arrived.

Cooperation

1. I have worked with others in committees or group activities.

2. I have been able to accept another person's decision even when different from my own.

3. I have been able to work for, or under, the direction of someone else.

4. I have been able to work with persons I did not like.

5. I have accepted criticism of myself without becoming defensive and angry.

Objectivity

1. I have understood the difference between evaluating the competency of a person apart from his/her personality.

2. I have recognized what was easy and what was difficult for me.

3. I have kept confidences.

4. I have argued or kept silent according to the needs of the moment.

102

Now go through the lists of functional skills presented in Figure 7-3. This will be your appraisal of the transferable skills you have. Try to be honest in your appraisal. As with the previous exercise, it may be helpful to find someone else to rate you as well. It is a rare person who can perform well in all areas. Furthermore, it is not necessary to be able to perform in all areas. This comprehensive list is provided so that you can begin to see specific skills you have. You may notice that some skills fall into more than one category. Mark the skill if you have used it in that category. Please feel free to add any that are not listed.

You have now completed a major part of your skills self-assessment. By combining your strongest personal skills with your strongest functional skills, what you can offer an employer should become clearer to you. After we consider your education and training you should be able to complete the picture of what you have to offer.

EVALUATING YOUR EDUCATION

Formal education can be a definite asset to you when seeking a career. Even if you do not take training in the specific area you eventually work in, formal education can provide you with the confidence and understanding necessary for a life-long career.

Assessing your formal education can be difficult because many people think of their education as courses taken, such as English 101 or History 250, instead of defining the skills learned and the knowledge acquired. If you have difficulty seeing how your schooling relates to an employment situation, you need to concentrate on this area.

Ask yourself the following three questions and jot down your answers on a piece of paper you can refer to again:

1. What parts of my formal education will be useful for a career? (e.g., English composition, mathematics, typing, etc.)
2. What other training have I had that could relate to a career? (e.g., leadership workshops, learning to use equipment, etc.)
3. What information or self-education have I acquired that would be valuable in a job assignment? (for example, how-to-do-it manuals, home study courses, TV courses, planned reading, and so on)

Formal training is not the only way to acquire job skills, but it is an important way. The combination of technical theory obtained in

Figure 7-3 Functional Skills

TYPE OF SKILL	Do Very Well	Some Ability	Limited Ability	No Ability
Manual Skills (Working with your hands)				
Constructing				
Assembling				
Fixing or repairing				
Finger dexterity				
Operating tools				
Operating machines				
Operating vehicles				
Typing				
Operating business machines				
Other:				
Follow-Up Skills				
Memory for detail				
Working well under pressure				
Making and using contacts effectively				
Following instructions				
Getting things done				
Implementing decisions				
Enjoy repetition				
Keeping records				
Recording information				
Organizing information				
Filing materials				
Other:				
Using Numbers				
Taking inventory				
Remembering numbers (eg. phone numbers)				
Calculating/computing				
Money management				
Keeping financial records				
Bookkeeping				

TYPE OF SKILL	Do Very Well	Some Ability	Limited Ability	No Ability
Budget planning				
Cost analysis				
Other:				
Influencing Skills				
Encouraging others				
Selling ideas				
Selling products				
Fund raising				
Getting groups to work together				
Promoting ideas				
Negotiating				
Other:				
Performing Skills				
Demonstrating products				
Modeling				
Public speaking				
Playing a musical instrument				
Acting				
Sports				
Lecturing				
Other:				
Communication Skills				
Reading				
Editing and proofreading				
Transcribing dictation				
Translating foreign language				
Writing letters				
Writing reports				
Writing speeches				
Writing promotional material				
Reporting accurately				
Taking minutes of meetings				
Instructing, explaining concepts				

Table 1 (left form)

TYPE OF SKILL	Do Very Well	Some Ability	Limited Ability	No Ability
Using visual aids				
Other:				
Helping Skills				
Caring for children's physical needs				
Caring for adults' physical needs				
Anticipating needs				
Exhibiting tolerance for others				
Helping with personal problems				
Listening carefully				
Conveying warmth and sincerity				
Problem-Solving Skills				
Researching				
Gathering information				
Analyzing information				
Diagnosing				
Putting things in order				
Testing				
Evaluating				
Other:				
Intuition Skills				
Using imagination				
Improvising				
Inventing				
Experimenting				
Showing foresight				
Quickly sizing up people/situations				
Showing insight				
Other:				
Artistic Skills				
Adept at coloring things				
Creating original designs				
Restoring				
Visualizing concepts				

Table 2 (right form)

TYPE OF SKILL	Do Very Well	Some Ability	Limited Ability	No Ability
Photographing				
Drawing				
Illustrating				
Drafting				
Other:				
Leadership Skills				
Taking initiative				
Searching for additional responsibilities				
Working without supervision				
Initiating change				
Problem solving				
Dealing with unexpected crisis				
Taking risks				
Making decisions				
Leading groups				
Motivating groups				
Making policy				
Developing programs				
Directing others				
Evaluating				
Other:				

1. What do you consider your most outstanding functional skills?

2. What skills do you want to improve?

Adapted from "Functional Skills," an unpublished document, by Kathleen Beem, Developmental Education Instructor, Edmonds Community College, Lynnwood, Washington.

formal education with work and general life experiences usually yields the most skill and knowledge. Many employers use educational criteria as a screening device to help sort through large numbers of job applicants. A college education is not a requirement for many careers, but it is a definite asset. It provides a formal, specific way of telling an employer what you know and may also be helpful when advancing or changing jobs.

Lifelong Learning

One of the best ways to stimulate personal and professional growth is to learn from and with other people. No longer is education something you pursue only when you are young. Our rapidly changing society with its expanding technology, complicated environmental problems, and everchanging laws and governmental regulations has brought about a commitment by many businesses and colleges to continuous training or "lifelong learning." This learning can take a number of different forms: independent study, in-service or "in-house" training, and more formal study.

Going Back to School

Continuing your formal education can be an ongoing process and an enjoyable one. Frequently, meeting and working with other people in a structured setting such as a classroom can discipline you in ways you could not do on your own. I truly believe one of the best ways to keep skills current, make good professional contacts, enhance your social life, and keep your mind open to new ideas is to return to the classroom. Many employers encourage this and will even pay your way. Others will recognize your initiative and willingness to grow even if they do not sponsor tuition-reimbursement plans. Continuing your education also helps to change conditions for you if you consider yourself to be underprepared and inexperienced. It helps people to change careers, deal with everyday problems, work to improve the community, and, most important of all, serves as a source of personal growth and pleasure.

One of the most enjoyable parts of my job is to watch students come together in a classroom and form relationships. Many of these relationships turn into good friendships and valuable professional contacts. They learn from each other's experiences and serve as supports for each other. Later on they may help each other find jobs.

Many long-established institutions of higher education, in addition to private firms and professional and community groups, offer a wide variety of courses. These, combined with opportunities for independent study, can meet almost any need. Even degree programs are now more available to persons with varied backgrounds, and, in some instances, independent learning and job experience may be credited toward a degree. In addition, more schools now accept part-time students, making it much easier for a woman with a family to pursue further education.

The college scene can be confusing, so once you decide to pursue a degree there are some questions you should ask to help you determine the quality of the program and the college.

- Is the college accredited?
- What resources are available in addition to the classes? (for example, placement service, counseling center, etc.)
- Are the credits earned transferable to other institutions?
- Are there requirements for a degree in addition to regular classes? (for example, internships)

Whether you choose a traditional program (such as those at colleges and universities leading to associate's degrees, bachelor's degrees, and graduate degrees) or nontraditional programs such as vocational certificate programs, community service or adult continuing education courses, or workshops and seminars, you will find a number of resources are available. Education can enrich your life in many ways. Returning to the classroom is an especially good way to improve your reading, writing, mathematics, and business skills, as well as learning about new equipment and procedures. Many adults discover that learning to read with greater comprehension, dealing with math anxiety, or giving an oral report is a much different experience as an adult learner than it was as a young student. Furthermore, the age range of today's college student is wide. I've had students ranging in age from 17 to 62 in the same class—and all enjoying each other very much. So don't ever think of yourself as "too old" to be a student.

Taking Tests

In some instances, employers may require you to take a test or a series of tests which indicate specific aptitudes, personality traits, and interest patterns. The tests most commonly given are those indicating intelligence or general aptitude. This testing may be part of the application procedure for a specific job.

If you have been to school recently, you are probably used to taking tests. If you have been away from school for some years, you may be apprehensive about the testing process. *Don't let tests scare you.* They are only one indicator out of many regarding your ability to perform on a job. None of the commonly used tests require advance preparation.

Many tests have time limits. When they do, you should be told how much time you will have to complete the test. Listen carefully to the instructions you receive. If you do not clearly understand what you are expected to do, be sure to ask questions. The time for questions, however, is *before* the test begins. Do not spend much time on any one question; instead come back to difficult or time-consuming ones after you have completed the others. Also, it is often better to follow your original inclinations on multiple-choice or true-false tests than to mull over the question a long time and possibly read into it implications that are not really there.

Once the test is over, do not reproach yourself for not doing better. Employers do not regard your score as an infallible measure of your abilities. A test is only one indication of your capacity to do the job.

PUTTING YOUR SKILLS TOGETHER

Let's do a summarizing exercise to put together what you have defined so far. Remember the "ideal" job you defined in Figure 7-1? Look at the job you indicated as closest to your ideal. What personal skills are required to do that job? What functional skills? What formal education? Write these down on one side of a piece of paper. Then across from these required skills and education, write down your outstanding personal and functional skills and your applicable formal education. Then answer the following questions:

1. What skills and education areas match as you compare the two columns?
2. What skills are required for your ideal job that you have not yet developed?
3. What formal education do you need?

Now you should have a fairly clear picture of what skills you have and need for your ideal job. Now let's consider how this matches the job market.

WHERE THE JOBS ARE

You have defined your ideal job and assessed your skills and education; now you are really looking at what is available. The job market is continually changing. New careers are opening up and others are being phased out. Keeping up with the changing job market can be difficult, but there are places where you can receive guidance.

Traditional Sources

Although most people are aware of traditional sources of jobs, sometimes we hesitate to use them. You may be hoping that a job finds you instead of the other way around. While that occasionally happens, you really can't depend on it. The most common places to search for jobs are:

1. Employment agencies, public and private
2. Career placement services—at colleges and some other organizations
3. Personnel offices of large companies
4. Newspaper want ads; ads in magazines and professional journals
5. Union hiring halls

All of these sources have advantages and disadvantages, but all have been good sources for people entering the job market. Some of the activities at the end of the chapter will help you explore these sources further.

Nontraditional Job Sources

When you say to a friend or relative, "I'm looking for a job—let me know if you hear of anything," you are using a nontraditional job source, sometimes called *the hidden job market*. Many career placement professionals estimate that more than half of all jobs are found through personal contacts—the "who-you-know-not-what-you-know" method of job seeking.

In the past, the hidden job market has been much more widely and effectively used by men than by women. Sometimes known as the "old boy" system, this method has been used not only by business executives but by men in all professions and trades. Women are now starting to see how similar cooperation among women can be helpful for career development. We will discuss this topic in depth in Chapter Fourteen but you should be aware now that personal contact systems can be one of the best sources of jobs.

In order to get started with the personal contact system, write down the names, addresses, and phone numbers of people who may be able to give you job leads. Don't limit this list to your best friends and immediate family; try to think also of neighbors, teachers, store owners, former classmates, etc.

Once you have in mind what you can do and the kind of job you are looking for, make your contacts. Keep in mind that you are not asking your contacts for jobs; you are really asking for suggestions of places to look and people to ask. Then when you contact their suggested sources, you can use your original contact's name for a comfortable opening. For example, you might say something like, "My uncle, Joe Brown, suggested I call you about a possible opening in your accounting department." If, at that point, the source does not have an opening, you can then say, "Do you have any suggestions as to where else I might look?"

After you have contacted an individual, make notes about your conversations so you will not get mixed up later. When you find a job, let your contacts know and thank them. Also, keep your list and add to it. You may need it again sometime.

Planning Your Strategy

If you have followed the suggestions and completed the exercises up to this point, you are probably ready to launch your new job campaign. The next three chapters will give you specific ideas for the tools and information you need to do this. Think of yourself as a skilled, competent person. A good employer somewhere needs your skills and talents.

chapter eight
PREPARING JOB SEARCH CORRESPONDENCE

Not Everyone Who Applies for a Job Is Interviewed

In today's market it is not unusual for more than a hundred people to compete for the same job. Preparing the written communications you will need for a job search is an extremely important aspect of the job search process and needs both time and careful effort. Professional-looking employment papers are a valuable career tool.

THE RESUMÉ AS A BASIC JOB SEARCH TOOL

What Is a Resumé?

Resumé is a French word meaning "summary." A job applicant's resumé is a concise, one-page (usually) presentation of the skills, work experience, education and other qualities which qualify him or her for a job. A resumé is usually accompanied by a letter of application, and the purpose of the combination is to get the writer invited for an interview.

A resumé is also sometimes called a data sheet, qualifications summary, or work history. The four terms are often used interchangeably, although technically, a slight difference in emphasis may characterize each. For example, a work history would emphasize previous work experience, and a qualifications summary interprets background in terms of qualifications for a specific job.

One minute is not a very long time. That's approximately how long it takes to scan a page of typing or a resumé. So, as an applicant you have about 60 seconds to get past the first hurdle of getting a job: to convince the person screening applicants that you deserve fifteen to sixty minutes of an interviewer's time.

A Hypothetical Situation

Imagine for a minute the task of the clerk in the personnel office of a large insurance firm. A supervisor in the Claims Department has furnished a list of minimum qualifications and requested the names of five candidates to interview for a secretarial opening. The Personnel Department files contain several resumés and letters of application for secretarial jobs, and several more are received in response to an advertisement placed in a daily newspaper. The clerk now has a total of 65 resumés and letters of application to review.

If you were the clerk facing this problem, what would be your first concern? Probably, "How can I eliminate 60 of the resumés in this stack?" Even if you gave each resumé-and-letter-of-application combination only two minutes, you would be working over two hours on this project of finding five candidates to be interviewed! It is obvious that your task is going to be *negatively* rather than *positively* oriented; you are trying to *eliminate* applicants down to a group of five.

Your resumé thus has a tough job to perform. It must convince the person who first reads it that you are deserving of a closer look. Your resumé may end up in the reject pile if it doesn't present the necessary qualifications; has errors in spelling, typing, punctuation; is poorly organized; looks as though it is a chore to read; and hides rather than highlights the requested skills. Your goal is to have your resumé end up in the "little" pile—to be one of those five who will be called for interviews.

Why Is a Resumé Valuable?

The task of preparing an effective resumé is not an easy one; a good resumé requires a great deal of thought and effort and time. Many people dread the thought of doing the work required. They tell themselves a resumé really isn't *that* important because the company will have applicants complete an application blank, and that nobody ever got a job just because of a resumé because *skills* are what really matter. They are kidding themselves! The truth is that no one in our hypothetical situation even got asked for an interview without a resumé. Remember, you have spent years living your life and acquiring the skills you have to offer; now you must present them effectively in approximately 200 words. It makes sense to spend several days preparing the device which is usually needed to get you an interview. Without resumés there are usually no interviews; without interviews there are definitely no job offers.

Telling someone who needs your skills that you exist is one reason for preparing a resumé. It's not enough just to have good skills; you have to make someone who needs your skills aware of you. Don't consider the resumé an unnecessary duplication of the information asked for on a company's job application form. On the resumé you are able to present the information in the format and in the order you want and with the emphasis that is best for you. You are not restricted by the printed application form.

Another useful aspect of the resumé is that it helps you organize yourself for job interviews. It can be very embarrassing to be asked by an interviewer the dates you worked for a company and find yourself trying to remember if it was from 1959 to 1963? ... or was it 1958 to 1964? ... (you know it was before your oldest son was born, but ...). Even though you are talking about your own life and not some obscure date in a history book, it's easy to get confused and find your interview jitters compounded by a small thing like forgetting exact dates. Preparing a resumé will help you mentally put your past in order and make those dates stand out in your mind. You can also have a copy of your resumé with you during the interview, just to be sure. So, an effective resumé does the following:

- presents your qualifications to a potential employer in such a way that he or she is sold on the idea of interviewing you
- makes you aware of your value as a potential employee
- organizes you for job interviews

That's a big order!

The work you have done in the previous chapters will now come in very handy. I will assume you have identified your values, skills, and talents and have matched them to the job market so that you now have a specific job in mind. Because you have a target, your resumé preparation task will be much easier.

What Do You Have to Offer?

Now that you have an idea of what characteristics a valuable employee would possess, you need once again to concentrate on what you have to offer. You may be like many other people in that your skills and abilities far exceed your own opinion of them. Take a good look at what you have done and what you can do. Don't be too modest; be fair to yourself. In Chapter Seven you evaluated your personal skills, functional skills, and education with a specific job in mind. Let's use those worksheets to prepare a resumé that will present this information to a prospective employer in terms of what he or she will consider most relevant.

Organizing and Writing Your Resumé

Resumés are as individual as the people who prepare them—there is no single correct way to organize a resumé. A thoughtful analysis of your strengths and weaknesses with respect to a specific job will help determine the general format that will work best for you. We will limit the types of format discussed to the most basic ways of organizing your resumé; there are many variations and individual touches.

1. *Chronological Organization.* Historically this has been the most commonly used organizational pattern. Previous jobs and education are listed by date, with the most recent given first. Figure 8-1 shows an example of a chronological resumé giving Amy Nelson's qualifications as a medical secretary. She chose to highlight her education by placing it first.

Her resumé looks easy to read because of the abundance of white space, concise entries, and variety in line beginnings. She includes the items on her attendance to indicate her dependability.

The gap of six months between her jobs is obvious when she uses the chronological resumé format. (She traveled in Europe before attending summer school as a full-time student.)

The advantages of the chronological format are:

- It appears "normal" to screeners because it has been so widely used
- When shown by consecutive dates, your previous work experience can

Figure 8-1 Chronological Resume Format

AMY NELSON
426 Second Avenue
Lynnwood, WA 98036
321-4630

Job Objective: Medical Secretary

EDUCATION

June, 1981   Medical Secretary Certificate -- Edmonds Community College

45 credit hours including the following specialty courses:

medical terminology   medical forms typing
medical office procedures medical transcription
medical law and ethics   first aid and safety
business letter writing

June, 1978   Diploma and Certificate of Proficiency in Office Skills --
Lynnwood High

(courses included general business and secretarial skills)

OFFICE SKILLS AND EQUIPMENT

ACCURATE TYPING: 60 wpm
SHORTHAND: 90 wpm
MACHINE TRANSCRIPTION: 25 wpm
ELECTRONIC CALCULATOR: by touch
IBM ELECTRONIC 60 AND MEMORY TYPEWRITERS

WORK EXPERIENCE

Sept., 1980 - present   Medical Records Center Clerk - Stevens General Hospital
Edmonds, WA 98020

Responsible for duplicating, filing, and retrieving
patients' records, staff and patient contact, typing
and telephones. Worked full-time while attending
school. Missed only one day of work due to illness.

June, 1978 - March, 1980   Sales Clerk - Sweet Sixteen Dress Shop
Edmonds, WA 98020

Responsible for sales, opening the store, daily cash
log, and inventory. Excellent customer relations
skills. Missed only two days of work due to illness.

Figure 8-2 Functional Resume Format

MALRENE PRATT
23064 - 32nd West
Machias, Washington 98201

331-6249

CAREER OBJECTIVE   Permanent position with growth potential in Traffic
or Transportation Industry in the Pacific Northwest.

EXPERIENCE

Physical Distribution   Responsible for receiving and unloading
activities, physical counts, processing and
expediting orders, loading, and shipping.

Traffic   Arranged for traffic transportation to
consumer locations (national and
international), scheduled shipments to
coordinated with production, coordinated
shipment with carrier, rated commodities,
traced shipments, and monitored "hot loads."

Customer Relations   Processed O.S. & D. claims and maintained and
promoted good customer relations.

OTHER RELEVANT SKILLS   Typing, Telex, office machines, payroll, accounting,
filing, timekeeping, switchboard communications,
two-way radio, inventory control records, rate and
tarrif maintenance, freight bill auditing, inside and
outside sales, tractor/trailor operation.

EDUCATION   Associate of Technical Arts Degree
Edmonds Community College
Major: Transportation
G.P.A.: 3.37

PROFESSIONAL LICENSES   Combination Driver's License, D.O.T. Medical
Examiner's Certificate, Advanced First Aid
Certificate, C.P.R. Certificate

appear steady and continuous, and regular increases in responsibility can be shown

- The interviewer gets an overall impression of your life based on what you were doing during specific periods
- You will find it easier to write because you won't have to analyze your experiences very thoroughly to pick out pertinent skills and abilities—just list them by dates

Some disadvantages of the chronological resumé are:

- Skills and abilities pertinent to the job may not be emphasized unless your last job also emphasized them
- "Holes" (non-working periods) will really be apparent
- If your previous work experience has all been in the same field, you may not appear qualified for a different field
- Your resumé may not be distinguishable from many other resumés because it's in a traditional format

2. *Functional Organization.* In recent years a new format has been used more widely. Rather than organizing entries by dates, previous employers' names or job title, the functional resumé is organized under headings which name the skills and abilities of the applicant. Names and dates of previous employment are not emphasized and in some cases are not listed at all.

The advantages of the functional resumé are:

- Your skills and abilities for the specific job are stressed
- "Holes" in your work history are not as apparent as they are on a chronological resumé
- It's easier to apply for a job in a new field because you are not "typecast" by your previous jobs
- The fact that some of your abilities were developed in non-paid employment is not emphasized
- A nontraditional approach to resumé writing may be what you need to set you apart from the other applicants
- The fact that you have had many short-term jobs won't show up so you won't look like a "job-hopper"

Figure 8-2 shows a functional resumé outlining Maurene Pratt's qualifications in the traffic or transportation field. Since she will use this resumé to apply for several different jobs, she has purposely written a very general job objective.

116

You may find several unfamiliar terms, such as "hot loads" and "O. S. and D. claims" because Maurene has used the vocabulary of the job for which she is applying. The industry person for whom this resumé was written understands these terms very well.

Before preparing this resumé, Maurene listed all her previous volunteer and paid work experience. Here is what her list, which covers about fifteen years, looked like:

child care	metal products shop, shipping and receiving
berry picking	Cub Scout den mother
nurse's aide	bowling league treasurer
dishwasher in a café	school room mother
Avon saleslady	political campaign worker
florist shop helper	church bus driver
clerk in sheriff's office	Sunday school teacher
truck driver	church secretary
paper shuffler	grocery checker
metal products shop, inside and outside sales	paper company purchasing clerk

Some of these jobs lasted several years, others only a few weeks because she was hired to fill in for a person on an extended vacation or out with illness. As it happens, some of the most relevant jobs were these temporary ones, so she wouldn't want to leave them out. If Maurene had used a chronological format, we would see a lot of space devoted to a very varied work history.

Maurene decided that the functional resumé would better enable her to show her skills in her new field. Although she told about her specific experiences in each of four broad skill areas, she hasn't listed employers' names or a single date. She decided the company application form and the interview would provide the opportunity to give these details.

Some disadvantages of a functional resumé are:

- Some conservative employers may not be comfortable with a "new" approach
- Employers are naturally interested in your previous employment experience and will want some details (although they may wait for the interview to get them)
- Your previous employment may be very relevant, and this format won't emphasize that fact (you could emphasize it in your letter of application)

3. *Combination Letter of Application and Resumé.* This is basically a sales letter highlighting your interest in and suitability for a specific job. It combines features of the letter of application and the resumé in one document. It is usually best suited to the person who hasn't had much paid work experience or who wants to pursue a new career. Some employers may not think that it fulfills the requirement when a resumé has been requested. Because you are not including a separate resumé, you must be careful not to make your letter too long and detailed. You are merely trying to whet the employer's appetite and make him or her want to interview you. The combination letter/resumé will not be specifically covered in this chapter, but many of the general suggestions given about application letters will help you construct your own.

Emphasizing What's Important

After you select the general format that will give you an opportunity to present your qualifications in the most advantageous way, you need to consider some other ways to emphasize them. Emphasis is achieved by:

Placement. The item which comes first on a page or first in a series usually receives the most attention. Begin the main part of your resumé with the most important information and the most convincing characteristics. On a chronological resumé that will be your education or work experience; on a functional resumé it will be your skills.

Length. The amount of space devoted to an entry is also an indicator of importance. If you are applying for a job as a bookkeeper, previous bookkeeping work experience or education in a junior accountant program should take up more space (have more detailed entries) than general education or nonrelated jobs such as work experience as a waitress.

Highlighting. Highlighting is another effective way to emphasize. Important items can be underlined, typed in all capital letters, indented in many different ways, or set off by unusual spacing (such as spread-typing which has one space between every letter and three spaces between words). Asterisks, color (such as red for certain words), and bold-face letters (made by typing over the top of previous typing) also attract attention. Because you want a professional-looking resumé, you would not want to use every one of these highlighting methods on the same resumé; but a few may be used to advantage.

Why are format, arrangement, and appearance of the resumé so important? Because, at this point, these are things which you have the most control over and can most easily change. You may never have worked full-time or may have been out of the work force for the past twenty years while raising your three children—these are historical facts that can't be changed. But what you can control is the emphasis given these facts. You can make something else stand out more, such as your recent education or the transferrable skills you acquired through volunteer work.

Writing the Heading and Job Objective

No matter which format you choose, you will need identifying information at the top of the page: your name, address, and phone number. Any attractive, easy-to-read arrangement of the information that will enable a prospective employer to contact you is appropriate. Using side headings such as "Address" and "Phone" are not necessary because an address and phone number are obviously just that. You avoid a cluttered look by leaving them off.

Next, a section to identify your objectives to the employer is appropriate. Your job objective should be a concise statement of your goal. It can limit the jobs for which you are considered, so if you are qualified for any one of several jobs, you may choose not to specify a particular job. You may want to be more general and say something like, "To meet an employer's need for general office skills, organizing ability, and work experience in real estate."

An alternative to a job objective (or sometimes in addition to it) is a "Summary of Qualifications" following the identification section. In this section you would state your background in general terms, such as: "Five years' secretarial experience in the field of real estate, organizing ability and recent brush-up on secretarial skills." The remainder of your resumé would give the details of these general statements.

Writing Your Entries—General Advice

No matter which format you choose for your resumé, your entries need to say what you can do. Your language should be crisp and to the point. Use specific words that convey action, tell what you accomplished, and speak in terms of the employer's needs.

Begin descriptions of skills or duties with action verbs. For example, say "Supervised three clerical workers," not "I was responsible for supervising..." Also avoid using words that play down your part. Don't say "assisted," "helped," or "worked for." Figure out a positive, forceful way to concretely state your own responsibilities, such as "prepared illustrations for a 100-page report on the use of parks for the Community Action Council," and not "helped prepare 100-page report on..."

If you can, use indicators of responsibility, such as how many people or dollars were involved, how much time was saved by your suggestions, or how big a project was. For example, say:

- Organized city-wide campaign which netted $25,000 for the March of Dimes Mothers' March
- Responsible for a service club membership drive which doubled the previous year's enrollment

Make your entries parallel and consistent in their organization. For example, if you begin one entry with a date or a company name, begin all others in that category the same way.

Matching the Employer's Needs

To fit the employer's needs your resumé should:

- be organized so that your pertinent qualifications are immediately apparent
- speak the employer's language
- not contain "eliminators"

If you are responding to an advertisement or job announcement that states the qualifications sought, your job is easier—simply "play back" your qualifications in the same order they were requested. If you don't have this advantage, you will need to use the insight gained from your research in Chapter Seven to determine which qualifications to emphasize.

Each job field has its own vocabulary. If you can speak the language of the field appropriately, you will appear more qualified. For example, if you are applying for a job as a legal secretary, refer to your ability to type briefs, judgments, and orders. You will appear more suited for the job than someone who refers only to the ability to type business letters and reports.

Since the task of the resumé reader is negatively oriented (remember, he or she is trying hard to *eliminate)*, the reasons for eliminating are numerous and as varied as the individuals who screen the resumés.

Eliminators can be as obvious as messy corrections, typographical errors, or a generally unattractive resumé. Or, eliminators can be as subtle as emphasis on the wrong skills, such as an overemphasis on "people skills" rather than typing or language skills for a word processing position.

Eliminators can also be based on personal bias, and are therefore sometimes unpredictable. For example, the screener might not have had good luck with divorced employees in the past because they brought their problems to work. So he or she may eliminate an applicant because a resumé states marital status as "divorced." Leave out any information that is not specifically job-related—don't let the screener eliminate you without a job-related reason!

Writing Entries for Your Chronological Resumé

If you are using a chronological format, decide whether your education or work experience is a stronger qualifier for the job you seek. If they seem equally relevant, put your work experience section first.

Work Experience entries on a chronological resumé are organized by date, with the most recent first. Highlight the most strikingly relevant aspect of your past experience. This would be the general field in which you have worked or your previous job titles. For example, assume you are applying for a job as a medical secretary. If your past experience has been in the health field, but not secretarial, list the company names first. If the company name doesn't indicate that it is medically related, either provide a brief description of the company or show the relatedness in the "duties" section. Show off your knowledge of the job you are applying for by listing those duties from past jobs that most directly apply.

The education section of a chronological resumé is also organized by dates, with the most recent first. You can emphasize the program you were enrolled in, the degree or certificate you earned, or the name of the school, depending upon which you put first and which you highlight with typing techniques. If your education has not resulted in a formal degree or certificate, but you have taken classes relevant to the job, you could use a general heading such as "Education Beyond High School."

Optional sections of the resumé include Awards and Honors, Hobbies, Community Activities, Personal Statement, and References, to name a few of the many possiblities. Use these only if they are current and directly related to the job. Don't include any of the eliminators talked about earlier, and don't dilute the effectiveness of your selling points and clutter your resumé by including irrelevant information.

It's debatable whether you should include the names, job titles, and addresses or phone numbers of persons who have agreed to act as your references. It is probably safe to assume their value to the employer is somewhat diminished by the fact that you are not likely to list persons who would evaluate you unfavorably. Many employers would prefer to choose for themselves whom they contact. If you don't include the names and addresses of references, the statement "References will be furnished upon request" at the bottom of the page will suffice. Most employers won't check references until after an interview anyway.

In outdated books you will often see a photo of the applicant and a "Personal Section" listing everything from height and weight to religious preference and nationality of ancestors. (Sometimes they are shown right under the heading where the job qualifications you want to emphasize should go!) It is illegal for an employer to request and use these for hiring, and most would not like this information forced on them via your resumé. Any information that is not directly related to your ability to perform the job is irrelevant—don't appear out-of-date by cluttering your resumé with it.

Writing Entries for
A Functional Resumé

Unlike the separate detailed Work Experience and Education sections emphasizing "when" and "where" that characterize a chronological resumé, entries on a functional resumé emphasize what you have done and can do. Choose four or five skills that are vital to the job you are applying for. Use these as main headings and list under them the things you have learned and done (no matter where or when) that would fit.

You may want to have separate sections listing your former employers and schools by date, but without detail. You know an employer will want to know—particularly about your previous work experience—but you may decide to wait until the company application form or interview to give these details.

The information about optional sections of the chronological resumé also applies here. Remember, relevance to the job is the prime consideration.

Typing Your Resumé

When your draft is typed you will be able to see if the information is attractively laid out, whether your margins should be altered, if the comparative length (and therefore emphasis) of entries is appropriate, and where you could use special techniques for emphasis.

Use the following guidelines for your draft:

- Try very hard to keep your resumé to one page, but not if doing so makes it appear "crowded."
- Single-space entries with double or triple spaces between them.
- Use headings to identify the different categories such as Job Objective, Skills, and Education.
- Leave as much "white space" as possible by using margins of at least one inch on all sides and appropriate spacing within and between entries.
- Keep sentences brief and paragraphs short (fewer than five lines) so the resumé doesn't look "solid" and hard to read.

Make any changes that are needed and retype your resumé in the corrected format. Before typing your final draft, have someone check it over for you. Your resumé is now ready for final typing. If you can't type it perfectly yourself, have someone type it for you. It must be absolutely error-free. As an applicant you are trying very hard to make a good impression. If you made errors at this time, an employer would wonder how thorough your everyday work would be.

Use a dark ribbon, preferably an electric typewriter, and good quality paper. Don't use erasable paper because it smears too easily, and don't use paper that is too lightweight because it is too hard to read.

Ideally, every resumé is individually prepared and typed for a specific opening. If this is not practical, you may have to gear your resumé to a specific category of jobs so it can be used to apply for several openings. If this is the option you choose, have your resumé reproduced by a professional printer who can give you high quality copies.

A Last Self-Check

Before taking your resumé to the printer or using the original, take one last look at it and ask yourself these questions:

- Did I limit my resumé to one page or do I have a good reason for not doing so? (Having too many directly related qualifications to fit on one page is a good reason; wordiness and inclusion of irrelevant information are not.)
- Am I aware of questions that my resumé will bring to the mind of a reader? (Such as: What was I doing during the ten-year "gap" shown in the Work Experience section?)
- Have I emphasized my most important qualifications for this job by putting them in a prominent place, making those entries longer, and highlighting with special typing techniques?
- Do I have a good reason for including every item?
- Have I left out possible "eliminators?"
- Is the paper and typing or reproduction of high quality?
- If I squint my eyes and look at the resumé, does it look too high or low or too far to the left or right?
- Do most lines begin at the same left margin and therefore create too "solid" a look with little variation?
- Do I have more than five solid lines of typing without a break?
- Are entries within the same section parallel and consistently typed?
- Have I avoided using "I," but instead started entries with verbs?
- Is my resumé absolutely error-free?
- Does my job objective stress what I can do for the employer and not vice-versa?
- Does my resumé reflect the "true" me so that an interviewer won't be unpleasantly surprised when I arrive instead of "super person?"

Now that you have in your hands the best possible resumé you can produce, put it to work for you.

The resumé has several potential uses:

- Mail it on request in response to a newspaper ad or other job announcement.
- Mail it to a firm that you know has an unadvertised opening.
- Send it to a list of firms which could logically use your skills.
- Give it to friends who may be able to pass it on to potential employers for you.
- Give it to placement officers, college instructors, or employment agency counselors who may be helping you find a job.
- Provide a copy to persons who have agreed to act as your references.
- Take two copies (one for the interviewer and one for you) with you to provide a focal point for the interview—the copy you sent to obtain the interview may have been misplaced.

Whenever you are mailing your resumé instead of handing it to someone, you should accompany it with a letter. The letter of application and other types of employment correspondence will be discussed next.

THE LETTER OF APPLICATION

The purpose of the letter of application is the same as that of the resumé: to get you an invitation to an interview. The letter itself introduces you as an applicant for a specific job, highlights a few of your most important qualifications, encourages the reader to find specifics on the resumé, and then requests an interview.

This is the basic plan for the letter of application:

First paragraph:	Name the position and possibly tell how you learned about it.
	Present some idea of what you have to offer. Try to come up with an interesting opening.
Middle paragraph or two:	Highlight or summarize in terms of this reader's needs those qualifications you have given details about on the resumé.
	Explain why you want to work for this company or why you are suited for this type of work.
Last paragraph:	Ask for an interview.
	Give a phone number so the person can contact you, or say you will call his or her office.

Some letters of application are merely brief cover letters or letters of transmittal that essentially say "here is my resumé" and then request the interview. This type of letter, however, doesn't accomplish all that it could. Since it doesn't do any selling or highlighting of what you are offering, I don't recommend you use it. Since resumés submitted for the same job tend to be similar, your letter of application can provide another opportunity to express yourself in a way that will make you stand out in the screener's mind.

Your letter should have a natural, conversational but businesslike tone; it should not sound stilted or be copied from a book. Let your personality and enthusiasm for the job show. You want to provide a spark that prompts the reader to recognize your suitability for the job and makes him or her want to discuss the job with you in person.

Focus On the Employer's Needs

Your emphasis should be on what you have to offer the company, so put yourself in the employer's position and focus on his or her needs rather than on your own need for a job. Remember this person's problem: to choose the candidate who will be most productive in the shortest possible time. Try to avoid beginning many of the sentences with "I" and making selfish-sounding statements such as "I want to get experience in this field." No employer wants to be your training ground.

When you focus on the employer's needs be sure not to make obvious or dogmatic statements or sound like you have all the answers to this firm's problems. Statements like, "Baxter, Inc. depends on sales for its existence. I can improve your sales by 30 percent" will not be well received by those who have spent years working to improve Baxter's market position. Remember, the employer is looking for a valuable and compatible addition to the existing team.

As you did in the resumé, use the vocabulary of the job, speak in terms of the qualifications of the job announcement or help-wanted advertisement, be positive, and don't include eliminators.

The closing paragraph is the place to ask for the interview. Unless unusual circumstances exist (such as the need to travel to a distant city for the interview), you usually leave it to the interviewer to set the time and place for your meeting. If you can't come at the time the interviewer wishes, say so when you are contacted about the interview; don't go into detail about your availability or unavailability for interviews in the letter.

Appearance and Format

Your letter of application should be written in personal business letter style on plain paper or on your personal letterhead; it should never be typed on a business letterhead. Your address and the date will be at the top, and the letter should be addressed to a specific person even if you must call to get the name and correct spelling from the company's switchboard operator. An exception, of course, would be your answer to a "blind" newspaper advertisement which lists only a box number. Most of the items which you used as a last self-check of your resumé can also be used for your letter of application.

THE COMPANY'S APPLICATION FORM

At some point in your job search you will be asked to complete an application form prepared by the firm. This form will obtain information the company needs for the screening process and may also become part of your personnel file if you are hired. In addition to the basic identifying information (such as full name, address, and phone number), the application form usually requests dates, names, addresses and brief details about education, training, work history, military experience, and sometimes references. It is a good idea for you to have prepared your own summary beforehand, so you will have this information handy whether you fill out the application form in the office or at home.

Since companies sometimes continue to use outdated forms that ask for information that is inappropriate or illegal, it is important for you to know the applicants' rights which apply in your state. Generally speaking, the information requested must be a bona fide occupational qualification. For example, a personal question such as, "Do you own your own home?" need not be answered if the employer cannot show that owning your own home is a requirement for the job for which you are applying. Simply draw a small line next to these questions.

As you have in your resumé and letter of application, be positive. Leave out those "red flags" that might label you as a person who is hard to get along with, someone who has many health problems, or someone who is a job-hopper. For example, if you are asked to tell why you left a former job, think of a true but less negative-sounding reason than "personality conflict with the supervisor." The supervisor may indeed have been a bear to work for, but there are usually many reasons for leaving a job. Pick one that doesn't cast you in such a bad light. You don't have enough room on the form to tell the whole story and a brief, one-sided view will not favorably impress the prospective employer.

Don't be surprised if the completed application form doesn't emphasize those items you think are your strongest qualifications for this job. That's why preparing a resumé is so valuable. On your resumé *you* determined the order and amount of space devoted to each item and, therefore, chose the emphasis.

The following guidelines should help you in preparing a good job application form:

- Get two applications if possible.
- Fill out the form in dark ink.
- Double-check all spelling (you may want someone to go over it with you if you are not filling it out on the spot).
- Take ample time (remember, this is a sample of your work).
- Take the following information with you: dates and names of all previous employment and education; phone numbers and addresses of employers and references; your Social Security number.

PREPARING OTHER
EMPLOYMENT-RELATED
CORRESPONDENCE

The Reference Request

Another letter you may need to write in your job search process is one to ask someone to serve as a reference for you. A reference may be called upon to write a letter on your behalf or to talk with your potential employer, so it is a courtesy to ask the person's permission before you use his or her name. It is a good idea to tell him or her a little about the jobs for which you are applying and to enclose a copy of your resumé. (He or she may hear of a job for which you are suited). A letter is also a useful way to bring up those pertinent facts about your association which you remember but which the reference may have forgotten. Coming up with ideas to mention in a letter of reference is often hard for people, so don't be shy about providing a little help.

Once you have been hired, it would be appropriate to send a brief note to thank those people who served as references and keep them informed as to what you are doing. You may want to use them as references again.

Here is a basic plan for a letter requesting permission to use a person as a reference:

First paragraph:	Tell why you are writing.
Middle paragraph or two:	Give specifics of your association and mention any special things you would like him or her to remember.
Last paragraph:	Express your appreciation. Enclose a resumé.

Follow-up Thank You for the Interview

After the interview, sending a letter to thank the interviewer can be a courteous as well as useful gesture. Since most people don't take the time to send a letter such as this, doing so may set you apart from the other candidates. In addition to thanking the interviewer for talking with you and for any special courtesies shown you, such as a tour of the facilities, you can remind him or her of your continued enthusiasm for the job. It would also be appropriate to summarize your most important qualifications, or to mention any relevant information you may have forgotten to mention in the interview.

Figure 8-3 is an example of a follow-up thank-you letter Maurene wrote after her interview. She used this opportunity to dispel the interviewer's doubts about her willingness to drive 37 miles to work every day. Notice the first-name basis; Jack had insisted on that during the interview.

Figure 8-3 A Follow-up Thank You Letter

```
                              23064 - 32d West
                              Machias, WA  98201
                              January 5, 19--

Mr. Jack Berglund, General Manager
ColdSpot Seafood, Inc.
3261 - 43rd West
Seattle, WA  98101

Dear Jack:

Thanks for a most informative and enjoyable interview and the tour of your
facility--everyone at ColdSpot was so friendly!

After hearing you talk about the growth plans for ColdSpot, I'm even more
eager to be your traffic coordinator.  If you are looking for a long-term
employee who wants a career and not just a job, I'm your applicant.

Jack, I know you were concerned about the distance I would have to travel to
work.  Let me assure you that I find driving enjoyable (remember I used to
drive truck), and my car is dependable.  Also, Sherry in the packing
department said something about the possibility of getting together a carpool
from Everett.  Who knows, we might even decide to move to Ballard!

If you need any other information to be convinced that I'm your best choice
for the job of traffic coordinator, just call me at 331-6249.

                              Sincerely,


                              Maurene Pratt
```

chapter nine
SUCCEEDING IN THE INTERVIEW

Now that you have assessed, planned and prepared for work, you should be able to go right to the employer you want and get the job you want. Right? Well, probably not quite. You have one more major hurdle to consider: the interview. Many people have found themselves in situations where someone else (perhaps even someone less qualified) got the job because the initial interview did not go well. The interview process can be frightening, but it does not have to be a disaster. If you know what to expect and are prepared, your chances of being successful in the interview are much better.

PREPARING FOR AN INTERVIEW

The Nature of the Hiring Process

If your resumé and cover letter were successful, your job contact came through, or some other factor has worked in your favor, you've been granted an interview. The employer wants to know more about you and whether or not you will fit a specific job. An interview is an exchange of information; the employer wants to learn more about you and you want to learn more about the employer. For the most part, the employer will want to know why you want the job, what you can do for the organization in the job, and how much it will cost. You probably want to know what advantages or rewards you will gain by working for this company, what is involved in this particular job, and how much you will be paid.

Why Prepare?

Being interviewed is one of the more difficult aspects of the job search because it is somewhat difficult to control. But do not treat the interview process casually even though there is an element of chance and luck involved. The better prepared you are, the more control you will have over yourself and the interview.

In preparing for an interview you will probably feel both excitement and apprehension, but the research you have done on yourself up to this point will now pay off in the actual interview. You will be taking risks; every interview is a risk. But you will also be closer to the goal you seek—a career.

Being prepared means knowing the answers to some important questions and being able to articulate these answers clearly to an interviewer. You need to be able to tell the interviewer:

- what personal strengths you have that could help you in the job you are seeking
- what weaknesses you have that would affect your work and how you plan to overcome them
- what you know about the job you are applying for and what skills and abilities will allow you to perform it well
- what you know about the organization you are applying to and why you want to work there
- what you want from your working life and what you can give to others

Impressing the Interviewer

An interviewer's first impression of you is frequently the deciding factor in whether or not you get the job. This reaction may not always be fair, rational, or professional, but it is *human*. No matter how many books you have read on how to prepare and conduct yourself in an interview, you must accept the fact that the interviewer is a unique individual with biases, quirks, competencies or deficiencies you can't necessarily know about. You will need to use all the judgment, intuition, and insights you can muster to help you meet each situation. No one knows for sure why a person may click with some

132

people and fall flat with others, but this is a factor you must reckon with.

Imagine that you are the person sitting behind the desk waiting for the next interviewee. As that person comes through the door the first thing you will notice is appearance—not just an attractive suit or lively eyes, but the total picture. If the overall impression is one of vitality, neatness, and professionalism, this person has probably passed the first hurdle. Now you can get down to the business of finding out what this person is like. The information provided in Chapter Five will help you attain the look you need for a successful job interview, but don't imagine that an attractive appearance is the only factor that will get you the job. Your appearance helps you to create a positive first impression, but once the initial reaction has registered on the interviewer, he or she will turn to your qualifications and your ability to answer questions and handle yourself in the give and take of the interview session.

One way you can determine what impression you make on others is to ask some people whom you trust for honest feedback. (Don't just ask your friends or family. They will usually not see you as an employer would.) This can be very risky, but it's better to know before the interview if you come across as too soft-spoken, or too overpowering, or too shy. The exercise in Figure 9-1 will help you know how you appear to others. Have someone help you set up a mock interview session and then rate your performance. If you are in a situation where this mock interview can be videotaped, that will be especially helpful. You can often correct nervous mannerisms and other possibly annoying traits if you have an opportunity to observe them yourself. What you learn from this may be invaluable to you in a real interview. When I have had students try this in a classroom setting, they usually find it frightening but enlightening. And most are amazed to find out how well they really can perform in an interview—even in front of a TV camera.

Setting up role-playing situations or having group discussions with friends and acquaintances who are themselves involved in job-seeking can be helpful and supportive, but you can also do this alone if you have to. Practicing in front of the mirror or with a tape recorder may also tell you what you need to know.

In thinking ahead to the interview, use the knowledge you have gained about yourself so far to assess your strengths, accomplishments and skills. Look again at your goals and values. They will help

Figure 9-1 Impressions

Instructions: Place yourself in a setting where someone is asking you questions and you are required to respond. If possible, have someone else observe and evaluate your performance according to the questions below. When the session is finished, have the person asking the questions evaluate the session also.

Did she appear energetic and vital? _____

Did she appear confident or ill at ease? _____

Did she appear calm? _____

Did she seem pushy or rude? _____

Did she exhibit a sense of humor? _____

Did she exhibit any nervous mannerisms (such as twisting a handkerchief or
tapping a foot etc.?) _____

Did she interrupt the person asking questions? _____

Did she speak too loudly or too softly? _____

Did she speak clearly and distinctly? _____

Did she use correct language? _____

Did she answer questions in detail without being repetitious? _____

Did she appear to understand what she was talking about and communicate in a
way the listener could easily understand? _____

Does she sound honest or phony? _____

Does she appear competent and responsible? _____

Did she seem appropriately dressed for the occasion? _____

you answer the questions the interviewer will ask you about yourself. If you have a good idea about what you want and what you can do, you will appear more confident and competent.

Preparing Answers to Interview Questions

Table 9-1 contains a list of questions asked frequently during interviews. While this not an exhaustive list, it will give you an indication of what kinds of questions may be asked.

Two common mistakes made by job-hunters during the interview process are (1) failing to listen to the question (which we will discuss later) and (2) attempting to answer questions with no preparation. You may simply annoy the interviewer if you answer a question that wasn't asked or give a rambling, overgeneralized answer.

When answering questions, there is a happy medium between being too brief and being repetitious, irrelevant and wordy. Use each question as an opportunity to make the points you feel are important

134

Table 9-1 Sample Questions Frequently Asked
at Interviews That Focus on You*

Tell me about yourself.

What are your greatest strengths and weaknesses?

What would you like to tell me that is not on your resumé?

Why are you leaving your present job?

What kind of people do you have difficulty working with?

How would you describe yourself?

What is your interpretation of success?

Why should we hire you?

How do you feel about being supervised by someone with less education than yourself or who is younger than you?

Why should we hire you instead of someone else?

Are you willing to travel and work overtime?

How well do you work under pressure?

How do you think a friend or a teacher or a former supervisor might describe you?

How long do you intend to stay with us?

Have you ever hired or fired people? How much leadership or supervisory experience have you had?

How did you improve each job you have held?

How much money do you feel you should be earning?

What can you do for us and how soon can we expect results?

What do you know about (a specific field)?

Why did you choose your particular field of work?

Why did you leave your last job?

---

*INSTRUCTIONS: Practice a response to each question until you feel comfortable with it. Almost all personal questions are variations of something listed above.

and relate to your ability to do the job. For example, assume you are applying for a job as an administrative secretary and the interviewer says, "Tell me about yourself." Don't respond as if this were a *social* question; direct your answers to the *job*. Some example types of answers follow:

A poor answer: "I was born in Idaho and worked as a secretary ten years ago."

A better answer: "I attended the University of Idaho and worked part-time to pay my way. Since that time I have worked as a secretary for the Black Company and also have taken time out to raise a family."

A good answer: "I attended the University of Idaho, where I took several courses in business administration and English while working part-time as a receptionist in the business office. Since that time, I've worked as a secretary for the Black Company, where I organized and summarized sales reports for the marketing division. I quit to raise a family but continued to perform volunteer community work which utilized my secretarial skills and organizational abilities."

By relating past experiences to the skills you need for the job, you can indicate that you have the personal qualities plus the right experience to handle a new job. For example, if you are a former elementary school teacher who is now looking for a position as a salesperson, it may not be very helpful to say, "I was a third-grade teacher." Instead, you might say, "When I taught third grade, a large part of my job involved persuading parents of children with learning disabilities to attend special classes. This was like a 'selling' job in many ways; I had to convince both the children and their parents that they could deal with this situation."

The well-prepared applicant knows how to answer questions confidently and naturally. Prepare especially carefully for questions in areas where your education or past work experience may be weak. Be able to stress your personal qualities or volunteer activities in these areas. Be honest but be positive.

As you prepare yourself to answer questions about your personal qualifications and experience remember:

- Don't make your answers too quick and short.
- Relate your past experiences to the skills needed for the job.
- Illustrate your personal qualities with specific examples from your past.
- Refer to the company and the job to make your points.

Learn About the Company

I remember sitting on an interviewing team for a college teaching position, where one of the out-of-state applicants had obviously read the college catalog and was already familiar with many of the department programs. The interviewing team was highly impressed. Most of the other applicants could talk well about themselves, but could not talk knowledgeably about the department's programs.

In addition to knowing about yourself—what you want and what you can do—you also need to find out about the company you are applying to. Remember, you are trying to convince a potential employer that you will fit in to his or her organization. Knowing the company's products—whether they be manufactured goods or services—is extremely important. It also helps to know how many people are employed there and what the names of some of the top officers are. You can frequently get this information from your local library. Such publications as *Moody's Industrial Manual, Standard and Poor's Register, Fortune* Magazine and *Business Week* may give you insights into the company. Another good source of information is the company's annual report. If the library doesn't have a copy, call the firm's public relations department and ask for a copy. While you have them on the phone, ask them to tell you about the company and to send you literature.

Pick the brains of any friends, relatives, or acquaintances who work there. Nine times out of ten you'll find such people glad to help. After all, you've placed them in the position of both "expert" and "Good Samaritan" by your questions.

Whenever possible, get a complete written job description. It will give you specific information on the skills required, duties to be performed, desired education and training, and pay range. Job descriptions can usually be obtained from the personnel department. Knowing about recent trends in the field will help you match your capabilities to the work that needs to be done. For example, if you are applying for a job as a records system supervisor, knowing that much of the equipment are being automated may allow you to say something like this: "I think my knowledge of computers will help in setting up your new records systems."

Completing the questions in Figure 9-2 will help you put together information about the company. And after you find out about the company, *use* that information in the interview. You will frequently be asked why you are applying to this particular company for a job. Answering "because there's an opening" may be truthful but not very impressive. A better answer might be, "Your bank has opened many new branches in the last several years, so I feel there may be a great deal of opportunity here." If you are not asked a direct question which gives you an opportunity to show what you know about the company, be prepared with questions you can ask the interviewer that reveal this knowledge.

Figure 9-2 Finding Out about the Company

```
Name of the company _____

Location _____

How many employees _____

Product or service of the company_____
_____
_____

Whom to see about interview _____

Description (qualifications and duties) of job you are applying for (name of
job, description of duties, equipment to be used, knowledge required, etc.)____
_____
_____
_____
_____

Pay range for jobs in this category (if you can get this information)_____
_____
_____

Advancement or transfer possibilities within the organization_____
_____

Any employment tests required_____
_____

What reasons do I have for wanting to work for this company_____
_____
_____

What are some challenges I might encounter while working for this company?____
_____
```

Preparing Your Own Questions

Prepare in advance questions you think you may want to ask the interviewer. Most interviewers will ask if you have any questions, and a well-thought-out question can help you make a positive impression. Ask intelligent questions about the job, company, industry, and the personnel if it seems appropriate. Typical kinds of questions you may include:

- If I were to maintain average progress, what kinds of responsibilities might I have in five years?
- Do you promote from within the company?
- Will there be overtime? Evening or weekend work? Is this job exempt or nonexempt?*
- What kinds of training programs does your organization offer?
- How flexible are the hours?
  *Exempt means that you are not paid overtime; nonexempt employees do earn overtime pay beyond a specified hourly day or week.

138

Be prepared to ask the questions whose answers will tell you whether or not you really want this job.

Whether or not you ask about salary and benefits depends on the situation. Usually salary issues are discussed after the first interview; however, some circumstances will allow this to be brought up during the first interview—particularly if the interviewer initiates the discussion. Stress that you want the salary commensurate with the job to be done. It may help to know the starting salaries in the field. If you can't obtain salary information from the company you're interviewing with, check other sources to get a "ballpark" figure. A current *Occupational Outlook Handbook* lists thousands of jobs and includes typical salary ranges. Don't forget your state employment department. One of their services is career guidance and they have data on local, state and national salary trends.

Handling Illegal Questions

Illegal questions about marital status, children, attitudes toward birth control and other areas of personal privacy are especially tricky during an interview. Such questions as "Do you plan to have more children?" or "Are you married?" may arise if you are interviewed by someone who is unfamiliar with the laws. Of course, you have the right to tell the interviewer that, by law, this question cannot be asked, but this may leave a negative impression. You might handle the question by asking, politely, what relationship that information has to the job you would be performing. Or simply be prepared to give an answer that will let the interviewer know you can solve the underlying problem. For example, if you are asked whether you can handle the job if you have children, you can explain briefly what arrangements you have made to handle the situation. The employer may simply want to be assured that you will be a stable, permanent employee.

Final Preparations

Now that you are ready to answer and ask questions confidently and you are informed about the company and the requirements for the job, here are some final suggestions to consider *before* the interview:

- Be sure you know the location of the interview and the name of the person you will be meeting.
- Be on time. In fact, be a little ahead of time! (5–10 minutes)

- Dress neatly and simply. If possible, dress the way you think the interviewer will be dressed.
- Practice your opening remarks.
- Bring an extra resumé and a pad and pen for notes.
- Get rid of gum and put out cigarettes before going in to the interview.

WHAT TO EXPECT DURING THE INTERVIEW

You have now arrived in the office of the interviewer; you may feel tense, but you are also prepared to answer questions. What are some of the things you should be aware of now?

Body Language

No matter how you answer questions, your nonverbal responses will be noted as well. Nervous mannerisms such as drumming your fingers, swinging your foot, or fidgeting may be very distracting to the interviewer. Some of the people who serve as interviewers are not trained professionals and may not know how to put you at ease; you may have to put them at ease instead.

Listening Skills

Active listening is as important a communication skill as speaking in an interview. Failure to listen may cause you to perform poorly in an interview. You need to listen to what is being said and how, so that you can make an appropriate response. Three basic principles of listening that would be helpful in an interview situation are:

- Have an open mind (try not to put negative interpretations on what you hear).
- Listen from the speaker's frame of reference.
- Be aware of the speaker's voice, eye contact, facial expressions and gestures (this will help you understand what is really being communicated).

If the speaker feels you are paying attention, this provides a better communication process. Asking for clarification indicates this and also gives you a little more time to form your answers on very difficult questions.

140

Silence

Don't panic during short periods of silence. The interviewer may be considering your last answer, taking notes, or possibly testing your poise. The tendency is to feel pressured to add more to your last answer. You may, instead, get into a waiting game with the interviewer. A better approach might be to sit back, count slowly to five, then ask, "Does that answer your question?" or "Is there anything we haven't covered?"

Coming Across Positively

Forthright statements about what you do well conveyed in an honest manner are the most appropriate way to communicate in an interview. You should speak with pride and honesty about your accomplishments, potential and interests. This is not the time, however, for exaggeration or excessive emphasis on how wonderful you are. Most interviewers do not respond well to bragging, overstatement or distortions of background and experience. Try to convey, instead, a readiness to learn on the job. Most employers do not expect you to have all the answers.

When dealing with questions about your future career plans, it may be good to appear ambitious but not necessarily wise to look like an opportunist. If you view the job you are being interviewed for as only a steppingstone to something else, and you convey that impression, an employer may not think you are interested in staying very long or doing this job very well. It is important to remember that you are interviewing for a specific job, not just a step on a career ladder.

If you are confronted with questions you cannot answer, don't try to bluff your way through. It's acceptable to say, "I have never considered that in those terms before," or "I believe I would need some time to think about that question before I could give you a good answer." Do not lie to an interviewer or "stretch the truth" slightly. Many of your answers can be checked, and if you are caught in even a small "white lie," your overall credibility may be ruined.

Closing Off the Interview

Most interviews are less than an hour—some are as short as fifteen minutes. You will probably be able to tell from the interviewer's style when he or she wishes to bring the session to a close. Before you leave, ask if there is any additional information you need to provide, thank the interviewer for the opportunity to discuss the job, and ask when you can expect to hear from the company. Although you may be tempted to do so, do not ask the interviewer "how you did." This puts the interviewer in an awkward position and may create a negative impression. Although it is an unusual situation, if you are offered the job on the spot, you are justified in asking for a few days to think about it.

What the Interview Is Not

Interviews can and will vary dramatically. There are, however, a few interview pitfalls that should be avoided:

1. The interview is not a career counseling session. Don't express interest in any job other than the one you're being interviewed for. If you're applying for a job in personnel, don't say, "I'm interested in this job, but do you have any openings in marketing?" If you've done your homework, you know what you're applying for. The question "Well, what jobs are open?" is not likely to convey an unwavering career interest.

2. The interview is not a true confessions session. The slings and arrows of outrageous fortune have no place in the interview. Tell your friend, your mother, or your goldfish about your fallen arches, your divorce, or the death of your cat. Do not tell the interviewer. The interview is your chance to display yourself at your best.

3. The interviewer is not a social worker. You may, in fact, be desperate for a job. Do your best to minimize this fact and emphasize what you can do for the organization.

4. The interview is not a place to get even with the last boss. No matter how unfairly you may have been treated by your last boss, you will not say so in this interview. Certainly, high praise is not in order, but neutral comments will reflect better than will character assassination. If this is a touchy area, be sure to think through your comments before the interview.

WHAT TO DO AFTER THE INTERVIEW

Once the interview is over, you need time to think about what you have just heard and what you have just said. At the first opportunity, write down what was discussed, what impression you had of the company, what interviewing techniques you think you may need to improve. Also, now is the time to remember some of the employment correspondence discussed in Chapter Eight. If you are interested in the job, send a note to the interviewer thanking her or him for the time and restating your interest in the job. If you are not interested in the job but are offered it, express your refusal without sounding too negative. If you receive an offer you are willing to accept, call the employer promptly and find out about the details for your first day at work. Follow this with a letter expressing your enthusiasm and eagerness to join the company.

What if you don't get the job and you really wanted it? Keep up your courage and remember that a positive self-image communicates itself to others. There may be any number of reasons why you did not get the job—some of these reasons may have very little to do with you personally. If you are concerned that your performance or qualifications were exceptional and you still did not get the job, call the person who interviewed you and ask for some feedback. You may be able to learn something that will be invaluable to you in your next interview.

Also remember that an employer wants to hire someone who has a fair chance of getting along well in the company. This means he or she is looking for someone who shares basic values about work ethics, standards of quality, or punctuality with other workers in the organization. This phenomenon is sometimes called the "clonal effect." The "clonal effect" is the tendency of organizations, groups, or individuals to duplicate themselves whenever they can. Most organizations replace members who have left with people who have similar characteristics, thus maintaining the status quo within the dynamics of the organization. Actually, this may be a much more subtle form of discrimination than discrimination based on race, sex or ethnic origin. An impression may be based on something as minimal as mannerisms, choice of words, sense of humor or lack of it. If you are not selected because of something like this, you may eventually see it as a blessing rather than a rejection.

ACCEPTING THE JOB

Listen to Your Feelings

With whatever time you have to think over the job offer you have now received, do a little research. You could be making one of the most important decisions of your life. You may want to think back to the decision-making process discussed in Chapter Four.

After the interview carefully think about whether or not you *really* want the job being offered—what are the pluses and minuses, does it fit your lifestyle, is it secure? How visible would you be in the job, and what are the possibilities for promotion? Be sure it would be the right job for you, and don't jump at it just because it's the first offer.

Talking Over the Terms of the Job

When a prospective employer wants you for a particular job, you are in a bargaining position. How strong the position is depends upon how much you are wanted and on the company's policies. This is the time to talk about specifics:

Salary. You need to know if there is an organizational chart with an already-prescribed starting salary of if there is some "room to bargain" on the salary placement. It may help to find out the salary of the person you are replacing. This is also a time when it is helpful to know what the industry is paying generally. You may wish to agree to a low starting salary if the prospects for raises will be readily forthcoming. Also, find out about raises. When and how they are given? Are they based on merit or on cost of living?

Job duties. The job duties should be made as explicit as possible; preferably the company will have a written job description. This is the time to clear up whether or not you are expected to perform such tasks as making coffee, watering plants, or other duties other employees are trying to avoid.

Title. It helps to know what your specific job title is. This will help you relate to the organization and to the industry as a whole. Be wary of titles that do not seem to have appropriate authority or duties connected with them. For example, the titles "administrative assistant" or "coordinator" or "specialist" may carry much responsibility and require much skill or they may be a fancier version of clerk. Check the job description.

Company rules. Many companies have a booklet that explains company policies, rules and benefits. If there is no booklet, get a verbal explanation so you will know what is expected of you. You may need to take notes.

Where you work and to whom you report. You should find out where your work station will be and who your supervisor is. This will help you to establish the chain of responsibility and the communication structure.

Benefits. Vacations, medical insurance, holidays, retirement, sick leave, and so on make up the benefit package of most companies. If you understand something about them when starting out, it may save you misunderstandings or possible loss of benefits later. Sometimes you do not have the option of changing your mind after you have signed up for a certain benefit. For example, if your employer offers several types of medical insurance plans, you may not be able to change your mind later about this until a specified "opening date" comes up later. You usually can't alter a company's benefits, but you can understand what they are before you take the job.

You may not be able to get all agreements in writing, so it is a good idea to jot down some of the things you are promised. Keep a record of what you were promised, date it and file it away. This may help you and your employer to refresh memories if that should become necessary.

Before You Start

Beginning a new job is truly an adventure. You need to keep on the track of reassessing yourself and evaluating your work. You owe your employer loyalty, honesty and good performance, but you also owe something to yourself. You owe yourself the right to an enjoyable life and fulfilling career.

chapter ten

JOB SEARCH CONSIDERATIONS FOR SPECIAL GROUPS OF WOMEN

Is being a woman an advantage or a disadvantage when seeking a job? Are there more barriers for some groups of women than for others? Are women creating greater unemployment levels for men? Does a working mother endanger the well-being of her family? These issues are now being discussed by many people in our society—employees, politicians, clergy, educators. You should think about these questions as you pursue your job search.

Women entering the labor force have many things in common, but there are some differences that are worth noting separately. Special circumstances may require you to think about choices, barriers, or attitudes that fit your particular situation but do not apply to other job-seekers or career-changers.

WHAT WE HAVE IN COMMON

To understand why women face some barriers in their job search, it may help you to know something of the history of women in the work force. Many of the traditional roles men and women are still trying to fulfill are based on an economic division of labor that occurred when families were required to take care of most of their needs themselves. In the early part of this century, the growing and preserving of food, the making and mending of clothes, the bearing and raising of children by necessity fell to women. Men usually engaged in physically demanding work in the fields or the factories. Both sexes usually worked long and hard and the life expectancy was much shorter than what we know today. Many women simply did not live beyond the time children were old enough to leave home.

Gradually, as technology eliminated some of the hard physical work and drudgery in both the household chores and the work in the factories and fields and people began to live longer, the old roles and the division of labor did not fit as well as before. In the crisis atmosphere of World War II, it became acceptable for women to take jobs in the shops and the factories. When the war was over, some women remained in the work force, but many returned to the previous roles for women—wife and mother. The men left the military and returned to the fields and factories. It was clear, however, that women could certainly perform the jobs previously held by men despite the popular myth of "men's work" and "women's work." But attitudes do not change as fast as technology. Society's disapproval of women working outside the home no longer fits the economic circumstances.

Many of the technological advances of the 1940s and 1950s had significant effects on the lives of women in their homemaker roles. For example, changes in the food industry now produced more processed and convenience foods; the invention of household appliances cut down on the time and physical demands of housework; perhaps most important of all, birth control methods allowing for "planned" child-bearing gave women more independence than ever before. Couple these changes with the increased lifespan for women, which allows for a possible career life of twenty or thirty years after children leave home, and it becomes even more apparent why so many women are entering the labor force; however, many men (and women) have simply not been prepared in their early life experiences to accept these changes. Many people, particularly husbands and children, continue to want the kind of comfort, attention, and status that resulted from a married women remaining at home. During this transition period, it is not always easy for people to accept the changes that require them to take on different responsibilities or change their views of how the world is supposed to work.

Today we find ourselves in the midst of a revolution of attitudes over the changing roles of women and men in our society. As a result

147

of these changes, there is a great deal of controversy and mistrust between many different factions of our society over the "proper" roles for women. Legislation, court battles and the introduction of such concepts as "equal pay for equal work," "comparable worth," and "affirmative action" have polarized people in and out of the work force. This has complicated the career lives of many women.

While each work situation will have its unique aspects, here are some of the realities a woman should be prepared to deal with when engaged in a job search:

- Although women make up more than half of the population in our society, they are still considered a "minority." Many of the people hiring employees hold very traditional attitudes about the roles of men and women.
- Men have had (and still have to a large extent) most of the power and control in our society. This is gradually starting to change, but you must remember that the assumption of power is a process, not an event. Most of the jobs that involve directing and leading are still filled by men.
- Many men fear that women's access to power and position will block or hinder their own career goals. Some men accept women as colleagues and equals; others do not and may feel the need to fight back directly or indirectly.
- Many women fear and distrust other women who seriously pursue a career. They may fear a loss of their own economic protection and support from a spouse.

These attitudes are not only realities on the job, but they may also be part of the hiring process. Despite the fact that many organizations are actively recruiting women, there is a good chance you will face some preconceived notions of what you can or cannot do. If you develop an awareness of these kinds of attitudes, you are less likely to become defensive when confronted with discriminatory attitudes when you are looking for a job.

CONSIDERATIONS FOR THE VERY YOUNG WOMAN

The period of transition from student to young-woman-with-a-career can be a very exciting and challenging time. Most of my young women students in their late teens and early twenties have been especially excited about the interviewing process and the subsequent "wonderful" job they are sure they will get. These same young women are often shocked and disillusioned when confronted with the realities of entry-level jobs, the demands of employers, and the workings of a business organization. Add to that the frequent attitude of employers that young people are not very serious about work and you have a very real barrier to getting a job and developing a career. So what can be done about this barrier? Recognizing some of the realities of your situation may help. Here are some possible attitudes you should be aware of:

1. *You may not be taken seriously because you are a "girl."* There is a distinct difference between being perceived as a "girl" and being perceived as a "young woman." (Some people consider all women in business to be "girls" but that is not the major consideration here.) If you are perceived as a "girl," employers may attribute to you such characteristics as being flighty, silly, shallow, and flirtatious. You may be thought to be unbusinesslike or not really serious—earning "pin" money until you get married and "settle down." You will have to work doubly hard to convince a prospective employer you are serious about a permanent position and career.

2. *You may be considered immature, unprofessional, or unable to handle sensitive situations because you are young.* The assumption is frequently made that because you are young you cannot properly deal with confidential or sensitive material. The assumption may also be made that because you are young you will not be able to deal professionally with outraged clients or irritated colleagues. Remember, this is a *perception*, not a *fact*. The truth is many young people deal very well with confidential material and some older people do not; the reverse is also true. It depends strictly on the individual regardless of age. But because of the perception, you will have to be able to convince an employer that you are capable of exercising mature judgment.

As you look for a job, you may need to do some of the following things to overcome the barriers of your particular situation.

1. Dress for the interview and for work in a conservative, businesslike fashion. This doesn't mean trying to look twenty years older than you are; it means adopting the more conservative of the dress styles for your age.
2. Your attitude during the interview and at work should be as businesslike as possible. You need to appear calm and confident.

3. You, more than any other category of women, need to appear deeply interested in something other than yourself. You need to express your knowledge, potential for growth, and stability.
4. Avoid, as much as you can, using the speech habits and phrases that may be part of your youthful culture and peer group. You need to express yourself clearly and straightforwardly in vocabulary that is not slang or language that would be inappropriate in a business situation.

Young women just out of school frequently expect to jump right into a responsible position. Even with high expectations, you should hold back a little at the beginning and learn what is expected by the organization before you seek a great deal of responsibility. You will be expected to "pay your dues" before gaining recognition and promotion. Develop some patience. Opportunities will come along for you.

Gradually, many employers are becoming aware that hiring a very young woman does not mean hiring a temporary employee. Even those who marry and have children are more frequently returning to work soon after the child is born. If you give the right signals that say you are interested in a permanent position and increased responsibility and then prove it with your job performance, you can overcome the barrier of being perceived as too young and immature for a serious career. Table 10-1 will give you some examples of the stereotypes—both good and bad—often applied to women of your age group.

Table 10-1 Frequently Held Attitudes About Young Workers

- Has the enthusiasm of youth
- Usually has recent, up-to-date training
- Seen as flexible, able to learn
- Has higher energy level
- Has no family commitments (may be more willing to work late)
- Has little life experience but knows latest developments in the field
- Willing to travel
- May be seen as demanding too much, too soon
- Seen as a risk; may want to marry and have children in a few years
- May be discounted because of youth—considered immature
- May not be permanent; sees herself as having options
- May be seen as a daughter or a sex object

You also have many advantages in starting your career at this early age. As men have traditionally been able to do, you will have more time to accumulate experiences, skills and knowledge which will help you with career success when you are older. Furthermore, because ordinarily you do not have the same kind of family responsibilities as some other groups of women, you can concentrate your energy and time on activities and training which will enhance your career.

SPECIAL PROBLEMS OF RE-ENTRY WOMEN

For our purposes here, let's consider *re-entry women* to be women who have held a job at some time and then left the work force to marry and raise a family. This type of woman then "re-enters" the work force after an absence of about five to twenty years. Many in this group will have multiple careers—continuing to be housewives and mothers in addition to their jobs.

Lack of confidence is often the major problem of this group as they prepare to return to work. If you are part of this group, you may, for example, feel that your skills are outdated or that you can no longer compete with younger and more recently educated job-seekers. In addition to these fears, women in this group also must deal with the feelings of their families as they return to work, and employers may also be interested in how the family feels about your absence from home.

Returning to work requires some changes in behavior as well as lifestyle: while working at home you were basically a consumer of goods and services; now you will be a producer of goods and services. You have been your own boss and set your own schedule; now an employer will hold you to an established set of standards.

Guilt and conflict over family responsibilities is the second major problem for this group. However, before you allow yourself to succumb to guilt and conflict because you have chosen a paid career as well as a domestic career, listen to what the Women's Bureau of the U.S. Department of Labor has to say about most of the working mothers in the United States:

> Many mothers work because they or their families need the money they can earn. Some work to raise standards of living

above the level of poverty or deprivation; others, to help meet the rising costs of food, education for their children, medical care and the like. *The majority of women do not have the option of working solely for personal fulfillment.*

Your family may need you to work more than they need to have you stay home. Besides, you also have responsibilities to yourself.

Even though questions about marital status and children are illegal and should not be asked during the interview, you need to answer some questions for yourself before you appear for an interview or accept a job. You may even wish to discuss some of these issues in the interview. For example:

- Have you made the kind of child care arrangements that are secure and stable enough to keep you from worrying while you are at work?
- Have you thought about how to combine your household duties and your job?
- Are you prepared to handle hostility from nonworking mothers, relatives, wives of your male colleagues and male competitors?
- Is your husband threatened by your new independence?
- Do you have people you can call on to help in times of emergency?

If you have thought about and have some answers to these questions, you will undoubtedly come across to an employer as more competent, confident and organized in the interview process.

One last word for guilty mothers—the "real mother" myth is still very much a part of the American culture in spite of the huge number of working mothers. This myth says that you are not a "real mother" unless you are at home caring for your family's needs. Because guilt can be harmful to you and what you are trying to achieve for your family, you need to combat it with fact. The fact is your husband and children are not necessarily worse off—and may even be better off—if you work. Many studies now indicate that the divorce rate is no higher in families where the woman is employed than in families where she isn't. In fact, having a second income may relieve some financial pressure and tension within a family. Also, studies comparing the children of working and nonworking mothers in areas such as school and social adjustment, grades and achievements, extracurricular activities, delinquency, etc. indicate there are few differences between children of employed and unemployed mothers. This is not to say your child will never have problems. Most of the problems, however, will have little to do with your working.

Household Management

While you plan your return to the work force, begin making arrangements with your mate for the realities of a two-career family. The woman should not carry the full burden of household management in addition to her work outside the home. Some steps you and your mate may want to take to devise a more equitable work distribution include the following:

- Decide what tasks need to be done and how often. (You may need to lower your "white glove" standards.)
- Involve your children in the process.
- Distribute the tasks among family members based on skill, interest and availability.
- Check your budget and selectively employ outside services.

Children and Child-care

Choosing the best child-care arrangement is frequently a challenging task. Even though many thoughtful fathers are accepting a greater share of the responsibilities and pleasures of raising children, most parents cannot provide for the total time needed for child care just between the two parents' schedules. (Some parents who feel particularly adamant about not entrusting their children to others have worked out part-time work arrangements or flexible time schedules—particularly when preschool children are involved. In some instances, this may also be less expensive than having both parents work full-time.) For those parents who choose child-care arrangements outside of the immediate family, there are a number of different arrangements that may be made.

Career Challenges

It is important that you talk to your mate about possible future issues and problem areas. Dealing with some of these will help you approach your own career plans more confidently. It is important that you understand the expectations you have of one another, your personal dreams and hopes, your concerns about the relationship itself, and the responsibilities each of you is willing or unwilling to assume. Here are some questions that may help you to deal with the issues facing two-career couples:

153

1. What is his current career standing (status, promotability, etc.)? What is yours?
2. How does your partner view your career? (necessary, something to make you happy, an interference, etc.)
3. What will you do if your vacations fall at different times?
4. Whose job has priority if the need for relocation arises?
5. Are the career goals of you and your mate compatible?
6. How will you handle your money?
7. Who will have the responsibility for child-care arrangements?
8. If you work in the same field, will you view your partner as a colleague or as a competitor?
9. Will a promotion of one partner cause admiration or resentment on the part of the other partner?

There are no correct answers to these questions; there are only individual solutions—many that may need to come from a compromise. If you anticipate some of the issues in advance, however, you may be able to negotiate a solution, so the actual event is not so traumatic.

Also, remember that a two-career relationship can offer a great deal to both partners: it gives women an opportunity to find satisfaction in a variety of roles; it offers men the chance to share the family financial burden, be more involved in family life, and potentially have more time for personal pursuits. A two-career relationship is not the easiest of choices but it does present challenges and satisfactions for many couples.

To give you some examples of stereotyped perceptions employers may have about re-entry women, look at Table 10-2. Prepare yourself to be able to answer questions in a positive way during the interview process.

To overcome some of the barriers to employment for your particular situation, try some of the following ideas:

- Dress for the interview in a conservative, businesslike fashion—preferably in a good-looking suit with appropriate accessories. You are trying to play down the "housewife" stereotype.
- Your attitude during the interview needs to be one of confidence, energy and enthusiasm. You must also convey the impression of seriousness about a career.
- Show the employer that your knowledge and skills are current and appropriate for today's work situation. If you use examples involving family or volunteer activities, relate them directly to business applications.

154

- Indicate, by your choice of words, that you understand the language of the business world. (Reading business sections of the newspaper or business magazines beforehand will help you.)

You have some advantages, too, in starting or changing your career now. Employers value maturity and life experiences. Many employers know that re-entering women are especially eager to prove themselves and do a good job. Deal with the barriers and emphasize the advantages.

Table 10-2 Frequently Held Attitudes About Re-entry Women

- Has wisdom, maturity, and rich life experiences
- Is more stable and reliable than very young workers
- Has competencies but does not know their value
- Will not relocate
- Will be grateful; will accept lower pay
- Will not move; does not see other options
- Willing but unable to work late; gets tired quickly
- Low self-esteem; pessimistic; does not expect promotions
- Family commitments may interfere with work schedule
- May be seen as office wife or "mother"
- Will be working only for "extras"—not seen as the main breadwinner

---

THE SINGLE PARENT

It is difficult to be a mother with a full-time job; it is even more difficult to be a single mother with a full-time job. Unlike the married re-entry woman, the single mother does not have to deal with conflicts with a spouse, but the single re-entry woman has double duty with child-care responsibilities. Add to this the possible emotions of remorse, guilt, anger, fear, and self-pity that may come when a woman loses her husband through divorce or death, and the dilemmas for job-seeking mount. Among the most striking changes that occurred in the work force in the 1970s was the sharp rise in the number of working women who had principal responsibility for the maintenance and welfare of their own families. Almost one out of every nine women in the 1979 labor force maintained her own family.

One of the major problems for this particular group is financial insecurity. A characteristic which almost all single-parent families share is lower-than-average income. Self-pity and a panic over how to manage can overwhelm you enough to make you want to run away and leave family and job far behind. This makes it difficult to present a positive, confident attitude to an employer when you are most desperate.

Before you begin your job interviews, deal with your finances. If you are already working when the separation or loss occurs, try not to undertake anything new for a while. If you are job hunting, try to find something interesting but not too demanding. After you are more used to your situation, then seek greater career challenges.

The second major problem a single working mother must come to grips with is interacting with her children. There are some traps in dealing with your children you should try to avoid if possible:

- trying to carry on just as you did when your spouse was there
- indulging your children to make up for the guilt you may feel
- unloading your problems on your children
- letting your children unduly influence your career decisions

Your children can learn to adjust to your new life and you should help them. They, in turn, may be able to help you cope with changes. Learning to be independent and responsible is important for children, too.

Here are some ideas to help you cope with your situation:

- Remind yourself that you are not alone in this situation; there are many women with the same problem.
- Develop an "extended family" of relatives and friends who can share responsibilities with you.
- Develop as many set routines as possible (such as calling home at the same time each day) to help your children feel more secure.
- If your children are old enough to perform household tasks, divide up the responsibilities as much as possible. Be honest with them about the help you need.
- Find someone (either a counselor or objective acquaintance) who would be willing to serve as a sounding board for your problems and frustrations and help you find productive solutions.

Basically, the single mother trying to find a career has many of the same problems and encounters similar attitudes to the married re-entry woman, but there are some distinctions worth considering when preparing for an interview. Table 10-3 lists some frequently held attitudes about single mothers.

Table 10-3 Frequently Held Attitudes About Single Mothers

- Needs to work so may put up with unpleasant or tedious environment more readily
- Seen as serious about permanent employment
- Will be concerned about pay, so may be willing to accept overtime
- Family commitments may interfere with work schedule
- May be absent from work a great deal
- Low self-esteem—possibly emotionally unstable
- May be seen as potential troublemaker for "available" men in the organization (may be seen as simply looking for another husband)

To overcome some of the barriers of your particular situation when seeking employment, try some of the following ideas:

- Dress for the interview in a conservative, businesslike manner. You do not want to appear dowdy, but you do not want to look like a sex object either.
- Your attitude during the interview should be confident and cheerful. You must convey the impression of a strong ability to cope. You must *not* appear desperate or bitter about your circumstances.
- Like the married re-entry woman, show the employer that your knowledge and skills are appropriate for today's work situation. Relate your experiences from family or volunteer work experiences directly to business applications.
- Indicate your seriousness about permanent work and career goals by using vocabulary indicating awareness of business and current events. This may also indicate interests outside of your immediate problems and situation.

Even though it is probably better to acknowledge your family situation to an employer rather than to pretend it does not exist, single working mothers need to emphasize what they can give an employer and de-emphasize what they need for their families. An employer does not owe you your family maintenance or help (even though many are understanding and very helpful). Of all job applicants, you in this category must give the impression of being able to cope in a confident manner. *And you will be able to.* Going to work can bring structure and normality to your life in very healthy ways. If you focus on the positive aspects of going to work—providing you with money, social contacts, and participation in something larger than the world of your immediate family—you will find satisfaction and a sense of self-worth. It takes someone with a strong sense of self to be able to carry off so many different and conflicting roles without getting lost in the shuffle. If necessary, go back to Part One of this book and concentrate again on *you*—what you think about yourself as a person as distinct from your roles as worker and parent. You and other working mothers are putting tremendous demands upon yourselves; and for the most part, you are doing it without the support of the society in which you live. Several years from now when someone asks you how you did it, you may not know quite how it happened but you will be able to say, "I just did it; that's all."

THE DISPLACED HOMEMAKER

If you are a divorced or widowed woman in your late forties or fifties, you're looking for a job and you have no job experience, you may fit into a group often identified as "displaced homemakers." You may also be categorized as a "late-entry" career applicant and may have to deal with the barriers of discrimination based on both your sex and your age. If you couple those factors with the expectation that you had chosen a career as a housewife and mother and now the latter two roles have been removed (or at least modified considerably), you may think you are in a "no-win" situation. But there is hope. In spite of the barriers, many women in this group are finding career satisfaction and success they never thought could be possible. So don't panic; let's see what you face and what you can do about it.

One of the major problems facing the displaced homemaker is understanding and adapting to the changes in the work world. Workers do complain about tedious tasks and overtime. Many office workers *are* becoming more militant and organized and are unionizing. Many workers take "mental health" days and charge it to sick leave. Much work is automated, produced under pressure deadlines, and may not receive the quality control you think is important. Today's work ethic *is* different.

A second major problem facing the displaced homemaker is lack of confidence and feelings of inadequacy based on having little or no work experience. You in this group need especially to review the transferable skills exercises in Chapter Seven and the assertiveness skills in Chapter Four. Identifying and gaining skills should help you gain confidence.

A third problem for displaced homemakers is overcoming society's attitudes and their own feelings about being "over the hill." It is true that many women 45 or older often are segregated into dead-end jobs with little chance of advancement. Some of this has come about because of direct discrimination by employers, but some of this has also come about because many women this age are afraid of asserting their needs and rights. Table 10-4 lists some attitudes held by many employers about displaced homemakers and late-entry women.

Table 10-4 Frequently Held Attitudes About Displaced Homemakers or Late-entry Women

- May be seen as having rich life experiences but little awareness of the latest developments in the field
- May be seen as rigid, set in her ways
- Has some competencies but does not know how to value them
- Low self-esteem, pessimistic; does not expect promotions
- Lack of energy and stamina; gets tired quickly
- May be discounted because of "sheltered life"
- Will be grateful; will accept lower pay
- Will be stable and reliable
- May be seen as "motherly"
- If not seen as motherly, may be seen as childlike
- May be seen as slow, unproductive and too perfectionistic

How do you come to grips with the barriers and discrimination you may find? First of all, don't swallow the myths you've heard about older workers or accept the frequently held attitudes. People are living longer. If you are 45 right now, you have a career life left of at least 15 to 20 years and very possibly more. Based on Department of Labor studies, many of the myths can be countered with facts.

MYTH: Older workers can't meet the physical demands of jobs.
FACT: Very few of today's jobs require great strength or heavy lifting. Labor-saving machinery makes it possible for older workers to handle most modern jobs without difficulty.
MYTH: Older workers are too slow. They can't meet production requirements.

FACT: There is no significant drop in work performance and productivity in older workers. Many older workers exceed the average output of younger workers.

To help you deal with preconceived attitudes, here are some ideas you need to think about when you are seeking employment:

1. Dress for the interview in businesslike clothing that is not dated or too dressy. Go easy on perfume, jewelry and makeup. You should not try to look as if you wish to recapture your youth. You want to look attractive and ageless.
2. Your attitude should be one of enthusiasm, energy and confidence. You need to convey the impression that you have a great deal to contribute and have ample time to make those contributions. Do not give the impression that your major goal is retirement.
3. Know what kinds of skills are required and be able to show how your skills are directly applicable to business.
4. Learn to speak assertively. Indicate your seriousness about a satisfying career. Let the employer know you are interested in professional growth and promotion and are willing to give the time or take the training necessary to achieve it.

The Handicapped (or Disabled) Woman

Disabled persons are not "charity cases." They are often willing workers with physical or mental limitations but not necessarily job limitations. Who are the handicapped? People with physical disabilities such as blindness or missing limbs are examples of the most visible group of disabled persons. But the term handicapped, or disabled, may also apply to the mentally retarded (those persons whose mental development has been arrested, but who may still have the skills or abilities to do certain kinds of jobs) or the "mentally restored" (persons who were mentally or emotionally ill but who are restored and ready for work).

If you are a handicapped or disabled woman, you may think that your chances for satisfying employment are especially slim. But as a disabled job applicant or employee, you have the same rights and benefits as nonhandicapped applicants and employees. Your ability, training and experience must be considered. Your disability must *not* be considered unless it keeps you from doing your job adequately. Because of the Affirmative Action requirements in the 1973 Rehabilitation Act, more and more employees are learning about handicapped workers. Affirmative action for handicapped workers covers a lot of jobs. Good health and possession of all limbs and faculties will always be an advantage. But it is no longer essential that a worker possess all of these in order to handle a great variety of the jobs available today.

But not everything is ideal and not all employer attitudes are enlightened ones. A list of frequently-held attitudes about disabled women is given in Table 10-5. You will need to convince a prospective employer that you will be an asset, not a liability, to the organization. Most handicapped individuals are aware that their handicaps cause no problems or only minor difficulties. The real problem is not in holding the job, but in getting it in the first place. You need all of the skills of the other groups plus some additional ones.

Here are some suggestions to help you in the interview:

- Dress for the interview in an appropriate, businesslike manner. Let the employer know you are serious and wish to contribute to the success of the organization.
- Do your homework about handicapped employees. Many studies show handicapped workers to be better risks than regular employees.

You need to convince the employer to look beyond the disability and say, "Yes, this person can do the job."

Table 10-5 Frequently Held Attitudes About Disabled Women

- Disabled persons will be sick more often than other employees
- Disabled persons will not be as productive as other workers
- Other employees may not accept the disabled worker
- The employer may have to make expensive accommodations for the disabled worker
- Disabled persons may not be ambitious
- Disabled persons may not stick to the job
- Disabled persons may need a great deal of supervision
- Disabled persons may be limited in the duties they can perform

---

What Does the Future Hold?

In spite of the barriers, we are in a time of growth and opportunity for women in the work force. Women of today are making important steps in changing the work world. We have to take the risks—barriers and all. If we remain on the outside, refusing to play because we don't like the rules, we will not get a chance to make or change the rules.

Only the people inside the organization have a chance to modify them.

We are in the process of attaining a new place in the world fostered by a deeper understanding of what women are, want, and can do. First, *you* must recognize this; second, you must make prospective employers recognize this. Even though you must concentrate first on yourself and your unique qualities in planning your career, it is good to be aware of what you share with other women. You can learn from the experiences of other women; then you can help other women learn from yours.

chapter eleven
FITTING INTO
THE ORGANIZATION

Beginning a new job is an exciting adventure. Your motivation and enthusiasm are high and your energy and enthusiasm are at peak levels. At least this is the way it should be. Sometimes, however, people approach the first day of work with dread and foreboding. They want to succeed, but somehow things don't go quite right. What makes the difference between the person who makes it and the one who doesn't? Getting off to the right start certainly helps. Knowing what to expect and preparing yourself for the challenges will help you to make a positive start so that you can find your place in the organization.

FIRST DAYS ON THE JOB

The Day Before

Plan your clothes, transportation route, and other personal organization needs the day before so that you don't have to start your first day worrying about anything except getting there feeling in charge of yourself. Wear something simple and basic until you find out what others in the organization usually wear. Even if it's summer, you may want to take along a sweater or jacket in case the work area is cold. Do not assume that the company will automatically have coffee or tea, tampon dispensers in the bathrooms, or any other items necessary for your personal comfort. You needn't carry a suitcase-full of things, but a tote bag or briefcase with personal necessities and a magazine or book to read in case you are not given anything to do for a few hours may help you through this time of nervousness and stress. If you don't need any of the items, great. If you do, you will be glad you planned ahead.

The First Day

Now you have arrived. You want to make a good impression because this first impression tends to remain for quite a while even if your behavior changes later on. In every new job there is a period of adjustment (sometimes called the honeymoon period) in which a new employee is allowed to make mistakes while learning the job, finding out the rules, and fitting into the organization. You can use this period to good advantage or abuse it foolishly. Just because you are receiving special privileges and attention now does not mean that this will always be the case. You are being scrutinized far more carefully than you may imagine. You should not be overly concerned about this but you should be aware of possible advantages and disadvantages during the "honeymoon" period. Although you may come in as a learner, it is important that you soon establish yourself as independent and reliable; you must become accountable for your actions. That is the only way you will be given colleague status in the eyes of the other employees.

Here is a list of suggestions for making it through your first days of work. Adjust them to fit your individual situation, of course, but most are applicable to all types of jobs and organizations:

- Try to learn your physical surroundings.
- Try to find time to sit down with your supervisor so that you find out right away what is expected of you.
- Find out whom you can join for breaks and lunch.
- Become knowledgeable about what is going on around you; listen carefully to what people are saying, the vocabulary being used, etc.
- Do not talk about personal matters since you do not yet know how that will be interpreted.
- Do not be afraid to ask questions about the company and your work.
- Do not jump to too many hasty conclusions about the people you meet; you may soon be seeing them in an entirely different light.

Becoming Part of the Group

One issue that has to be approached carefully is how and when you become included in the various informal groups within the organization. Some of this will depend strictly upon your own needs. Some people need to take their time and observe; others need to jump right in and participate. Either way may be appropriate depending upon the situation. But whatever you do, you need to be aware of your behavior and what kind of responses you are getting from others. For example, are the people in the organization formal or informal? Is the contact and socializing only horizontal (among workers of equal status) or is it also vertical (mixture of bosses and subordinates, professionals and staff, and so on)? Are the social relationships casual and mostly on the surface or are they indicative of long-standing and deep friendships? Are there unwritten rules about status and titles? One irony of the need for belonging to a group is the fact that most people are more likely to be accepted into a group if it seems that they are *not* trying to get in. Many people are turned off by new workers who seem too eager, opportunistic, or desperate. At the same time, however, you won't be accepted if you don't make any attempts to make contact.

If you make a good impression the first few weeks on your new job, the personal contacts and admiration can serve you well for years to come. Use your honeymoon period to learn as much about the company, the business, and your boss and colleagues as you can. Make sure you work hard. This is absolutely important for acceptance. You can relax a bit later but not during those first few weeks and months. Honeymoons are usually over much more quickly than we would like. Make yours a good one.

Visibility and Competence

Many books and articles dealing with how to be successful in an organization stress *visibility*—in other words, how well-known you are to people who can directly affect your career. Visibility is only an asset, however, when it reveals competence. Visible incompetence scares both bosses and colleagues and it certainly does not create much challenge, fun, growth or security in your job. Incompetents don't always get fired. Most of us can cite examples of people we've seen in high-paying jobs who weren't competent. Most of them got the job (or kept it) through someone else's mistake or because that individual and the manager became friends and the manager now finds it difficult to face the situation realistically. Depending on "friends" to give you a good job or keep you in a good job is pretty risky, however. As one person put it, "It's easier, safer, and less fatiguing to be competent."

What is competence? One dictionary definition is "having requisite ability or qualities; rightfully belonging; legally qualified or capable." Translated to the world of work, that basically means (1) knowing how and what to do on the job, (2) doing your work in a timely fashion, (3) being thorough and accurate, (4) being prepared, and (5) being efficient and attentive. Some organizations would add "being able to get along with others and being loyal to the organization" as additional components of competence. Quite frankly, one of the main reasons for finding a job you enjoy is that it's so much easier to be competent that way. People who spend a lot of time doing what they don't like frequently end up not being very good at it.

FINDING OUT THE RULES

Until you know what kind of behavior is expected of you, you cannot make the choice of going along with or not conforming to this behavior. While most organizations have written rules and procedures that employees are expected to follow, most also have many unwritten rules. It is the unwritten rules that determine, to a large extent, what is correct behavior in your place of work. These unwritten rules of accepted behavior are called "norms" and these norms establish what people should or should not do as good members of the organization.

What are some of the norms you may have to confront? Where and when people smoke, what kind of joking takes place, acceptance or lack of acceptance of profanity are examples of norms. It may be the norm to come early to meetings or it may be that talking about the boss may be accepted in certain circumstances but frowned upon in others. Many of the norms of an organization are arrived at consciously; others come about by default. There may also be varying degrees of awareness among other employees about what the norms are.

In Table 11-1 there is a list of behaviors you may look for in order to figure out the norms of your company.

Table 11-1 Types of Informal Behavior

Employees in the organization:

dress alike	dress individualistically
talk about personal matters	do not discuss personal matters
treat each other formally	treat each other casually
leave their office doors open	close their office doors
discuss salaries openly	do not discuss salaries
leave on time	stay late
arrive on time	arrive late
do assigned tasks only	are self-starters
tease and joke with each other	frown upon teasing and joking
use telephone for personal calls	use phone for business only
accept profanity	frown upon profanity
are patient with each other	are pushy and demanding
are expected to socialize with other employees	socializing with other employees is discouraged
have clean offices	have cluttered offices
accept women at men's informal gatherings	do not accept women at men's informal gatherings
address bosses formally	call bosses by first names
go through appropriate approval channels	communicate directly with each other
cooperate and reward teamwork	compete with each other
stick together within a department	seek and meet new people outside of their departments
discount women	treat women as equals
are expected to use company products	are not expected to use company products
write memos to each other	call or see each other in person

It is very important that women entering an organization be able to identify and understand the norms. It has been observed by many researchers and management consultants that women are generally at a disadvantage because they do not know many of the unwritten rules about organizations that men learned through such experiences as the military or athletic teams. Furthermore, there may be different unwritten rules for women than for men. For example, aggressive behavior may be an accepted behavior for a man but not for a woman; a display of emotion may be accepted behavior for a woman but not for a man. But don't *assume* anything; *observe* many situations before you come to any definite conclusions about your organization's unwritten rules.

As you become more aware of what is accepted behavior in your organization, you may discover that some of the norms do not fit your values or goals. You may wish to "break the rules" or attempt to set new rules. There are prices to pay for doing this, but there may also be rewards if you can successfully carry it off. To what extent you can break the unwritten rules or establish new ones depends upon your ability to depersonalize criticism. Since many women have been taught to avoid conflict, facing criticism is difficult. To avoid bad feelings created by conflict, some women always play it safe and never go beyond the expected. You will have to be the best judge of whether or not it is worth expending the energy to change a rule or deal with the possible negative consequences of going against the norm. Most leaders are initiators and risk takers, but they also need to know when the risk is worthwhile and when it is not.

Let me give you an example. In the early years of my teaching career it was an "unwritten rule" that women teachers did not wear pants to work, only dresses or skirts. Several of my colleagues and I taught in a rather cold part of the campus and especially during the winter months we thought it would be nice to be able to wear wool slacks and stockings instead of skirts and nylons to work. Three of us showed up for work one Monday wearing wool pant suits. Throughout the week we received feedback from other faculty and staff—some of it questioning and, in some cases, mildly hostile. We believed in our cause, however, and persisted. Within a year, it became common practice throughout that school district for women teachers to wear pants. Several years later, many people couldn't believe that it had ever been an issue. The norm had changed. The new norm fit the needs of employees within the organization and it corresponded with changes outside as well.

There are other times, however, when "breaking the unwritten rules" may have negative effects. You need to learn the limits of flexibility in your organization.

OFFICE PROTOCOL

When to Talk and When to Listen

"Talk is cheap," according to the old saying, but talk may be expensive if it costs you your reputation as a serious, reliable employee.

Learning how to talk in your organization becomes a question of knowing what to say when (and knowing when to keep quiet).

Because there is less formality and more assertiveness on the part of employees in today's organizations, you may feel you have the right to comment on everything. Although times have changed, human nature is much the same as in former years when "yes, sir" was the safest phrase to say to a boss. Most bosses still prefer some deference and respect. Also, your peers appreciate consideration as well.

Sometimes you need to ask yourself, "Do I really need to say this?" before speaking up. Women frequently get caught in the stereotype of "talking too much," even though this can be a characteristic of both sexes. In many instances you may need to make a deliberate effort to restrain comment. As the old saying goes: *Far better to remain silent and be thought a fool than to speak and remove all doubt.*

On the other hand, if you never speak up, you may be thought to be unintelligent, indifferent, or overly shy. Furthermore, you can't get what you want if you are afraid to tell people what you want. You need to put forth your ideas if you expect to get credit for them. Here are some guidelines to help you analyze whether what you are saying is appropriate:

1. Does what you say contribute to getting the work done? This doesn't mean you never engage in social remarks; it means that most of the time you are talking business.

2. Do you speak about the organization's wants and needs, not just *your* wants and needs? You may express your feelings, but this should relate to the effect on your work.

3. Does the way you talk enhance the image you wish to transmit? Do you sound girlish or tough, engage in self-put-downs, use slang expressions, or have other speech habits that may detract from what you are trying to say?

4. Would you be able to put what you're saying in writing? In other words, would the message be clear with supporting facts and a constructive tone? This is especially helpful if you are about to make a complaint about something.

5. Did you really have the opportunity to speak or did you "push in"? Be careful about interrupting people inappropriately.

6. Are you brief and concise or do you ramble?

7. Do you *know* what you are talking about? Don't be guilty of expounding on something you really know very little about.

You confidence will grow as you become increasingly able to respond appropriately in many situations.

Exercising Discretion
Outside the Organization

It is remarkable how many individuals risk their own welfare, endanger the reputation or career of others, and ruin friendships because they lack discretion. Almost every employer from time to time will make confidential statements in the presence of intimate staff. Many businesses also have trade secrets which, if revealed to outsiders, could result in severe losses.

Discreet employees recognize their responsibility and exercise restraint with respect to sensitive information. Telling your family, your bridge club, or your neighbor may bring a momentary thrill, but that thrill could be costly and have far-reaching effects. The discreet person avoids taking unnecessary risks. The list below provides some examples of topics that call for some discretion on your part.

- Discussing an employer's social contacts or habits.
- Accepting gifts from someone in a competing organization in exchange for information about your organization.
- Discussing your employer's business appointments with his or her spouse.
- Pressing for information about a co-worker's medical, financial or other personal problems.
- Revealing the contents of an unfavorable evaluation made of another employee.
- Discussing your marital or family problems with other employees who are not close friends.
- Asking questions about other employees' salaries or benefits unless this is public knowledge anyway.
- Discussing your negative opinions of the boss with other employees.

Handling Names and Introductions

The way you use others' names also contributes to your ability to get along in an organization. The simple courtesies of introducing people and addressing people you meet both personally and professionally are important in making others feel comfortable. Do not be overly worried if you make a mistake with form, as long as you do not make the other person feel awkward.

The formality of the occasion governs the formality of the introduction. It is helpful if you are familiar with proper titles. Also, it has become the accepted practice to mention *first* the person you are honoring. This is why older people are mentioned before younger people, visiting dignitaries before other guests, and so on. Here are some points to consider when introducing people in a business setting:

- All business introductions should include first and last names. For example, "Mr. Roberts, I would like you to meet Jane Richards. Ms. Richards, this is Donald Roberts."
- When a guest comes to your office for an appointment, you stand and offer your hand. (Many women feel uncomfortable doing this, but this is now an accepted practice for women as well as men.)
- Do not use phrases such as "shake hands with" or "I want to make you acquainted with."
- When making an introduction, you may want to add a bit about the person you are introducing to serve as a conversation starter.
- If you have not been introduced, feel free to introduce yourself. Simply say, "We have not been introduced. I am Jane Jones." Or you may say, "My name is Jane Jones. I don't believe we have been introduced."

If you feel confident and comfortable when you are making introductions, you will make the people you are introducing feel comfortable as well. Graciousness and good manners are always appropriate in a business situation—even when the people you are introducing are arch competitors.

Office Telephone Courtesy

When calling on the telephone, give your name immediately. If the person you need to talk to is unavailable, state briefly the reason for the call if it is a business matter; otherwise state that you're calling on a personal matter.

When answering the office telephone, simply state your name. If you are answering someone else's phone, say "John Jones's office." Be as helpful and courteous as you can on the phone.

If you need to transfer a call, tell the caller what you are doing. Do not allow him or her to feel forgotten. If you evaluate your behavior in terms of courtesy and thoughtfulness, you will never go far wrong.

Smoking

Smoking in the office is almost always a topic of controversy. Health warnings regarding smoking not only have brought greater awareness of the problems caused by smoking, they have also brought a change in our social attitudes about smoking. Before lighting up, find out what is acceptable in your organization. Nonsmokers are entitled to consideration and have the right to speak firmly but politely when a smoker causes them discomfort. By the same token, the smoker should not have to submit to a righteous harangue by a smug nonsmoker. They should agree which one should move to a different location. If you are a smoker, ask if those close to you mind if you smoke and be sure to clean up your own ashtrays.

Other Office Courtesies

A woman should no longer assume that during the regular working day men will accord her such courtesies as holding the door for her, standing when she enters a room, or offering her a chair. The men you work with may see you solely as a business associate and an equal.

Just as men aren't standing back to let women through the door first, men should no longer presume that a woman in business will naturally take on jobs once traditional in both the home and the office. If getting the coffee or taking the minutes is not part of your job description, you may politely refuse. Many offices have worked out systems so that these chores are taken care of on a more equal basis.

The business world may thrive on progress and innovation, but social situations are still largely traditional and based upon fairly conservative customs in dress, speech, and manners. The "civilized" manners of the office usually prevail even when many of the activities resemble guerrilla warfare.

POWER AND POLITICS
IN AN ORGANIZATION

"Power" and "politics" are words that often get a negative reaction from people, but if you are to be really effective in an organization, you must develop an understanding of these concepts. The cliché "it's not what you know but who you know" is as true in the organizational world as in the rest of life. Power and politics are realities of all organizations. Awareness of them will make you more sensitive to the unspoken needs and feelings of others. For years, power and politics have worked against women. They have been used to dominate, control, and limit our advancement. When you depend upon someone else for a sense of identity and self-worth, you have little real personal or professional power or authority. It is important that you now learn to deal with power and politics in order to achieve the success you want in your career. Power is not bad. All the strengths and skills you have previously identified will be underutilized unless you have the power to put them to effective use.

Knowing the Organization

Regardless of your career aspirations, you should know and understand as much about your organization as you can. Know who reports to whom; then open your eyes and see how much power each position (or person in it) really has or doesn't have. Do not let titles fool you. Many people with wonderful-sounding titles have little power or influence.

Most organizations have a hierarchy (like the military) that makes up the formal structure of the organization. This formal structure is depicted on an organizational chart and most organizations have this kind of chart. (Some very small companies may not.) The formal chart tells you the way things are *supposed to be*—who supervises whom, who has authority for certain decisions, and so on. The chart does not tell you, however, the way things *really are*.

Informal Structures

The informal structure of the organization does not come on a preprinted chart; you have to draw this one yourself. The informal structure has the real lines of communication, influence and power. How do you find out what this informal structure is? Observations, questions, experience, and awareness will give you this knowledge. Observe who is friendly with whom, who sees whom after hours or on weekends, who goes to whom for information and advice, who leads the more prestigious projects, etc. Pay attention to what gets rewarded and what gets disapproved. After a period of time, you will begin to see a pattern.

If you have no particular desire to move up in an organization, you may not think it is necessary to pay much attention to the politics of the organization. But opportunities, benefits, and security are enhanced even for those who do not want power positions if they have a good understanding of what is going on within the organization.

The Office Grapevine

Office gossip is a mixed blessing for many new employees. Listening to what workers who have been around for awhile have to say can be very helpful to you in learning about the organization, but it can also be dangerous if you begin passing along the information right away, or worse yet, adding your own interpretation to it. You need to discover what kind of "credibility" the person giving the information has—how much of the information is pure speculation or outright falsehood and how much is genuine information.

When you are learning about your organization, keep this motto in mind: *You may pick the grapes but don't fertilize the vine.* Your own credibility may be at stake.

Sometimes rumors or ideas are planted by people who have a particular axe to grind. Sometimes management itself will plant rumors in order to gauge the reaction among employees.

Office gossip can be a powerful resource. Gather all the information you can, but be careful not to malign anyone. You can expect to be quoted. Gossiping about personal relationships—who's dating whom in the office, and so on—is a favorite pastime of most employees. Unfortunately, this kind of gossip is usually far more damaging to women than to men. Take much of this information with a large grain of salt. Also, what people choose to do in their private lives should not be something you make judgments about at work. Judge your colleagues on their competence, not their private lives.

BUILDING TRUSTING RELATIONSHIPS

Developing a Relationship
With Your Boss

Getting along with your boss is a very important part of fitting into an organization. You do not have to like or admire him or her, but you should try to work with this person as well as you can. Regardless of how skilled you are technically, getting along with your immediate superior will have an important effect on your career success.

174

People working together must be concerned with each other and with what happens as they work together in the office environment. It is important that you let your boss be human. You then hope he or she will extend this same courtesy to you.

To start building a personal relationship, find out how your employer wants to be addressed by you. If her name is Jane Smith and she wants you to call her Jane instead of Ms. Smith, then do so. However, when you are talking to others—particularly people outside the organization—you should refer to her as Ms. Smith (or Mrs. Smith or Miss Smith, depending on her preference). By doing this you permit a personal relationship between you and your boss that also shows respect for his or her position. If your boss wishes to be treated formally, you may wish the same treatment in return.

No one can tell you exactly how to develop a good personal relationship—it must be sensed. But you can take the initiative of creating an atmosphere of trust. If your boss learns that you do not betray confidences, that you understand the goals he or she is working to achieve, and that you are not discussing his or her personality quirks or office activities with other people, you will probably be considered trustworthy. From this type of trust relationship a sense of loyalty can develop. Loyalty and trust should be mutual in an employer-employee relationship. At least, that is the ideal situation.

Conflicts With Your Boss and Co-workers

Most of the time it is possible, with a little work and a tolerant atttitude, to develop a good boss-employee relationship. Occasionally, however, you may find yourself in a situation where you and your boss just do not get along. This may come about because of very different values, temperament or work habits. When that happens, you owe it to your employer to do the best you can and to try to do things the way you are asked to do them, but at the same time you should think carefully about transferring to another position, or, if necessary, finding a job in a different company. Don't let the situation deteriorate to the point where you are either asked to resign or you are under constant stress. How much you can tolerate will depend upon how much contact you have with your boss. If it is a great deal of contact, you owe it to yourself and your boss to try to get out of the situation with as much dignity for both of you as possible. Good communications skills may help you solve the problem without going to the extreme of resigning or transferring. Some of these skills are explained in the next paragraph.

You need to expect that some conflicts will arise with your co-workers. Conflicts usually occur in the following situations:

- People have different standards or expectations.
- People compete with each other as they strive to perform well or be recognized.
- Misunderstandings arise from poor communications.
- People become defensive about who has the authority to make decisions.
- Disagreements occur over how to best handle a problem.
- Interpersonal conflicts (or personality clashes) occur.

If you try to suppress conflict, you don't really eliminate it. It is best, in most cases, to get the conflict out into the open and then use good communications skills to help solve that conflict.

Developing Communications Skills

What are effective communications skills? In her book, *The Woman's Guide to Management Success: How to Win Power in the Real Organizational World*, Joan Koob Cannie describes four trust-building communications skills: listening, attending, stroking, and reflection.

Let me describe each skill briefly:

1. *Listening.* This is similar to what we talked about in the chapter on interviewing techniques. Think about what you hear. Try to figure out what the speaker really means. (You will have to pay attention to such things as tone of voice and body language in addition to the words.) Listen for assumptions. Are these assumptions accurate? Why is the speaker saying what he or she is saying? Try to determine the speaker's goal. When you listen with a purpose in mind, your attention will be more focused.

2. *Attending.* This is basically a nonverbal skill whereby we show others, physically and psychologically, that we are paying attention to them. When you show people you are interested in them, you are meeting their self-esteem needs.

a. *Physical attending.* For good "physical" contact as communication, be aware of the following things: (1) remove physical barriers (such as desk or counter) unless you definitely want to establish

176

distance; (2) don't violate personal space—in other words, don't get so close to people that they become uncomfortable; and (3) stay on the same level as the person you are listening to. If the person is sitting, you sit. If the person is standing, you stand.

b. *Psychological attending.* In psychological attending, you encourage others to relax. You convey a sense of their worth as human beings.

3. *Stroking.* "Stroking" is a term originally developed by psychologist Eric Berne; it basically means saying things to others which show you value them. You "stroke" others by giving them your attention, respect, praise and warmth. This is not the same as empty flattery or phony compliments. Real stroking should be genuine.

4. *Reflection.* Reflection is repeating, in your own words, the content and feeling of what the other person has just said. Reflection immediately shows people that you are listening, that you are trying to understand, and that you care. This tends to build trust and reduce defensiveness. Also, it does not judge, evaluate or question what the other person is saying. With this skill minds meet, needs are understood, and emotions are expressed.

Developing good communications skills can help you resolve conflicts with other employees. This skill may require considerable practice. It is not just a matter of being "naturally nice." If this is an area you feel you need to improve, you might wish to take a course which would help you learn and practice these skills. Communications skills courses are often available both within companies and through local colleges or private agencies.

Understanding Territory

You must define the limits of your domain within the office. In the home, members of a family usually agree among themselves who will handle certain matters. In the office, similar domains exist. Sometimes in trying to find the limits, you may make mistakes. That is not bad. It is better to get into trouble early on the job when you are still "feeling your way." As you press to find limits, you will find them. Individual "territories" are not necessarily defined in the job description; many of them come about through habit, personal prerogative, deliberately taking or giving up territory.

You need to develop good relationships with your co-workers and your boss—both to gain visibility and to gather information helpful to performing your job. The research on the subject is not complete, but we know more about relationships all the time and what makes good ones happen. Good office relationships seem to have the following ingredients:

1. You value others and you show it.
2. You are open and honest in your dealings with others.
3. You are considerate and thoughtful of others' needs and feelings.

Getting along with others is one of the major factors in career success. It is not something that just happens, however; you need to work at it.

Fitting into the organization can be as important to your career as learning the technical aspects of your job. It is frequently the part of your career presenting the greatest challenge.

chapter twelve
OVERCOMING SEXISM AT WORK

President, senior vice-president, director, chief executive, top administrator. Less than one percent of the women in the work force today are in these positions. This chapter is addressed to the women who want that percentage figure to change even if they have no personal desire for a top management position.

Sexism is a part of society which also affects the workplace. Traditionally, patterns of work for women have been very different from patterns of work for men. The more favorable patterns for men are examples of sexism in action. You as an individual may have escaped it, but you do need to be aware of its existence and how it works.

WHAT SEXISM IS

Basically, sexism is the practice of the double standard—treating people differently because of their gender. Another way of describing it would be to say that sexism is giving unfair advantage to one sex over the other. In Chapter Eleven we talked about the division of labor and other historical incidents which led to sex-role stereotyping of work. Although a great deal has been written about the development of sexism, our concentration in this chapter will be focused on the workplace. This is in no way an exhaustive discussion of sexism but rather an overview which will introduce you to some of the major elements of this controversial topic.

Sexism In the Workplace

The division of labor in many corporations is based on the notion that there is "men's work" and "women's work." The idea that women may be active and busy but the *real work* is carried out by men is commonplace in many organizations.

Where do we see the greatest inequities between men and women in the workplace? Chiefly in the following areas:

- pay
- promotions
- discounting of capabilities
- display of emotions
- language
- nonverbal communications
- sexual involvement with a co-worker

Why is top management only one percent women when women comprise close to half of the labor force? Is it because of the socialization process girls go through which reduces their motivation, ambition, and achievement needs? Is it because men have traditionally held these positions and have been reluctant to share them? Is it because women are considered to be "less equal" and therefore not deserving of such positions? Whatever the reasons, the reality is there and it is up to us to overcome our own attitudes toward women in the work force and help men overcome theirs. Our culture has dictated that men be high achievers; women are expected to support and value achievement in men.

You may feel very ambivalent about the roles of men and women. You may feel caught in a conflict between society's (and perhaps your own) idealized image of femininity and the traits of a successful working person. The traits of a successful working person, as accepted by our culture, are basically characteristics usually ascribed to men—enterprise, independent, self-confident, assertive. Our society, on the other hand, has frequently rewarded passivity, dependence, and underdeveloped emotional skills as characteristics of a "healthy" female or a "healthy" child. So when women adopt the more "masculine" characteristics and assert their own competence, they may be rejected even in the workplace. They are considered "deviant" and labeled as deficient. They do not exhibit the idealized "normal" female personality.

Sexist Attitudes

Sexism begins with attitudes. What are some sexist attitudes? Well, how often have you heard the following comments: "She doesn't need to work; she has a husband to support her." "We can't put her in sales; what would the wives of the other salesmen say?" "Now that she works, her family must be suffering." "She is too emotional to handle a supervisory position." "If she didn't dress that way, she wouldn't attract so much flirting and gossip." All of the preceding statements reveal sexist attitudes and suggest separate standards for men and women.

Volumes could be written about the many ways men discriminate against women. Some acts of discrimination are merely annoying; others are quite destructive. Many are so deeply ingrained in people that they are often not aware of their sexist behavior. Many men will deny being male chauvinists, for example, and will then tell or laugh at a joke that degrades women. And it isn't only male attitudes and biases that constitute obstructions for the career woman. Forces within a woman herself may pose threats to her own career success and the success of other women. For example, as many young girls grow up they find their worth measured by their attractiveness to the opposite sex. A girl's worth is measured by popularity; she has to be pretty. Frequently, to be accepted by boys, she has to subjugate herself; if she has intellectual ability, she has to explain it away or underutilize it. This process does not magically change once a woman becomes an adult. The socialization process stressing nurturance and supportiveness of males is very deeply ingrained. The role of mother in our society also emphasizes the nurturant and supportive aspects, the "servant" role. As a result of this conditioning, both men and women are suspicious, intolerant and unsupportive of women who challenge the "servant" role in the workplace. This attitude then reinforces the woman's feelings about herself so that she is right back where she started—passive, dependent, nurturing.

Many sexist attitudes may come not in the form of statements but in the form of actions taken. For example, a supervisor may shield a woman worker from criticism for fear she will suffer hurt feelings; heavy physical activity is part of a particular job so women are assumed to be incapable of performing the job; women are assumed not to want the demands of a management position because of the family responsibilities a supervisor may think they now have. These attitudes may then lead to sexist behavior which can put a woman in the position of being directly discriminated against in such areas as pay and promotions or simply discounted in importance or competence. Let's look at some of the areas of inequity.

SPECIFIC AREAS OF SEXISM

Discrimination in Pay

According to studies by the U.S. Department of Labor, the average pay of those women who work full-time the year round is only about three-fifths of the average for men who work full-time the year round. A great deal of the pay differential results from the fact that women have traditionally had access primarily to low-paying jobs, have often had limited opportunities, or were simply paid less than men for the same work. While the law is now helping to change this, there are still many situations where outright discrimination exists. The Equal Pay Act of 1963 prohibits unequal pay for men and women who work in the same establishment and whose jobs require equal skill, effort and responsibility. Applications of that "equal" standard, however, have frequently been based upon the way jobs were evaluated in the past or on other cultural considerations. Many women are still trying to identify "equality" for purposes of the act. In addition to actual pay, women are frequently discriminated against in benefits and other "perks" as well. Sometimes these additional benefits can amount to a significant dollar value.

Comparable Worth

Whether formally or informally, the monetary value of jobs is identified through a process called "position evaluation." Do existing systems measure the worth of jobs in an unbiased, objective, quantifiable manner? *Business Week* Magazine has predicted that *comparable worth* will be "the civil rights issue of the 1980s." *Comparable worth* has become as important a phrase for women and minorities as *equal pay for equal work* was in the 1960s and 1970s. Equal pay for equal work seems to apply only to women who have managed to break into male territory; whereas *comparable worth* measures different jobs but compares them on the basis of comparable factors such as knowledge required, amount of responsibility, etc.

To give an example of how comparable worth works, let's consider a primarily female-dominated job, such as surgical nurse, compared to a male-dominated job such as airplane mechanic. When the factors of (1) skills required, (2) effort, (3) responsibility, and (4) working conditions are considered for both jobs, they may be very similar—in other words, they may have *comparable worth*. But the pay differential may be very great—largely because of the gender of the employees due to cultural bias based on traditional roles.

One of the reasons why comparable worth systems of job evaluation have been resisted is the tremendous initial costs of implementing such programs. This has become a controversial question because many men fear that the implementation of comparable worth programs will bring their wages down rather than raise women's wages to the present level for men. But the overriding attitude (often unspoken) is that women are not "worth" as much as men. They are usually not seen as breadwinners. Their work is often not as valued. That is the *real* problem to overcome and that may be a slow process. Only time, commitment, and tenacity on the part of career women and others who sympathize with them will reduce the earnings gap and bring about equity in pay.

Discrimination in Promotion

It is a violation of the Civil Rights Act of 1964 to deny equal opportunity for promotion. Nevertheless, many women have found it difficult to get on a job track that puts them in a promotable position. Why does this happen? Part of the problem comes from the assumption that women themselves fear taking the risks required. Sometimes women simply do not know how to "play the game" or are not allowed to play the game. You are the one who must change the assumptions. If your present company offers the opportunity for advancement, you must make sure that you let those involved know that you want to advance and that you are able and willing to take the risks involved to do so. That will not solve all the discrimination problems but it will help.

Discounting of Capabilities
By Emphasizing Appearance

Many times men discount the capabilities of women by concentrating on their physical attributes instead of their job competence. Because an attractive appearance in women has long been valued in our society, many men consider it a compliment to acknowledge a woman for her attractiveness rather than for her abilities. Furthermore, as mentioned previously, women are socialized to compete on the basis of appearance. I remember hearing a top executive officer introducing two members of his administrative staff to a large group of people. One administrator was a man; one was a woman. The two administrators were of equal rank in the organization. In an attempt to compliment each administrator, the executive stated that he would like to be able to give speeches as well as the male administrator and wished that he were as attractive as the female administrator. In another instance, I witnessed a professional woman giving an intelligent, forceful presentation to a group. One male member of the audience commented to the other, "Well, it's too bad she isn't much to look at."

This attitude about appearance versus competence constitutes a large part of the double standard encountered by capable women. Furthermore, many personnel experts agree that an attractive appearance is even more important for women than for men.

Women often receive less praise and fewer financial rewards than men do for similar performance. Unfortunately, many women have bought this concept as readily as men have. Thus they tend to belittle their own accomplishments and the accomplishments of other women. It is important to remember that while attractiveness is important for both women and men, rewards for ability are also important for both women and men.

Display of Emotions

Women have often been told that they are more "emotional" than men, but in the workplace they are actually not allowed the same display of emotions that men are allowed to have. Women are not supposed to become outraged or exhibit anger; they are not supposed to swear or pound desks. Likewise, crying is considered to be unacceptable behavior in the workplace, so women have not even been allowed this traditional method of dealing with anger and frustration. Women are supposed to be naturally nice even when confronted with the most outrageous insults. According to the unwritten organizational rules, women are supposed to be able to take the putdowns and keep smiling. This has been one of the most difficult areas of sexism to combat. Because of this, many women are adopting a cool, reserved exterior which may mask what they are really feeling at the time. Remaining silent has been one of the few ways women can adhere to their roles and also exercise some control over themselves in tense situations. This can be highly stressful and will be dealt with at greater length in the next chapter.

Sexism and Direct Power

Sexism most often occurs in situations where power relationships are operating (such as manager/subordinate, leader/follower). We discussed the need to understand power in organizations in Chapter Eleven. Power is the main component of sexism and it is important for you to understand that a woman in a power position can use sexism to hold down other women just as men in power positions can hold down women or other men.

Because men hold most of the top, middle, and supervisory management positions now, however, they determine to a great extent who is allowed to come into these ranks. Thus, much that is known about sexism concerns the "powerful" male versus the "submissive" female. Men may perpetuate their advantages and favor only the men and women who go along with them. You will have to determine what kind of actions will best allow you to overcome the sexist attitudes that may prevent you from being promoted or realizing your full potential. You must realize that sexism is connected to dominant/dependent power relationships. Men or women in power positions can hold someone down by discrediting the person in the less powerful position. If you are the victim of this kind of maneuver, you may have to find ways—direct or indirect—to deal with the situation. We will discuss some ways to do this at the end of this chapter.

The most common way to exercise power is through verbal and nonverbal communications.

Sexism and Language

Sexism in language comes in a variety of forms. Some sexism is inherent in the language itself—such as the use of terms like *mankind* to describe all people or the pronoun *he* when she is also implied. Most sexism in language, however, does not come just from using "he" or "him" as the universal pronoun or "man" or "mankind" to describe all people. The real sexism in language comes in the form of implications and hidden messages. Statements which appear just fine on the surface may carry a hidden message that serves as a putdown. For example, statements such as "You do that job very well for a woman" or "What does your woman's intuition tell you about this problem?" may not be as flattering as the speaker wants you to think. The purpose of a hidden message is to maintain power over another person. This power of language should not be taken lightly. Language can control behavior and is used by some people to manipulate or put others on the defensive.

Male and Female Vocabularies

Researchers who have studied language have determined the existence of male and female vocabularies. This can become another aspect of sexist communication. For example, the use of harsh language by women is still considered by many to be unfeminine and in bad taste. Also, certain elements of the language are considered appropriate for men whereas other, less valued, usages are regarded as proper for women. The issue of language has kept some women out of certain all-male jobs with such excuses as, "We can't have women in here; we wouldn't be able to talk freely." In addition to this, words such as "blood," "guts," sports terms, military terms and many obscenities are considered to be male terms. Women who use them may be seen as coarse. On the other hand, words such as "cute," "tummy," "darling" are seen as female terms. Men who use them are considered weak and effeminate. Words expressing power and action are usually "masculine"; words expressing niceness or passivity are "feminine." Most of the language of business is "masculine" and women who don't "speak the language" may be left out.

De-Sexing Language

As women, it is to our advantage to de-sex language whenever we can. As mentioned before, we often fall into the trap of describing women by how they look and men by what they do. For instance, we might say, "John is a lawyer." "Mary is an attractive blonde." Also, job titles are frequently sexist: salesman, mailman, policeman etc. These could be translated into salesperson, mail carrier, and police officer. Many women now are correcting men who call them "girls" (the men would certainly not call men from a similar age group "boys"). In order to de-sex language, we must first start with ourselves and de-sex our own language. Many people are simply not aware that their own speech reflects unconscious sexism. Some examples of ways to de-sex written communications are given in Table 12-1.

Table 12-1 Ways to De-Sex Written Communications

Examples of Commonly Used Terms	Alternative (Non-Sexist) Terms
workman's compensation	worker's compensation
manpower planning	staff resources planning
mankind	humanity; human beings; people
man-made	artificial; synthetic
authoress, poetess	author, poet
the girls (or the ladies)	the women
businessman	business executive; business manager
chairman	chair; chairperson
stewardess	flight attendant

Powerless Language

A further example of sexist communication can be found in "power-less" language. Sometimes women belittle themselves by repeatedly using phrases such as "I'm not sure about this, but..." or, "I may be wrong, but..." or, "May I say something about that...." These kinds of qualifying statements or statements asking permission may diminish your credibility if used a great deal. Phrases that apologize when you don't need to, or words that justify your actions or ideas more than is required, are examples of powerless language.

Guidelines to follow for de-sexing language:

1. Reword to eliminate unnecessary gender pronouns.
2. Replace the masculine pronoun with *one, you, he or she, her or his,* as appropriate.
3. Alternate male and female expressions and examples.
4. Women should be identified by their own names. (They should not be referred to in terms of their roles as wife, mother, sister, etc.)
5. Job titles should be nonsexist.
6. Males should not always be first in order of mention.

Conversational Practices

Even the way people acknowledge each other in conversation can be sexist. For instance, one study of conversation in mixed groups of men and women indicated that men interrupt women in conversation far more than they interrupt other men and more frequently than women interrupt anybody. The more powerful conversational partners tend to interrupt the less powerful ones. I am not suggesting that you take up the practice of interrupting people to assert your power, but you might observe how often this happens to you and let the interrupting person know that you do not like to be continually interrupted.

Perceptions of Authority

Perceptions of authority may also cause discriminatory behavior. A man and a woman can make statements with the same meanings, and the man will frequently be given more credibility. He may be seen as more authoritative and factual. Studies of male and female college professors have revealed that male professors were considered more authoritative in situations where they delivered the same lectures as their female counterparts. Many women have had to "plant" their ideas with a male colleague in order to get the "powers that be" simply to listen. Furthermore, argumentative statements are also seen as male behavior, and women may be at a disadvantage when engaging in this style of communication.

Sexism in Nonverbal Communications

One way in which sexism can be indicated nonverbally is by touching. Typically, there is more touching of women by men than the reverse.

Our culture has given those with status and power the right to touch those of lower status without seeking their permission.

Another way in which sexism can be indicated nonverbally is by invasion of a woman's "personal space" by a male colleague. This personal space is the invisible boundary around each individual that we do not allow others to breach unless the relationship is an intimate one. For example, if a male co-worker puts his arm around your shoulder as he introduces you to a client, he has immediately lowered your status in the eyes of that client.

One final example of nonverbal sexism is through direct eye contact. While mutual eye contact indicates a sense of confidence and mutual trust, if turned into a stare it can become a form of manipulating behavior and can make the other person uncomfortable. Women have been conditioned to look down or away in the presence of a stare. Sometimes it is possible to kill a stare by simply returning it, however, and many women are becoming more comfortable doing this rather than looking away in embarrassment.

Women in working relationships must appear confident and become comfortable in facing male co-workers directly. As you observe sexist behavior in verbal and nonverbal communications, become aware of how to overcome some of your own habits and try to learn new actions. You can do this without hurting others.

WAYS TO OVERCOME SEXISM

The woman who wants to be successful in an organization, to compete with men for positions and wages, cannot afford to let the men she deals with judge her according to stereotypes. Men and women have adopted prejudices against each other for the simple reason that such prejudices can be self-serving. Prejudices are also less demanding. When you automatically resort to stereotypes, you don't have to think. But in the long run (and frequently in the short run as well) sexist behavior is both self-destructive and destructive of others. The best reason for organizations to overcome sexism is to be able to utilize all available resources and talents—not just half of the resources and talents.

Once you become aware of sexist behavior, you must begin to learn new behaviors and actions for yourself. Some of this also includes learning what risks are involved and developing some strategies to deal with the risks. Women who wish to change sexist attitudes must become very perceptive about how far to push the norms and how fast. You may need to walk a tight line: you want to avoid behaving in a way that confirms stereotypes about how women should behave; you don't want to upset people to such an extent that you don't reach your objective.

What Are the Risks?

Although many men and women within organizations are beginning to speak out more on the rights of women, many are still not able to deal with this concept on a personal level. The intellectual commitment may have been made but the emotional commitment to the idea is not yet there.

Lack of awareness about what constitutes sexist behavior may also bring about a defensive attitude. A person may simply not understand his or her own sexist behavior; yet understanding and acceptance of the concept is necessary before behavior changes can occur. This lack of understanding probably accounts for much of the negative reaction to "uppity" women. Many people are totally unaware that they are perpetrators of sexist language and actions, and may become hostile if you point out this lack of awareness in front of others.

As a practical matter, a man's bad will may stop a woman in scores of ways that would be difficult to prove as discriminatory. Legal remedies, such as lawsuits and grievances procedures are frequently slow, expensive and unpleasant. Can you imagine working for a boss you had beaten in court? Sometimes this route may be necessary, but it should not be your first strategy in changing the situation.

The double bind in which many women find themselves in organizations is: *To succeed, you must play by the rules, but you are not supposed to use the same rules!* So, you take risks. Risk-taking may be more hazardous for women—but you must do it if you wish to change anything.

Ways to Change Your Thinking

Before you can do anything about sexism in organizations, you must examine your own behavior. *Step one* in your plan to overcome sexism is to refuse to sanction sexism. For example, don't laugh at jokes that demean women. Don't use sexist language yourself or engage in putdowns. Consider yourself to be an equal member of the group.

Step two requires you to get off the defensive and choose the behavior you think is most appropriate for the situation. Self-acceptance instead of role acceptance is one of the first steps toward doing just that. When others determine our personal worth for us, we become dependent on their judgments and thus lose our sense of identity. You must accept yourself as a valuable, worthwhile person. If you can go into a situation with the expectation of being accepted, of being able to handle what comes up, then you can help make that expectation a reality by your own attitudes.

To deal with sexist behavior, you must determine what seems most important to you and take responsibility for yourself but not for the behavior of others. In other words, pick your battles. If you do what you can in the areas over which you have some control, gradually, working with others, you can help to influence others as well.

Dealing With Others' Sexist Behavior

If you decide to deal with sexist behavior in others, you should do so in an assertive way. Remember the discussion of assertiveness in Chapter Four? You defend yourself without demeaning others.

It is important to adopt an assertive style when dealing with sexist behavior because this projects an image of self-confidence. This style comes about via your general manner, your physical appearance and actions, your way of speaking and your manner of relating to others. Let's consider some examples:

Situation One: A male colleague says to you: "Don't tell me you're one of those women's libbers!"

If you adopt an *aggressive* stance, you may angrily say: "What's it to you?" or "You'd better believe it, buddy."

If you adopt a *nonassertive* or passive stance, you may timidly say: "Oh, not really. Why would you want to think that?"

If you adopt an *assertive* stance, you may say calmly: "Don't you believe in equal rights for women?"

Situation Two: Mr. B calls in Mary Jones, one of the firm's new sales personnel, and congratulates her on landing an account he has been pursuing for two years. He says to her, "Mary, you did a first-class job on the Brown account. You really surprised everyone. How did you manage to get old man Brown to sign—well, never mind, we won't go into that."

If Mary decides to take this on as a way of showing Mr. B his sexist innuendoes, there are several things that can happen. If she decides to be *aggressive*, she will probably say, "How dare you insinuate that I used my body to get that account? I'm just a lot smarter than the average salesperson around here!" If she decides to be *unassertive*, she probably will not even mention this putdown—she will simply seethe about it when she returns to her desk. If she decides to be *assertive* about it, she may say, "Mr. B, I have worked very hard on this account. And I think my success shows that I have good abilities as a salesperson for this firm."

Other Ways of Changing Sexism

Pressure through numbers is one way to deal with sexist practices. The formation of support groups or coalitions may be helpful when confronting the person or persons in power who are practicing discrimination. The visibility and strength of groups can be illustrated by labor unions. Their power comes from collective action. The real power of the powerless is in *numbers*. Women must help each other combat sexist prejudices. Having other women help you present the problem as a group will bring greater visibility. Also, enlist the aid of sympathetic men. For example, a labor union (male-dominated) recently came to the aid of seven women union members who had been sexually harassed by a supervisor. The workers went on strike until the issue was settled. This may seem extreme to you, but sometimes extreme measures are called for in order to correct a really serious problem.

Finally, by gaining control of resources such as budgets and information channels and gaining access to influential people, you can also bring about some changes in attitudes and practices. The person who controls resources has power—whether those resources are money or information. Getting to know people who have the power and authority to make decisions and changes will help you in your pursuit of equal treatment. You can use the power of working relationships to influence discussions and actions.

Whatever avenues of change you pursue, please remember that patience and persistence are required. You cannot change attitudes overnight, or by simply standing up for your rights every now and then. But change will come if you are determined to make it happen.

SEXUAL HARASSMENT

Sexual harassment is an example of sexism in one of its more destructive forms. This topic has become one of increasing concern in organizations as the magnitude of the problem has emerged through information from rape crisis centers, research surveys and other agencies dealing with women's problems. Charges of sexual harassment are serious. This section of this chapter is offered to make you aware of problems which can exist. Do not take this new awareness to mean that your male co-workers should be feared or that every gesture or conversational exchange is a sign of sexual harassment. Instead, become aware of what sexual harassment is, why it is a problem, and what the consequences are.

What Sexual Harassment Is

What is sexual harassment? There have been numerous attempts to define the problem. Basically, sexual harassment is best described as unsolicited, nonreciprocal behavior that asserts a person's sex role over his or her function as a worker. In other words, the employee cannot choose freely to say yes or no.

Examples of sexual harassment behavior may include verbal abuse (such as sexist remarks about a woman's body), patting or pinching, demand for sexual favors in return for hiring or promotion, or even physical assault or rape. For many reasons, women are often reluctant to speak out about sexual abuse on the job. The fear of reprisal is great. Worries about possible loss of raises and promotions and even loss of the job itself have kept many women from fighting back in situations where they feel sexually harassed. Other problems of sexual harassment include credibility: Whom do you believe? It may be easier to replace an inexperienced young subordinate than an influential manager.

Myths About Sexual Harassment

One of the reasons sexual harassment has been difficult to fight is because of the myths surrounding it. So many people accept these myths as reality that problems have been difficult to solve. Some examples of the myths are:

- *Sexual harassment only occurs in a few select industries and positions.* Several studies have indicated that sexual harassment can occur at all levels of an organization. In addition, lawsuits filed indicate that many different types of organizations are involved in sexual harassment cases.
- *Sexual harassment is simply a fact of life and is no cause for concern.* Just because something is a common occurrence is no reason to perpetuate it or refuse to deal with it. Illness may be a fact of life too, but most of us try to combat it.
- *Women should simply ignore sexual abuse when it occurs.* This may not be as simple as it seems. It is difficult to ignore continual abuse. It is also difficult to ignore abuse or threats related to promotions, job security, or job performance.
- *Most charges of sexual harassment are false. Women use charges as a means of getting back at men.* In fact, women have little to gain from making false charges. They may be further harassed, demoted or fired. Also, they may damage their work references and potentially ruin their careers if they file false charges.

Getting rid of the myths about sexual harassment is not easy, but as more findings emerge from research and court cases, it will be easier to fight attitudes with facts.

What Sexual Harassment Is Not

Although the definitions given for sexual harassment may seem pretty clear, there are many situations where the definition is not so simple; definitions are highly subjective and are open to interpretation. Not every person is going to take offense at the same behavior. And there are many situations where the behavior is simply in the category of bad taste—in other words, a lot of questionable behavior simply falls through the cracks in the definitions. You may have to work with men (or women for that matter) whose language you find objectionable, whose mannerisms annoy you, or whose jokes offend you. This is not necessarily sexual harassment—especially if it is not directed specifically at you. You simply may not be comfortable in the environment.

Sexual harassment is most likely to occur when a person has the power to hire and fire, grant raises and promotions, or in some other way affect another person's economic situation. The most common harassment situation features a powerful man and a powerless woman.

Sexual harassment is not practiced by men who genuinely like and respect women. Good, decent men are not users of people for selfish gain. This kind of man appreciates your contribution to the organization and treats you with dignity and respect. Look for this kind of boss and co-workers and you are far less likely to find yourself in a harassment situation.

Finally, it is important to remember that sexual harassment is *not* funny. Sexual harassment simply perpetuates that notion that women should be considered in sexual terms and detracts from their contributions to their organizations. It assumes women are less serious about their work and that their prime function is to please and serve men.

Groups of Women Most Likely to Suffer From Sexual Harassment

Although all women may be potential victims of discrimination and harassment, some are more vulnerable than others. The following examples may give you some idea of what groups of women are most likely to be the targets of harassment:

- *The woman who accepts the definition of female as that of a sex object.* A woman in this category may actually believe that men have the right to treat her this way.
- *The woman who is insecure about her abilities.* This type of woman believes that she cannot compete with a man on the basis of her performance at work.
- *The woman who is the head of her own household.* She may be seen as a woman who needs her job very desperately and is willing to do anything to keep it.
- *The ambitious woman who may be viewed as a threat to less secure or unenlightened men.* This woman may be harassed by peer rivals who want to keep her "in her place" or to get her to leave the organization.
- *Women in a protegée/mentor relationship.* If the woman is the protegée and the man is the mentor, this may lead to a harassment situation— particularly if the protegée begins to grow professionally and develops other attachments in the organization and this "threatens" the mentor.

Sexual harassment is primarily a game of power and intimidation, not of attraction. It is one of the main power games when men and

195

women work together. Harassment has been a fairly effective tool for getting rid of women who provide too much competition.

Who Are the Harassers?

Although people who sexually harass others cannot be as easily stereotyped as the categories of women most likely to be harassed, there are some "types" who seem more prone to harassing behavior than others. Although a sexual harasser is usually referred to as "him," the "he" could just as well be a "she." There are female managers who have sexually harassed young male and female subordinates; there are male managers who harass male subordinates; and there are women employees who have tried to seduce their bosses. Generally, however, the harassers are male and they are in positions to retaliate if their demands are not met. The categories of men most likely to harass include:

- *A man who is insecure about his own abilities.* A man who lacks confidence may not want to compete with a woman for a particular promotion or other career move, so he engages in harassment to reduce the competition.
- *Men who are insecure about their sexuality.* If a man does not believe he can attract women on his own merit, he may resort to pressure to convince himself that he is really masculine.
- *Men who have a very low opinion of women and see them primarily as sex objects.* This is the man who truly does not see women as any kind of equal and wants them to stay "in their proper place." This is the classic male chauvinist.
- *Men who manipulate others for selfish gain.* This is the category that may very well include women as well. For these people, sexual harassment is simply a tool for getting rid of the competition.

Sexual harassment will continue as long as those who use it get the results they want. This can do real damage to a career. Sexual harassment will not stop unless women stop it.

How Can You Deal With Harassment?

You do have some rights when it comes to harassment and you may have to be prepared to exercise them. Effective handling of harassment must occur at several levels. Here are some guidelines for dealing with the situation:

196

1. Never give in to the demands of a harasser; also do not take the blame for the harassment. If you respond to the harassing, be assertive.
2. Keep careful documentation of your job performance. This should include performance evaluations, statements of co-workers about your performance, and, if possible, statements of co-workers who have experienced similar coercion. Harassment charges almost always involve only one person's word against another's. If you are coerced into quitting or end up being fired because you won't submit to the harassment, you will have better evidence for a defense.
3. Help set up an internal grievance procedure within your organization. To be effective, this procedure must be well-known throughout the organization, must ensure confidentiality, and must be under the authority of a powerful individual.
4. Contact an organization for background materials, for information and support.
5. Find a support group or a powerful woman in the organization in whom you can confide.
6. If you are dealing with a client (as opposed to a co-worker), inform the harasser in a matter-of-fact, nonthreatening voice of his possible legal jeopardy. Keep informed about the legal process.
7. Be firm and consistent about dealing with remarks and situations.

The consequences of sexual harassment on the victim, harasser and employer are great. Not only does sexual harassment result in high turnover for the company, but the stress symptoms for both the victim and the harasser may have a noticeable effect on performance and productivity. Harassment should be opposed on moral, ethical, and financial grounds.

OVERCOMING SEXUAL DISCRIMINATION

The federal government and many state and local governments, through laws, executive orders, and ordinances, have sought to provide enabling services if you are seeking employment, or trying to assure equal access to jobs. Laws such as The Civil Rights Act of 1964, the Age Discrimination in Employment Act, the Equal Pay Act of 1963 and many others may help you in the pursuit of your rights. To obtain more specific information, write to the U.S. Department of Labor, Equal Employment Opportunity Commission, Washington, D.C. 20506 and ask for additional information. If you think you have been discriminated against, they can help you file a complaint.

Lawsuits can be long, unpleasant, and expensive, so many women do not pursue their grievances through the courts. We can be grateful, however, for those who have. They have helped us all immensely. Equally helpful are those groups of people willing to lobby and work in the political system for legislation on sex discrimination or other means of bringing about fair and equitable treatment for women.

Once we accept the principle of equal opportunity, we must begin to think about implementation. The major first step toward that implementation is believing in the principle yourself. The real payoff will be the improvement in the quality of life for women and their families. Perhaps one of the most positive contributions of action to end discrimination will be to give all women and men a broader view of women that encompasses their role as human beings. This will help both individuals and organizations to be successful.

chapter thirteen
COPING WITH JOB STRESS

There is a phrase from a famous poem which goes: "The world is too much with us." For many working women, that phrase describes how they feel as they cope with the many demands in their lives—work demands, family demands, personal needs. As more and more women enter career positions, they are finding that success in the business arena may bring with it stress as well as money and prestige. Although stress can also be caused by family problems, financial worries, and so on, the most common source of stress seems to come from the workplace. This chapter will focus on work stress and how to cope with it.

WHAT IS STRESS AND WHAT DOES IT DO?

A common definition of stress is "a physical, chemical or emotional factor that causes bodily or mental tension and may be a factor in disease causation." A *stressor* is an event, environmental factor or person causing stress. These definitions will be used throughout this chapter as we discuss stress relating to work.

Stress in and of itself is not bad—in fact, it can be good. Most of us, however, are familiar with stress as a factor which can cause or aggravate a variety of body problems and illnesses. In addition, stress can play havoc with thinking and reasoning abilities. This, in turn, affects job performance and work productivity. Stress may also affect our relationships with people. So stress is a very important issue as it relates to our work lives.

Stress brings about physiological changes. Sometimes this is harmful; sometimes it is not. It is important to make some distinction between stress and simple nervous tension: stress is actually a condition which imposes demands for "adjustment" on a person. Usually when we say someone is under stress, we actually mean excessive stress or distress (damaging or unpleasant stress is distress). For example, a dry mouth or a tight stomach before an exam may help a student get good grades. Too many "tight stomachs" and the student may end up with an ulcer.

Researchers from many different disciplines—psychology, medicine, anthropology, management—are studying occupational stress, particularly that stress associated with the psychological aspects of work. Work stress and worker "burn-out" can be very costly to an organization. The pressures and conditions of our work environment, our interactions with others at work, other contributors such as fear of unemployment or resistance to change may all bring about physiological changes which may, in time, bring about illness. Indeed, stress at work is so commonplace that we tend to accept it as a part of the necessary frustration of daily living and do very little to systematically deal with the problem.

There is substantial evidence to show that stress can build up and accumulate in our bodies. Physical symptoms are often the first indicators of how much stress we are experiencing. Sometimes we receive warning signals: headaches, indigestion, other small physical flare-ups such as frequent colds, skin rash, backache, and so on. All of us have our own individual, recurring warnings of too much stress. In fact, before we go on, make a note to review your body's warning signals. You may wish to relate them to particular causes as we explore this subject further.

The Positive Side of Stress

It is important to emphasize that stress is not always a negative thing. A certain amount of tension and stress can, in fact, be healthy. Most of us have experienced normal excitement when we've solved a difficult problem or received some kind of unexpected reward. We need this kind of "stress" to be motivated, to keep active and to put forth constructive effort in the pursuit of our goals. While tolerance for stress varies from person to person, some stress spurs our productivity and creativity. It provides the "spice of life," and many people thrive on a high level of stress. The crucial factor is the degree of stress: too much stress can be incapacitating, too little can be not motivating enough.

Each of us has an optimal stress level. To keep from becoming "distressed," we need the right amount and the right kind of stress for the right duration. This is not so easy to attain, but it is worth working for.

Activity versus Inactivity

In trying to find your positive balance of stress, do not fall into the trap of thinking that stress is reduced by the absence of work or physical activity. As a matter of fact, vigorous physical activity may help relieve excessive stress, and we will discuss that more later in the chapter. Also, work we enjoy can be a very positive kind of stress even if the hours are long. On the other hand, continuous enforced leisure or boredom may be highly stressful.

Since work seems to be a basic need of most people, the question is not whether we should work, but what work suits us best. Successful activity, no matter how intense, leaves you with comparatively few scars. For many women, going to work while continuing to pursue the activities of family and home have been very positive. Problems occur when frustrations, failures, conflicting demands and unmet expectations are operating.

Let's look at some of the areas which may produce excessive stress or distress:

WHAT PRODUCES WORK STRESS?

Change In the Work Environment

New technology, as it eliminates some jobs and creates new ones, contributes to rapid change in the world of work. Promotions, demotions, and job transfers are further examples of change in the work environment. All change involves loss of some kind. Familiar people, procedures, places, organization supports give way to new places, people, or procedures. While this can be challenging and exhilarating, it can also be stressful. Let me give you a specific example: I became acquainted with a woman who had been a legal secretary for twenty-five years. Her shorthand and typing skills were superb. But in keeping up with the changes in technology and procedures, her law firm installed a word processing system complete with machine dictation and editing typewriters. With this new equipment, each secretary was now expected to produce more work in the same time. Procedures changed. Reporting relationships changed. She felt her skills had become obsolete and she was not valued. Work lost its meaning for her and she finally quit after a bout of repeated illnesses. *She did not want her work to change.* Another individual might have considered the changes to be challenging and found the effects to be positive and stimulating. The changing nature of work is a signficant stressor for many people. Learning to accept change can go a long way toward relieving stress in the workplace.

The Changing Work Ethic

Work has a different meaning for each individual employee. Some people view work as simply a necessity for putting food on the table; others see work as an opportunity for personal fulfillment. Some see work as a moral obligation of our society; others see work as a prison which keeps them from pursuing non-work activities. Some see work as a refuge from boredom and depression; others see work as an opportunity for creativity.

However defined, work is a key to good mental health. It contributes to self-esteem by making people feel competent through mastery of the challenge of their jobs, and they feel competent when they think others consider what they do to be valuable.

Sometimes you and your family have high expectations about your employment prospects and you find that there are no jobs available in what you want to do. If you take something simply to "get by," you may find yourself in a high stress situation. Or if you grew up believing "hard work pays off" only to find out that you can be laid off along with others who do not work as hard, you may feel stressed until you can resolve your feelings.

The Puritan work ethic has undergone some changes in contemporary society. There is no question that many of today's workers do not feel the same guilt about absenteeism that they did several decades ago. Furthermore, many employees feel entitled to more benefits than in previous years, including the right of job satisfaction. There appears to be an increasing acceptance of the notion that it is all right to put family needs ahead of business needs or to say no to a transfer. Our attitudes toward work are changing. These changed attitudes may collide with employers' demands and produce more stresses. Sometimes the overall work environment is hard to pin down in terms of stress. But many broad environmental factors— health and safety practices, attitudes of management toward employees, morale, overall economic influences—may all serve to produce stress in an individual worker.

How Well Does Your Job Fit You?

It has been suggested that some occupations by their very nature are more stressful and may lead to greater incidence of illness. In general, however, a more demanding job does not necessarily produce more stress. What seems to be the key element in job stress is *worker satisfaction*. When a worker is dissatisfied (for any number of reasons), this may produce some excessive stress levels. Let's consider some elements of worker dissatisfaction:

1. *Role conflict.* Such conflict occurs when incompatible demands are made by two or more persons on one individual. If you do work for two different people and each wants you to give his or her work priority, you may find it stressful to determine whose work is more important. In other words, you become the "person in the middle." One way to deal with role conflict is to try to anticipate it and communicate the difficulty to those making the demands before the situation gets out of hand.

2. *Boredom.* Boredom is a significant factor in stress. It may come about because of monotonous and repetitive tasks or because of the pace of the work. Lack of activity, particularly when it is necessary to *look busy*, may be more stressful than too much activity. Since most jobs have some tedious activities, most workers can plan on being bored from time to time.

Workers may overcome the stress of dull jobs in various ways. For some, the solution is to put other things at the center of their lives. Others find their rewards in the social interaction with other workers rather than the job itself. For still others, a strategy to bring satisfaction is to be creative when doing the work activity—find ways to vary the routine, compete with oneself, and so on.

3. *Ambiguity.* Ambiguity in work occurs when the description of the work is not clear and the worker is not sure how the job responsibilities can best be met. This may bring about a sense of futility and low self-confidence. Workers suffering from this condition should seek information from their employer which can help them formulate a clear-cut mission or set of directions.

4. *Overwork.* How much work is too much? Again, this stressor is relative to each person and the type of work being performed. *Quantitative overload* comes about from the feeling that there is too much to do in the amount of time given to do it. *Qualitative overload* comes when workers are confronted with problems they are not equipped to solve. Learning to set priorities is vital for relief in this category. Sometimes overwork stress can come about when a person plays the role of "indispensable" employee. It is one thing to fulfill an obligation to your organization; it's quite another to get in a position where they could not function without you. Making sure that others can provide back-up or take care of some of your duties if necessary is really a good idea.

5. *Crossing boundaries.* Closely related to role conflict, this category of work stress means having to deal with people inside and outside the organization who have different needs and philosophies. Persons in this situation frequently feel caught between the demands of the outsiders (clients and customers) and the requirements of their own management whose interests they must represent. For example, a student may want a certain course to be offered because of a particular interest, so he approaches an instructor about it. The instructor pursues this with the administration but they say "no" because there is not enough overall interest to cover the costs of offering the course. The instructor feels the stress from the conflicting demands. Again, sorting out priorities and values is extremely important for relief in this category.

6. *Job competition.* In many jobs the element of competition is very real. You may need to compete with others to get customers, or a promotion, or the boss' attention, or just to obtain a job. Work competition can set the pace for a healthy stress level, but if things go badly, the anxiety can add to stress and overreactions may become extreme. Self-monitoring is really important in this category. Some ways to minimize stress in this area are:

a) Don't put more competition in the situation than is necessary.

b) Eliminate competition from some of the other aspects of your life. Do some activities strictly for fun.

c) Be aware of "sneaky" competition in such stress-relieving activities as team sports, running, golf, etc. and don't succumb to it.

7. *Co-workers or clients who are stressors.* Sometimes the unreasonable or excessively demanding behavior of other people spills over onto us and produces our own high stress level. I think of these people as "stressors." Their irritability, anxiety, and irrational moods, may make it difficult for others and create a high level of tension in the office. I have seen students who could produce this high stress effect on a whole classroom; I've also seen teachers who have this effect on students; I have seen bosses who have this effect on employees. If you are working for someone who continually exhibits the behaviors of someone under excessive stress, you must try not to let this affect you or your attitude. Don't take on the other person's problem.

8. *Stressful work conditions.* In addition to stressful events, some aspects of the work environment may lead to worker dissatisfaction and high stress levels. The stressfulness of particular occupations has been debated for years. Air traffic controllers, police, and assembly-line workers are examples of workers whose jobs are considered quite stressful. What conditions bring about this high stress level?

a. *Assembly lines and piece work.* Assembly lines are often considered stressful because of the fragmentation of the work and the lack of worker participation in decisions about the work process.

b. *Physical environment stresses.* These consist of job hazards such as high noise levels, hostile crowds, dangerous conditions, and so on.

c. *Responsibility for people.* Workers who have direct and indirect responsibilities for many lives (physicians, teachers, social workers, and so on) may be vulnerable to stress reactions.

Workers with these conditions must continually find ways to put their jobs into perspective.

9. *Lack of job security, thwarted ambition.* A number of researchers have linked frustrated work aspirations to mental disorder. The stress reactions seem to be a consequence of frustration over the disparity between an individual's perception of where he or she should be in the organization and the reality.

10. *Stressful events.* Even for people who have good "job fit" and overall satisfaction, there may be events which are stressful at work. Most of these events do not lead to seriously high stress levels, but some can. Certainly the ultimate occupational stress—the loss of a person's job—can bring about serious reactions. Let's consider some other examples of threatening or stressful events:

a. *Evaluations of job performance.* Because evaluation serves as both an opportunity and a barrier to advancement, it is usually a stressful event. People who find evaluation the least stressful are those who have confidence in themselves and have accepted their own strengths and weaknesses.

b. *Changes in top management.* Many people feel threatened by fear of unknown policy changes or by fear that they will not measure up to a new set of standards. The feeling of being "on your guard" passes eventually.

c. *Changes in personnel procedures.* This change may threaten our feelings of security—again, fear of the unknown. But, like the change in top management, this stress usually disappears in a few weeks.

d. *Hiring of new employees.* The necessity of dealing with someone new often rouses our competitive feelings. It causes us to reassess our own position in the organization.

e. *Promotions.* Promotions can be stressful because of the large number of changes involved—new jobs and skills to learn, new people with whom to interact, old routines to abandon. For example, a classroom teacher who became a supervisor found herself very distressed because now she had to deal mostly with administrators and had little contact with students. Fortunately, she found a way to adapt: she began teaching seminars for other teachers and thus utilized her teaching skills and created an opportunity for "student contact."

f. *Retirement.* For many people this represents a loss of productivity and potency. Some may feel they are losing their identity—particularly if their own self-esteem is defined by occupation. To reduce this period of stress, it is helpful to have interests and hobbies outside of work.

Further Thoughts on Worker Satisfaction and Job Fit

Ideally, having a good job means doing interesting work, using acquired skills or developing new ones, supervising others or being permissively supervised. Even more important may be the need to feel appreciated, important, and useful. Other determinants of work satisfaction are good pay, job security, advancement opportunities, good personal relationships at work, and successful completion of a job.

REACTIONS TO STRESS ON THE JOB

Reactions to Frustration

Given any stressful situation, such as one of the continuing job stress situations described previously, most people go through a series of reactions in an effort to minimize the situation.

First, we look for an intelligent solution. Our feelings are playing a minor role here. Usually in the case of less serious stressors, this works very well. When no satisfactory solution develops from the first approach, we look for other ways to solve the problem.

The second level of reaction leads to an increase in random activity. One good example of this is the way we look for lost items. If the initial search does not locate the item, our behavior becomes more erratic and frantic. We may look repeatedly in the same places while becoming increasingly disturbed. This behavior is not logical, but sometimes we do find the lost object. Thus, our behavior operates as a stress-reducing solution.

If the second level of reaction does not work, we may become unrealistically angry. This often leads to aggressive behavior directed against the source of the stress; sometimes it is directed at a substitute (as when one takes out work problems on one's own family). Sometimes the only way to deal with stress at this level is to remove yourself from the situation.

Let's relate these reactions to job frustrations, through an example. I knew a good word processing operator who had been promoted to a supervisory position because of her job performance as an operator. She soon became aware, however, that the skills she had used to perform as an operator and the autonomous environment she had enjoyed were drastically changed in the supervisory position. Now she had to get others to work instead of performing the work herself. She had to handle all the complaints and demands from the customers. She became so frustrated and angry with herself for not being able to perform these new roles, she began to have severe headaches—so severe that she often could not come to work, let alone perform her job. Finally, recognizing this, she requested a transfer to a different position in another part of the company. After the transfer, the headaches, anger, and frustration disappeared. There may have been many other solutions to the problem as well, but removal from a stressful situation is one extreme solution that frequently works pretty well.

Burn-out

"Burn-out" is a term used for a transition period in a worker's life when he or she experiences apathy, lack of interest and motivation, cynicism, and loss of productivity when formerly the worker had been highly motivated and productive. Burn-out is frequently thought to result from overwork, frustration, and lack of external reward for performing well. It is particularly characteristic of those occupations that require high productivity and competitiveness, such as sales, or professional occupations such as teaching, law, medicine, or social work where it is necessary to deal continually with other people's problems.

Life Stress

In some instances, work frustrations are not a function of the job, they are a function of events and life habits that go beyond the workplace.

Just as we do not function at our best when we are running a temperature, our brains don't work well when we have an emotional temperature. It is difficult to face the fact that there are times when we are irrational and unreasonable. We are not always sensible and pleasant to be with. This behavior may come from a very high stress level, and then may cause the arousal of distress in others. In a work situation, the impairment of our intellectual functioning directly affects our job performance and productivity. Table 13-1 contains a list of some of the specific changes that people report in their job and performance behaviors as stress levels mount.

When we are angry, dissatisfied, or resentful, our emotion is all we are aware of. The more emotional we are, the less clearly we can think. Even while experiencing grief or joy, we are not particularly sensitive to others or aware of the consequences of our behavior. Many people who are not dealing honestly with emotions and behaviors in their personal lives may carry over these feelings and behaviors into the work situation where unreasonable behavior is frowned upon and not tolerated as well. This may then bring about even more stress as employers and co-workers react negatively to our "dumping" our feelings on them.

Table 13-1 Specific Behavior Changes
During High Stress Levels

People may ...
- behave less sensibly than usual
- make more mistakes of all kinds
- lose creativity and the ability to solve problems or complete complicated tasks
- do things they are later ashamed of
- narrow or highly restrict their point of view (tunnel vision)
- act irrationally or unreasonably
- waste time ("spinning of wheels")
- see fewer alternatives or options
- waste time on fruitless self-accusations
- waste time on searches for missing items (running around in circles)
- lose perspective
- appear fragmented and anxious
- become unaware of the consequences of their behavior

General Health Habits

Much has been written about nutrition, exercise, and other habits relating to our physical health. While your eating and drinking habits may not *cause* high stress levels, they can certainly contribute to the way you cope with stress. The old-fashioned word *moderation* is an important one in the context of stress. Generally accepted health practices such as getting enough sleep, eating breakfast, being moderate in one's alcohol consumption, not being seriously overweight, and avoiding smoking are lessons we were supposedly taught when very young. Unfortunately, when we become distressed, we tend to forget these early health lessons and try to overcome the stress by engaging in many negative health practices: too much coffee, not enough sleep, too little exercise, using alcohol to relax, and so on.

The Coffee and Cigarette Syndrome

For many people who work, there is a great temptation to "get going" in the morning with coffee and cigarettes. This may give a temporary "high" but, unfortunately, leads to an energy low in a few hours. Similarly, people may offer themselves a "pick-me-up" in the afternoon—a candy bar, coffee and doughnut, or a cola drink—and, again, get a quick "high." I have watched many students become junk food addicts as the pressures of the academic quarter mount—skipping meals and grabbing a bag of potato chips or a candy bar out of a vending machine to "save time." Unfortunately, the bad effects of these habits often do not become apparent until later.

If your diet, coffee drinking habits, cigarette smoking, and alcohol consumption have ceased to be *moderate*, you are contributing to the stress you may already be feeling from other events.

Stages of Life

Recently researchers have been paying greater attention to the various stages of life and how these stages relate to individual vulnerability to stress. Each period in a person's life has its own kind of vulnerabilities. The fear of aging brings about some stress in many people's career lives. There is a myth that people who have a title, substantial length of service, and good performance are safe and secure in their careers. Many middle-aged people become scared by their organizational roles and begin to question their career goals and expectations. The fears may range from worry about being replaced by a more youthful worker to concerns about the choice of careers and values. This has sometimes been termed a "mid-life crisis" and has been related primarily to men, but now that women are choosing lifetime paid work careers, we may see similar patterns for them.

Special Stressors for Women

The changes in women's roles in society may be a stress producer—both at work and at home. People in ambiguous situations are likely to be anxious. While the old rules are breaking down, new ones have yet to be firmly established. This tough transitional situation creates a double bind for many women. They may feel pressed by society, mate, and peers to be nurturing and supportive, but also to be independent and striving. As in role conflict on the job, women need to be able to assess priorities and get the people making the conflicting demands to be more reasonable.

LEARNING TO COPE
AND ADAPT TO CHANGES

Up to this point we have centered our discussion of stress on the causes of stress, with some isolated suggestions relating to particular causes. Let's turn now to a more general discussion of how to cope with stress.

Effective action against some of the causes of stress requires the efforts of the employer, employee associations and unions, and the individual worker. Let's concentrate on the individual worker—in this case *you*.

Looking at Your Particular
Working Conditions

By now you are aware of many different conditions and events which may cause a high stress level. I must emphasize again, however, that what may prove stressful to one person may not to someone else. The reason you need to know what kinds of conditions can be stressful is in order to have a greater degree of *awareness*. Awareness of what is causing stress is the first step in trying to overcome it. A word of caution: *Don't seek to explain every illness or uncomfortable situation as being caused by work or life stress.* Also, do not use stress (or "distress") as an excuse for nonproductivity or poor job performance. Your employer may be far from sympathetic. Instead, learn to identify stressors so you can correct them for yourself.

Determining If Your
Stress Level Is Too High

Sometimes we are not aware of just how stressed we are. Our stress level may rise slowly, not rapidly. Let's consider a specific example: Margaret's week has not been going too well. She had an argument with her husband about their fifteen-year-old son, who wants to buy a motorcycle. The argument degenerated into a fight where each blamed the other. She has been restless at night with several work projects on her mind. Upon awakening she is clearly not rested and is quite irritable. She arrives late at work because of traffic problems, and immediately on arriving confronts several irritated co-workers who need items from her. Throughout the morning she finds it difficult to organize her thoughts and focus on problems. She drinks a number of cups of coffee and has a couple of doughnuts. By noon she has a headache and would love to take a long lunch but instead works at her desk through the lunch hour so she can be ready for the 1:30 staff meeting. During the meeting she feels indigestion and has a difficult time concentrating on what is happening. By the time she reaches home, she is weary, tense, and feeling generally out of sorts. She would like to sit down with a drink and complain to someone about her rotten day, but her family wants dinner right away so they can go about their activities. Later that night she reflects back on the day, noting that nothing particularly unusual has occurred, but that nevertheless it had been an extremely stressful day.

Because Margaret's stress level built up rather slowly, it was not obvious to her what was happening until she had time to reflect back on the situation. She kept going even though she was not functioning at her best and was not very pleasant to be around.

According to Herbert Greenburg, author of *Coping With Job Stress* (Prentice-Hall), there are at least three elements at work in a slow accumulation of stress that prevent us from taking control of our situations:

1. Slow changes dull our awareness; they are insidious. Until someone points out the changes in us or we suddenly become aware of them ourselves, the stresses may continue to grow.
2. As our stress rises, our intellectual awareness drops. Emotions get in the way.
3. As we try to gain awareness, we rationalize or "fool ourselves" about our feelings.

Understanding how this develops, then, let's look at one of the first "tools" for dealing with stress: self-monitoring.

The following questions may help you determine whether or not your stress level is too high:

1. During a crisis, do you become nauseated?
2. Are you chronically tired with no great physical exertion to account for it?
3. Do you catch yourself gritting your teeth, clenching your fists or tightening your lips?
4. Are you plagued by indecision with a substantial amount of work piled up?

5. Do you become furious at inanimate objects?
6. Do you sit stiffly at your desk, hold a steering wheel in a tight grip, or lean tensely over your desk?
7. Do you increasingly reach for a tranquilizer or an alcoholic beverage?
8. Are you showing irritation over petty things? Feeling neglected or left out? Becoming increasingly impatient to get things done?
9. Do you have frequent headaches?
10. Do you have difficulty sleeping?

If you answer yes to several of these questions, and if these symptoms persist over weeks or months, you may be operating at dangerously high stress levels.

Breaking Stress Patterns

Self-monitoring, as discussed previously, is one way to become aware of stress levels, but once we determine that our stress level is too high, how do we break the pattern? Again, remember that you as an individual may need an individual solution, but the following guidelines may help you to find ways to cope with your particular situation:

1. *Take an exercise break.* Pursue some kind of vigorous activity three or four times a week. Choose something you like and do it regularly. Walking is a cheap and very healthy exercise. YMCA's, health clubs, and other organizations in your community may also help you find the right kind of exercise program for yourself.

2. *Slow the pace.* Rushing emphasizes getting the work done, not the quality of the product. Speed also interferes with the ability to concentrate. In fact, slowing down can often increase productivity. This is not an invitation to goof off, fail to fulfill your responsibilities, or avoid making decisions! The purpose of slowing down occasionally is to make you more productive.

3. *Try relaxation and meditation techniques.* There are many philosophies about deep relaxation and meditation. It is not the purpose of this book to recommend a particular kind. Rather, I wish to suggest that this whole area is worth looking into for stress management. These may include such techniques as yoga, biofeedback, meditation, massage, etc.

4. *Find support groups.* Church groups, sports groups, social groups, or any other kind of group made up of people whom you know and trust and see regularly can be valuable sources of support in times of stress.

5. *Seek solitude.* Removing oneself completely from demands for a period of time may work as a stress reliever. Taking a walk, reading the newspaper uninterrupted, or taking a short nap may be ways to remove oneself from interaction. I am convinced that everyone needs some time *alone.* This is not the same thing as being *lonely.*

6. *Plan.* Personal planning processes such as the ones you are learning from this book will help you assess situations and identify priorities. This can be a good coping strategy.

7. *Modify your diet.* Watch your diet: not only calories but content. Cut down on sugar particularly and limit alcoholic beverages and beverages with caffeine (coffee, cola drinks, and so on).

8. *Develop interpersonal skills.* Good communications skills and problem-solving skills practiced assertively are tools for tackling many stressful situations. These are learned skills (different from personality traits) such as we discussed in Chapters Four and Eleven.

9. *Seek professional help.* Members of the clergy, psychologists, physicians, and counselors may be the people to turn to if you have difficulty working out your own stress solutions. Someone who is a good listener is always a source of help in times of stress.

10. *Pleasurable activities.* Singing, poetry, laughter, you name it. If it is enjoyable to you, it is a kind of therapy.

One of the main considerations for stress-relieving activities is to find something that *works* for you and fits with your values, lifestyle, and habits.

Healthy Coping at Work

None of us is perfect and this is an important concept to remember in stress management. But if we were to consider a model of a person who copes ideally and adapts well, the following traits would be very important:

- The healthy, coping person knows herself or himself and understands and accepts his or her strengths and weaknesses.

- Such a person is one who has developed many interests outside of work as well as interest in her work.
- Such a person doesn't always react in the same way to factors he or she finds stressful. Also, this person can bounce back fairly quickly from stress reactions.
- Such a person acknowledges that others have different value systems and different ways of doing things, and he or she accepts this as a fact of life.
- He or she is active and productive at work.

While it is not possible to measure up in all five areas all the time, this model does give us a goal to aim for, so we can establish new coping techniques or modify some of the ways we now cope.

The more you know about your body, the better off you are in learning how to increase stress tolerance and maintain high levels of energy and vitality. Not only does your organization benefit when you are an energetic, vital worker, but you personally benefit as well. The basic reality is that we can, with some effort, learn to prosper in difficult, tension-producing environments. Then the stress becomes a positive rather than a negative factor in our lives.

chapter fourteen
EXPLORING CAREER GROWTH

To most of us, working is much more than something we do to get out of the house every day or to put bread on the table. A career may contribute to our self-esteem and give us enormous personal pleasure. And when we think of "getting ahead," our fantasies may include everything from becoming president of the company to starting our own business.

People have always had careers. But only recently has serious attention been directed to the way careers actually develop. According to a study completed by the National Bureau of Economic Research, most workers hold about ten jobs in their lifetimes. We live at a time when many different types of lifestyles are realistically available. But as possibilities expand, so does the necessity of choosing. Exploring and choosing from various career paths is what this chapter is all about.

AN OVERVIEW OF CAREER GROWTH

Once you are past your initial job-search campaign and situated in a position, you may find yourself beginning to think of what your next career move will be. Samuel Gompers, the first president of the American Federation of Labor, said that one of the things workers wanted was "more opportunities to cultivate our better natures."

Much of the recent research on employee satisfaction reveals that most workers do indeed want *more*—not just money and benefits, but *more* psychological satisfactions, *more* opportunities to learn and grow, *more* chances to use talents and skills to the fullest extent, and *more* possibility of accomplishing something worthwhile. All of this emphasis on personal growth can, at times, be a little overwhelming, but just how does career growth come about?

Have a Plan

Two or three years after you start a job, you should have some idea of where your interests lie and what you want to accomplish. The connection between where you are today and your future career goals is the *path*; in other words, this career path is what will allow you to reach tomorrow's career goals from today's situation. This path may involve additional education and training, professional licensing, contacts with resource people, moving to a new area, or some changes in lifestyle. Just like your original job search, your path is built around your values, interests, skills, goals, and opportunities. And also as in the original job search, you set short-term goals within a definite time period and take on whatever activities are necessary to accomplish those goals.

Career aspirations are usually long-term goals involving chosen job responsibilities and characteristics. Your path may take you to a position with greater responsibility and authority in your organization (a vertical move), to a similar job in a different company or department (a horizontal move), or to a change in the activities of your present job (enhancing or upgrading your present position). These three types of career paths will be discussed more completely in other parts of this chapter, but let's look now at a general example of a career path. Let's imagine that Joan has been hired into a company as a records technician and now wants to apply for the assistant supervisor's position which will be available in six months. Her long-term career goal is to be office manager. She knows she needs to improve her communications skills and her financial skills for this position because the responsibilities include budget maintenance as well as supervision and training of technicians. In this case she may set several short-term goals such as completing a course in budgeting or cost accounting, taking some communications or assertiveness training classes, and talking to several resource people in the company who can give her more ideas about the requirements for the position.

For each step of the career path, whether the move be horizontal or vertical, Joan will need to set specific plans.

This may seem a little confusing or vague to you right now, but throughout this chapter I will use Joan, our hypothetical career woman, as an example, taking her along the various paths that she might follow. The career paths available to her in her present company and department are shown in Figure 14-1. All of the positions shown are in the Records Department, with the exception of the Administrative Office Manager, who manages other departments too. Even without going outside the department, Joan has several career paths she can follow here.

Figure 14-1 Possible Career Paths for Joan

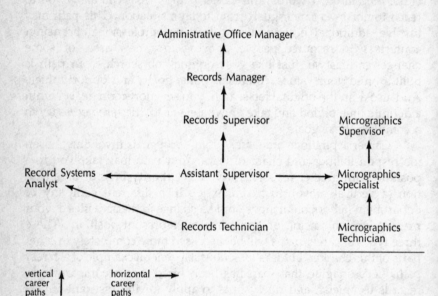

Understanding What Planning Means

Everyone has engaged in some kind of planning, even though the quality, the methods and the results may vary a great deal from person to person. But when it comes to planning a lifetime of career paths and goals, this can be a frightening proposition. One thing is certain, however; simply sitting by and waiting for something wonderful to happen is not the answer. Most opportunities do not come about by chance (although some may appear to) but rather through observation, exploration, and planning.

According to the authors of the book *Growing: A Woman's Guide to Career Satisfaction*, the fundamental components of career planning may be put in the form of six questions to ask yourself:

> WHAT qualifications are necessary for the career change I want?
> WHY are those skills necessary or important for me to build?
> HOW, specifically, can I acquire those skills or abilities—what alternatives are available to me?
> WHERE can I get the necessary resources, training, or experience?
> WHO can guide me along the way, give me feedback to help me stay on track?
> WHEN will I begin?

By answering these six questions, and converting the answers into short-term goals and activities to pursue, you are able to turn planning into action. That doesn't mean that your plans will always turn out just the way you had initially hoped, or that you won't change some of your goals along the way. But planning does pay off. Sometimes we don't see the results for years and sometimes the changes may seem very slight, but overall, planning is your best tool for developing career goals.

Considering Some Practical Problems In Career Planning

Career moves may affect your personal life in ways you may not have considered before. Promotions and other changes may affect your social relationships, your family relationships and your own self-esteem. Let's look at these three categories more closely:

1. *Family relationships.* Career plans may be somewhat complicated if you have a mate and/or children. If you are part of a two-career couple situation, your career goals must be discussed with your partner so that you both understand and support the necessary activities. Children's schedules and plans must also be taken into consideration. This does not mean you sacrifice your plans for theirs;

this means you anticipate the problems and come up with compromises and solutions. I heard a woman banking executive refer to this idea as "having your ducks lined up at home first."

2. *Social and work relationships.* Career moves can lead to important changes in your circle of business associates and friends. For example, getting a promotion may change the attitude of your present associates toward you and, perhaps, your attitude toward them. This can be quite painful for some people, particularly if it means giving up some friendships among work associates.

3. *Your self-esteem.* Seeking career moves may give you new confidence and vitality or cause you to become dispirited and frustrated. If you do not move as fast as you would like, you may wonder whether career planning is really worth it. Sometimes fears, such as fear of responsibility or fear of failure, may have an effect on your self-confidence. Moving to a new position you do not like or cannot perform well can be damaging to your self-esteem. On the other hand, achieving some of your goals can be tremendously confidence-building and can even improve family, social, and work relationships.

While women have frequently been guilty of underestimating themselves and their successes, it can be equally damaging to overestimate yourself. If you assess your abilities incorrectly and set your sights unrealistically high, the failure you experience may detract from your capabilities.

Being Visible and Developing Allies

As mentioned earlier in this book, if you want to move in an organization or even change some of the responsibilities of the job you are in, you must let someone know about it—someone who can help you. In addition to making your plans known to the right people, you need to cultivate their respect and interest. All the good work in the world will not help you move in your career if no one knows about it. Your boss must notice that you are doing your job well and must be informed that you aspire to move on.

One way to find out the steps necessary to get to the next position you want is to ask people already there to tell you how they made it. Most people enjoy talking about themselves and will be flattered that you have asked them. For many women, admitting ambition is almost shameful. They think being openly ambitious is being too competitive or being "power hungry." If this is how you feel about ambition, you may have a difficult time talking about it to others. However, if you look upon ambition as an opportunity to fulfill your potential and learn about new things, this may help you when you ask your boss or someone else what your next step should be. Very few people ever make it alone. We all need someone to lead the way as well as to encourage, support and make it easier for us. Developing a good relationship with your boss will help a great deal, but developing relationships with others inside and outside of the organization may be helpful too. Sometimes these people are referred to as "mentors" or "sponsors," and they can be tremendously important to your career growth.

Organizational Career Management versus Individual Career Planning

Up to this point, we have been talking only about the careers of individuals. But organizations also have concerns about career paths and career management and you need to be aware of this. Organizations have priorities just as individual people have priorities. The organization's priorities usually include such things as providing a service, making a profit, or meeting the requirements of the law or other charter. The organization needs people in certain types of jobs in order to accomplish these things. The organization can offer no more to an individual than the types of jobs it needs to satisfy its purposes. Thus, the organization may not be able to meet every employee's individual career expectations. One of the concepts you must understand is that *you* have the responsibility to find the kind of organization providing the environment, people, and work that fits your career plan. An individual's career plans work best when they mesh with the organization's career planning system.

ASSESSING YOUR CAREER MOVEMENT POTENTIAL

What Skills Are Necessary for Career Movement?

Regardless of your career plan, there are a number of overall skills needed by women who wish to advance in their careers. Most of these are personal skills (such as those discussed in Chapter Eight) which can enhance the technical skills required in many jobs. Mastery of these skills will not automatically move you up the ladder of the organization, but it will be extremely difficult to advance in your career if you do not have them. Here are some skills identified by personnel professionals as necessary for career advancement:

You will need the ability to

- solve problems
- manage time effectively
- make decisions
- speak effectively
- write effectively
- express feelings appropriately
- listen
- see what should be done and initiate appropriate activity
- learn new tasks
- accept company demands which may conflict with personal prerogatives
- understand and carry out organizational objectives
- work productively

Because some of these skills are developed over a long period of time, you may be concerned that you will be held back if you are deficient in any of them. No one can be perfect and whether or not you can improve skills such as the ability to make decisions or learn new tasks will depend a great deal on the attitude you hold and your desire for improvement. All skills can be made better.

Each job has its own particular knowledge base and skills and you need to be competent at whatever job you have been hired to do. But you must go beyond competence to be effective, and it is *being effective* that is most necessary of all for career advancement. You must perform *beyond* the minimum requirements of your job. Do not do just what is meaningful to you in the present, but also learn what is significant for your department (or your organization) in the future. The ability to look to the future and the flexibility to change with the times will help you to be effective and thereby help your career advancement.

How to Know When
a Career Move is Needed

People who are well educated, experienced, energetic, and creative are also typically ambitious. One way to act on this ambition is to seek promotion—that is, moving up to a more complex, challenging position. Promotions, typically, have been a way of recognizing worth and allowing unused abilities to be tapped. When you feel it is time to take on more challenging tasks, you will probably seek an upward, or vertical, career move. Sometimes, however, you may not want a more complicated job; you may simply want a *different* job. Regardless of what kind of move you want, it is helpful to have the kind of job that offers a base for advancement.

Much has been written about the so-called "dead-end" job. Generally speaking, a dead-end job is one where there is no possibility of career advancement. But this may be too simple a definition, because many careers may be "dead-end" in the sense that there is not a next "rung" on the ladder to move to, but they may still be very exciting, fulfilling and "growing" jobs. For example, in my job as a college instructor there is no next "rung" on the ladder without changing to a different career, but I never think of it as dead-end because there are so many possibilities for new projects, programs, experiences, and growth. Perhaps a better description for a dead-end job is one that will get you nowhere in terms of career fulfillment. This way of looking at dead-end jobs would personalize the term for each individual. If you are satisfied with your job and it provides you with the necessary income, challenges, friendly co-workers, and self-esteem, then it is not really dead-end. Not everyone finds it necessary to be upwardly mobile. But if your job takes on some of the following characteristics, it is time for you to think about moving out of it and into something else:

- The work is exhausting and stressful but not challenging.
- You are both tired and bored.
- You do not feel like a valued member of the team.
- You have lost respect for your co-workers and/or your boss and you no longer enjoy working with them.
- You do not believe in your company's products, policies, objectives, and values.
- You see other things you would really like to do.

As mentioned before, there are several ways to move yourself out of a career rut. Chances are, your path will *not* be a straight line. Successful career advances usually follow a zigzag path to growth. You may be on a constantly "correcting" course, somewhat like a computer-guided missile. This means that you may try one of several alternatives: (a) try to enhance your present job, (b) move to a similar job in a different part of the organization altogether, or (c) try for a promotion.

One final thought about the need for career moves. Some people are not particularly satisfied with where they are, but if they have no career goal in mind, they really have no criteria for recognizing satisfaction when they see it. Their fears of leaving their present position may be so powerful that they simply do not allow themselves to look in other directions. People like this usually stay where they are and grumble. Then there are others who simply don't care about on-the-job growth or achievement. They'd rather spend the minimum amount of work required for survival and spend most of their time and energy on outside interests or personal pursuits. (That may be fine if their actions are conscious, deliberate and what they really want. That can even be a career plan!) But for those of us who wish a lifetime of career satisfaction, it becomes necessary to understand when and how to make the necessary moves.

TYPES OF CAREER PATHS

The Vertical Move

For most people, the most common type of career advancement involves the *upward move*—in other words, advancing to a higher position in the organization with more responsibility, authority, recognition and pay. This kind of career move is also called *promotion*. For most people the path upward is long, arduous and carefully planned. It is not always exciting or dramatic, and it sometimes requires considerable sacrifice and many risks. Few really successful people ever stop working at it, even when they have reached the top of the organization.

Let's follow Joan on her first vertical step of the career ladder. She has decided to try for the Assistant Supervisor position.

Joan has been a records technician for fifteen months. There are five other records technicians in her department and she has helped the present assistant supervisor train two of them. Also during this fifteen-month period, she has taken on increasingly complex assignments, and she knows the work of several different work stations within this department. Assuming that Joan has already completed the assessment of skills in Chapter Seven for her technician job, she may now want to look at her assessment again as a resource for this next step. She will also want to consider the following questions:

1. What qualifications are necessary for the new job?
2. What additional skills must be acquired or enhanced?
3. How and where can I get the skills I need?
4. Who can help me?
5. What are the time considerations or constraints?

Is There Life After Promotion?

Joan has passed the test! She has been promoted. Everything should be euphoric and wonderful.

Although she is not yet a manager, movement to the Assistant Supervisor position will change Joan's relationship to the other records technicians. As an assistant supervisor she will be the liaison between the workers and the management. Now she will have some control over their work; she will also be doing work that is different from what she has been doing, and she will be meeting new people and learning new skills. Some feelings of jealousy and envy on the part of the other workers—particularly if any of them were competing for the same position—is almost inevitable. This is the beginning of a new self-concept for Joan. This concept now includes the issue of authority. She now has the right to make some demands, to check for quality, to help, to teach, and to supervise. The advantage of being from within her unit is that she knows it well and she knows the people well. However, those same strengths may cause problems if some of the technicians are either close friends or people she disliked. If she has anticipated some of the "people" problems which may arise, she will be better equipped to deal with them without losing her self-confidence. Readiness to assume new responsibilities and the risks involved is a crucial element in a successful career move.

Moving Into Management:
The Long-term Goal

If Joan is to make it beyond the supervisory level into management, her long-term goal, there are some additional skills she must have besides those identified earlier for successful career advancement. The following list focuses on some skills and attitudes she needs to be successful in a management position.

- *Willingness to take risks and make changes.* Every time a manager hires someone, delegates a task, or suggests a course of action, she or he is taking a risk. By figuring out the desired outcome, predicting negative and positive consequences, and determining specific action, a manager can better control risk-taking.
- *Managerial skills.* It is important to have an understanding of finance, operations, information systems, etc.
- *Competitiveness and assertiveness.* You need to take the initiative—not wait to be asked. You need a drive to achieve. And since there are usually fewer jobs than people who want them, ability to compete is an important factor.
- *Technical ability in a specialty field.* Specific technical knowledge about areas you will supervise is especially important at the supervisory and middle management levels.
- *Understanding your own behavior as well as the behavior of others.*
- *Willingness to invest in further training.* You may have to get a specific college degree or some other type of formal training.
- *Political awareness.* You need to be aware of politics within and between organizations.
- *Acceptance of yourself plus acceptance of roles you must play within the organization.* This includes understanding differences between your personal value system and that represented by your organization.

Many people want recognition and authority without having to be accountable or make difficult decisions. For such people, the role of manager may prove to be very uncomfortable. Management involves motivating, handling, and controlling personnel, machinery, money, and procedures. It means accomplishing work through the talents and skills of others. Many people opt for a management career because of the financial rewards, power, and prestige. As a manager, you can control your own work to a large extent—both what you do and when you do it. But as a manager, you also have real responsibility and accountability to the company and the people for whom you work. If you decide that the managerial track should be a career goal, ask yourself the following questions:

- In a group, do I tend to exert leadership?
- Can I listen openly and fairly to someone who disagrees with me?
- Can I tolerate public and private criticism of my decisions?
- If I have a difficult problem am I willing to seek the counsel of others?
- Am I willing to shoulder the responsibility for a team effort that fails?
- Am I willing to share the glory for a team effort that succeeds?

If you answer yes to all six questions, you should be able to handle the "people" aspects of supervision. Coupled with the appropriate technical skills and education, you may be on your way to a leadership role. Role-playing the position of "boss" may help you decide whether this kind of career is for you. Some people like this role; some do not. There is no question that management positions are continually challenging, and for people who thrive on stimulation and certain kinds of stress, vertical career moves into management may be the best way to achieve career satisfaction.

Is There Another Way to Move Up?

There may be opportunities in your organization that do not appear on the organizational chart. Once you have some idea of your needs and goals, the next step is to see what is available in your organization. You cannot do that very well, however, unless you know how your organization operates. As you look at the organization chart, you may be tempted to stay away from some areas that you feel offer little opportunity. Do not give in to that temptation. There is an old phrase that goes "The long way 'round may be the shortest way home." Even planned vertical movements are not always straight up and you may be missing some important opportunities.

The Horizontal Move

As we mentioned before, sometimes you don't want a more complicated job, you simply want a different job—the opportunity to learn other skills and experience new situations. In recent years, the emphasis has been on vertical moves for women—opportunities for women in management positions. Much less has been written about horizontal opportunities as an avenue for career growth. This type of move should be given greater consideration, because there are not very many openings at the top. A horizontal move can also be a very personally satisfying kind of career move for many people.

Sometimes the move can take place within the organization. If you are considering such a move, you should reassess your functional, transferable skills. For example, one woman who had worked as a legal secretary for twenty years used some of those skills to get an executive assistant position in a large public utility. The horizontal move also put her in a position where she could eventually move vertically as well. Her former position did not afford the same opportunities. This is an example of the zigzag approach we discussed earlier; you may need to move sideways in order to get the opportunity to move up.

Let's return to Joan and take her through a horizontal career move. Assume that she either did not receive the assistant supervisor position or decided not to apply at this time. She is now considering the position of micrographics technician, which is considered to be on the same level as records technician. In this position, she could acquire more specialized knowledge which would help her move to micrographics specialist. This position requires different technical skills; whereas the assistant supervisor position dealt more with training and people supervision. However, by doing this she may be able to increase her skills and experience in order to qualify for the assistant supervisor position or the micrographics supervisor position. A horizontal move to micrographics technician may also be helpful in the sense of broadening Joan's knowledge about another facet of records management.

Basically, horizontal moves are usually considered for the following reasons:

The move may give you

- a more pleasing work environment
- a better chance for vertical moves later
- an opportunity to learn about different types of organizations
- a broader background of technical skills and knowledge
- better pay
- a position better suited to your lifestyle
- a chance to "start over"

The horizontal move can figure in various ways in your overall career plan. If you make too many horizontal moves you may be seen as a "job hopper," but carefully planned horizontal moves may tell a future employer that you are a dynamic, growing employee. Before deciding on the move, Joan should ask herself the following questions:

1. What qualifications are necessary for the new job?
2. What additional skills or knowledge will be needed?
3. Where can I get the new skills?
4. Who can help me?
5. What are the advantages and disadvantages of taking this job?
6. What are the time considerations or constraints?

Enhancing Where You Are

Sometimes a person may find herself in the situation where she is not really dissatisfied with the organization she works for or the people she works with, but she still feels the need for something to do that is different from the ordinary day-to-day routine. Pension plans, movement on salary schedules, and so on frequently make it costly to change organizations (particularly after a long period of employment), so the person in this position may need to look within the job she now holds to make the right career "move."

Enhancing the job you now hold may actually be one of the most creative and satisfying career decisions you can make. Sometimes we are not very good at seeing things that are right before our eyes! You may be able to change some of your job duties and responsibilities while basically keeping the same position. Let's see how this would apply to Joan.

If Joan decides to remain in the records technician position she now holds, she needs to see what opportunities for growth can be obtained within that position. For example, maybe she would like to learn more about the legal aspects of records; she can check with her supervisor to see if there is something she can do in that area— perhaps trading duties with another technician for a period of time or being allowed some time to do some research in that area.

Sometimes you have to go outside the organization in order to see what opportunities are inside. Becoming actively involved in a professional association or other group where employees have similar interests may give you a new perspective and allow you to be involved in new projects and ideas. Most employers encourage their employees to pursue interests which may help them in their jobs. This may also be seen as a sign of initiative and bring about greater

229

visibility and opportunity within the organization where you work. We will discuss this further at the end of this chapter.

Joan needs to consider these questions:

1. What are some needs or trends I see for my department and my organization?
2. What are some types of projects I would like to do?
3. What are some "outside" activities that would enhance my job?

The Total Career Change

It is becoming increasingly common for people to have second and even third careers. In other words, you may take a path leading in a totally different direction. Sometimes this comes about because of necessity—a job becomes obsolete or there are simply no jobs in your field. Sometimes it comes about as part of a long-term plan. Either way, the total career change is another possible move to consider in your overall lifetime career planning.

You may long for something totally different, but in order to achieve it, you must again consider transferable skills and the regular job search process. Skills can transfer across industries or within organizations. Sometimes these same skills may even help you start and run your own business. This move calls for creative thinking and willingness to risk. You are in somewhat the same position you were in when you searched for your first job in your first career, except that now you have some valuable work and life experiences behind you that you did not have before. You have a better idea of what you can do well and like to do. You will have to explore such areas as (1) education/experience requirements, (2) hiring practices, (3) number of available jobs and employment trends, (4) pay levels and benefits and (5) chances for advancement and growth in the new career.

Again, let's look at our friend Joan and see what she will do in this situation. Joan has discovered while working in the records area that she is interested in talking to people about new equipment, forms, etc. One day a sales representative from an office products firm talks to her about becoming a sales trainee. Joan is excited by this opportunity, so she begins to examine her skills to see what she can do that would qualify her for this type of position. The pay is better than in her present position and there is good growth potential besides, so there are other advantages to the change besides her interests. Here are some questions to consider before making a decision:

1. What additional skills are required for this new career?
2. What skills do I now have that are directly transferable?
3. What skills must I improve?
4. What is my plan to do that?
5. How does this fit my long-term goals?

ORGANIZATIONAL FACTORS IN CAREER GROWTH

As you concentrate on your personal needs, skills, and goals in considering career moves, you may forget that there are frequently other factors that must be considered. These factors, mostly relating to traditions and informal structures, may set up barriers or slow your progress. Irritating as these may be, you must recognize some factors that are beyond your control and learn how to manuever around them or accept them as part of the overall scheme.

Boundaries

Understanding organizational boundaries is a very important part of career development planning. Unlike a nicely printed road map, an organizational boundary may be both visible and invisible. Organizational boundaries for jobs include such factors as kinds of knowledge, experience, or credentials necessary for a person to move to certain jobs within the organization. Additional boundaries may include seniority, what part of the organization you were originally hired into, educational background, and possibly age, gender, ethnic or racial background.

Keep in mind that although most organizations want to practice equal opportunity employment, organizations are made up of people, many of whom have biases that may work against you. Many of these same people control the formal and informal power structure in an organization. For example, Joan may discover that all the office managers have traditionally come from the accounting area, not from the records area. This may be an important consideration if she is to reach that position eventually. More education and other horizontal moves may be in order.

"Tokens," "Queen Bees," and "Self-made" Women

Many successful women love the fact that they are "special." They may feel they have unique qualifications that allow them positions which were normally denied to women. This group may not be particularly helpful to other women, believing that it should be no easier for others than it was for them; thus the title "Queen Bee" or "Self-made" woman.

While it is true that individual endeavors are important for success in business, if women do not help other women in the same way men have helped men, women will never be truly equal in the business world. That doesn't mean you have the right to expect another woman to champion you just because you are a woman, but you should be given equal consideration. Beware of the woman who will allow no other woman a good position on the team.

Another phenomenon related to the Queen Bee syndrome is the "token woman"—the lone woman in an almost entirely male group. This woman may have been picked by a group of men to show their "affirmative action" compliance or as a gesture to compensate for past injustices against women. If the token woman is totally noncontroversial (and not necessarily the most competent but the most acquiescent or willing to please), you can be pretty certain she is a "token." Some women consider being a "token" better than nothing; others stay away from this situation completely because the position may have very little real power and other people may resent it.

Traditional versus Nontraditional Jobs

Some jobs in business have traditionally been held by women, others by men. Certain assumptions have customarily been made that are not necessarily true. For example, women are thought to be good at detail, so they have had fewer problems getting into such jobs as bookkeeping, purchasing, support services, etc. Another assumption is that women have "intuition" about people; thus personnel departments have not been as difficult to get into as finance or production. Women have held the majority of elementary school teaching positions, but most college and university teachers are men.

Although many "old boy" networks may also contain "old girls," it is a fact of organizational life that some people get positions because they are part of an "in group."

Attributes such as sense of humor or ability to amuse others may become more important than technical skills. In order to get along in this climate you will need to figure out what skills and characteristics are valued by this "in group" which controls the informal power structure. If you can cultivate these characteristics without compromising your own personal value system, you may be able to benefit. If not, you may wish to seek a more compatible organization. What you may need is a large dose of tolerance.

Comfortable Achievements

Ultimately, whether or not you are comfortable making career moves depends in part on how you see yourself. By accepting yourself and your uniqueness, you will be more comfortable as a member of a team, you will be accountable for your successes as well as for your failures, and you will like yourself regardless of the results.

It is essential that you find some kind of balance in your life in order to keep on even footing in your career. You cannot do everything and achieve everything at once. You must look at career growth as a process—you take one thing at a time. You may have to rearrange some life habits. You may have to deal with obstacles. You may need to slow down or speed up or adopt alternate plans on occasion—but don't stop. Keep your balance and keep your life priorities in perspective.

CAREER GROWTH OUTSIDE
OF THE ORGANIZATION

Professional associations, community groups and other organizations may be another avenue of personal and professional growth. Volunteer activities and civic duty should not necessarily be considered things of the past when you embark on a career. They may even take on greater importance. While it is true that you will probably not have many daytime hours to offer and your evenings may also be limited, selected involvement in a group you enjoy can provide pleasure, stimulation, and a sense of accomplishment. Another spinoff may come in the form of professional contacts and opportunities to learn skills helpful to your career growth.

Working and Volunteering

The United States has a great many diverse voluntary organizations in such areas as health services, education, civic affairs, legal assistance, senior citizens' services, drugs, corrections, ecology, and consumer education. These voluntary organizations do a great deal to improve the quality of life while also giving the participants a great deal of personal satisfaction and opportunities to develop personal, functional and leadership skills. A working woman whose job may be routine or limited can seek satisfaction in the many volunteer activities to be found in most communities.

Some volunteer jobs require work on weekends and evenings; many can even be adjusted for women who have irregular working hours. Sometimes an employer will even allow some time off from work for participation in such activities. The important thing for the working woman to remember is to find volunteer work that is rewarding. Taking on tasks that you really don't like to do will only leave you frustrated and tired. This is not a "have to " situation, as your paid job is.

Experience in certain types of volunteer activities may be very helpful in getting or changing jobs. This is one area where women have often been allowed to develop management skills because they were not being paid to do it. For example, if you have ever been elected to direct an organization, you probably have developed some competence in areas such as planning and coordinating activities, running meetings, writing reports, delegating tasks, working with a budget, and following up on committee assignments; all of these activities are examples of jobs performed by paid managers. More and more employers are considering volunteer experience when hiring—particularly if you can show the direct relationship to the job you are trying to get. Also for the young, inexperienced woman or the displaced homemaker with little work experience, volunteer work can be a place to develop experience and confidence.

Professional Organizations

Another type of "volunteer" group which can be directly helpful to your career is the professional association. Although somewhat related to the "networking organizations" we will discuss later in this chapter, the professional association is a group of people with similar job responsibilities who get together for exchanging their ideas, furthering their profession, and socializing with people like themselves. Almost every kind of occupational group has some kind of professional association, whether it be accountants, nurses, secretaries, teachers, librarians, or various jobs in business and industry such as purchasing agents, word processing supervisors, etc. If you are in a job that does not have a professional association, you may want to consider more general professional associations such as business and professional women's clubs, Toastmistress groups, Chambers of Commerce, or other service organizations.

For many women, the professional association has been the means to comfortably integrate into formerly male territory. Furthermore, most employers consider affiliations and memberships to be a plus when seeking new employees.

If you are not sure whether or not you would eventually like to have a paid leadership or management position, finding out via the volunteer route may be a good way. There is no particular loss of status if you decide you do not want to be a leader for an extended period of time, as there might be in a paid position. One word of caution, however. Do not say you will do something that you are not really willing to carry out. Just because the work is for a volunteer organization does not mean that this is "lesser" work or that you do not have to behave responsibly. If you are simply not going to have as much time for the volunteer activities as you thought you might, explain the situation to someone in charge in enough time so that someone else can be found to do the work. In my own experience as a leader of several volunteer organizations, I would much prefer that a person say no to a request than say yes and then not complete the task. You have your reputation to protect here as well, and you should be just as professional as you are in your paid work.

Responsibilities as a Leader

Most democratically-run volunteer groups have a high turnover of leaders. Leadership of any organization takes time and energy, and most people cannot continue in that role for long periods of time because of career and family demands. Also, many groups need the vitality and energy brought by new and changing leadership in order to keep the voluntary organization vital and dynamic.

Depending upon the circumstances, you may find yourself thrust into the role of leader simply by displaying an interest. In that role you will be expected to reconcile disagreements, keep communication channels open among members, encourage contributions of talent and time from the membership, compromise or modify positions when necessary, and tell others in helpful ways how their contributions to the group are received. To be able to do all of this takes a good deal of self-confidence and persistence. That's one reason why volunteer organizations are a good place to learn leadership skills. You may be less inhibited about taking risks, thus allowing yourself to succeed and fail more often.

If you want to be a leader, there are ample opportunities in volunteer organizations.

Leadership Out of Necessity

Women who want to see organizations and societal values change are frequently compelled to get into leadership positions in order to act out these values. For example, women in business organizations, labor organizations, and political organizations have found it necessary to seek leadership positions in order to get these organizations to really deal with obstacles facing women. As long as most men see women as uninterested in leadership positions, it will be more difficult for the women who want such positions to get them. Numbers, however, are convincing. It is up to us to produce these numbers.

Just because you do not want a management or leadership position where you perform paid work is no reason for you to shun leadership positions in your professional association, or union, or church. Leading can be a very satisfying experience and a confidence-building activity for many women who want to do it and who are willing to accept the responsibility.

NETWORKS, CAUCUSES, COALITIONS, AND POLITICS

What Is a Network?

A network is a group where you can make contacts, gain information, or seek advice and support for your career advancement. There are many different kinds of networks and support groups. Some are formally organized; others simply evolve as informal groups. Because of their socialization, men may grow up knowing how to network without ever defining it as that. They often have played team sports or learned to fight together. They may have learned not to hold grudges. Somewhere early on they have absorbed the fact that they *need each other*. Women, on the other hand, are frequently taught to distrust each other and to operate on their own or to depend on a man.

Men don't talk about networking very much; they just do it. Women haven't come quite that far yet, so we are still *consciously* assessing ways to help each other and learn the team skills needed for career success.

Many women have now joined together to help other women find out about job openings, to get legislation passed, to help other women through emotional crises, and many other types of activities. Unlike the professional association or civic club, a women's network offers more opportunities to let feelings be known by communicating informally and seeking direct help and support. For most networks the major goals include increased communication among women leaders, sharing information and support, and increasing the visibility of women. In addition, networks can serve some of the emotional support needs of their members. Finding out that someone else has experienced problems similar to your own can be comforting. Even though we are talking primarily about women's networks, you should also look for ways to network with men as well. This broadens your base of resources.

Networking includes the informal ways people relate to one another. You are not networking by just joining groups. You have to utilize the contacts you make. You use other people to help you (and I don't mean misuse), and you, in turn, will help someone else. As someone jokingly put it, "Business is a contact sport." At the same time, you need to understand that "support" does not automatically mean favors or preferential treatment. You do owe it to yourself to explore the possibility of networking. You may find the suppport group you need, or information about what is going on in other businesses (and in your own company, too), or what jobs are opening up. It may help you achieve the career growth you want.

Caucuses and Coalitions

Many organizations now have separate subgroups within the larger organization that deal with problems of women—both within and outside the organization. Many labor organizations have separate women's caucuses which work to get women into union leadership positions and encourage unions to take stands on women's political issues. Some churches and large organizations like the American Civil Liberties Union or state bar associations may have a specific group that studies and deals with women's issues.

As this movement to recognize women has occurred, many all-women's organizations have now begun to include men in their membership. For example, the League of Women Voters now accepts men. Some other large groups do likewise while, at the same time, keeping the title of "woman" as part of their overall identity. Perhaps someday there will be no need to have "old boy networks" and "old girl networks"; there will simply be organizations with the expressed purpose of supporting both men and women with mutual interests.

Making a Political Impact as a Woman

According to some, politics may be the last and most difficult area for women to enter and make a substantial impact, but ultimately it may be one of the most important areas. It is not enough just to work for equal opportunities in our organizations; we must have some say about our government's policies as well.

There is no question that women have encountered many difficulties as political candidates, but that should not stop women from getting involved in the political process and finding out more about how our political system works. You should try to understand what politics is—a contest of ideas. Some of the ideas might as well be your own.

Many of the women suffragists believed that voting was the key to power. They believed that once women had the vote, their other rights would follow. But it is not enough just to have the vote. You must learn how to use the vote. Remember in Chapter Four when we talked about decision-making? A decision will always be made. If you don't participate in that decision, someone else will make it for you. Political decisions are part of your rights also; becoming more politically aware can be a very important part of your personal and professional growth. Consider some of the following ways you can make political contributions:

- Learn about the issues, both locally and nationally.
- Give financial help to a candidate you believe in.

- Volunteer some time to a candidate you believe in; don't wait for someone to ask you.
- Express your views on major issues in conversations with other people.
- Write or telephone your elected representatives, expressing your point of view. Communications do have an effect.

Some Final Thoughts on Career Growth

Career growth comes in so many forms that it is sometimes difficult to recognize it. It is always a good idea to sit down and take stock of your experiences from time to time so you can determine what really is contributing to your career growth. One good way to do this is to update your resumé on a regular basis—even if you are not considering a job change. The changes do not have to be monumental, producing new titles or great salary increases; even the small changes can have a cumulative effect which is very satisfying.

CONCLUSION

We live in challenging and difficult times. But we need to live life to the fullest, not hide from it. As you continue to explore areas for your personal and professional growth, you will find your experiences building on each other. If you tried the exercises and suggestions in this book, we hope you found some workable processes. We also hope you will continue to use them and expand on them in ways that fit your individual needs.

Writing this book has been a time of personal and professional development for the authors too. If the ideas and exercises we have presented work for you, we hope you will share your new knowledge and skills with other women. The impact can be great indeed.

APPENDIX

SUGGESTED READINGS

The following list of book titles, with a brief description of content, is provided for those who wish additional resources and information about the topics discussed in this book.

Deciding and Preparing

ABARBANEL, KARIN, and SIEGEL, CONNIE MCCLUNG, *Woman's Work Book*. New York: Praeger Publishers, 1975. Although some of the information in this book is now out of date, many of the ideas, suggestions, and resources listed will still be very helpful. The book has an excellent appendix containing information about everything from women's centers to newsletters and periodicals helpful to the working woman.

CAMPBELL, DAVID, *If You Don't Know Where You're Going, You'll Probably End Up Somewhere Else*. Niles, Ill.: Argus Communications, 1974. This is a short but important book on finding directions and setting goals for a satisfying life. The illustrations and quotations sprinkled throughout the text are both thought-provoking and entertaining.

CATALYST, *What To Do With The Rest Of Your Life*. New York: Simon & Schuster, 1975. This book is an excellent guide to career planning. It not only explores the process of career planning, but gives specific information about the preparation needed for careers in the health field, science and engineering, government and law, skilled trades, general business (including management, sales, finance and production). This is a valuable resource if you are unsure about what field to enter or are considering changing careers.

CATALYST, *Your Job Campaign: Self-Guidance Series G2.* New York: Catalyst, 1975. Written for women with at least some college education, this workbook provides guidance in examining wishes, goals, personality, experience, interests, and education.

GOODMAN, ELLEN, *Turning Points.* New York: Fawcett Columbine, 1979.This book takes a provocative look at people "in transition" as they deal with personal crises and changes in their lives. This is not a how-to guide but rather a study of contemporary life using many interviews and histories of women dealing with personal changes.

KNAUS, WILLIAM, *Do It Now: How To Stop Procrastinating.* Englewood Cliffs, N.J.: Prentice-Hall, 1979.If procrastination is your major time management problem, this book may give you a great deal of help. The book contains many suggestions and plans for overcoming procrastination patterns.

LAKEIN, ALAN, *How To Get Control of Your Time and Your Life.* New York: Peter N. Wyden, Inc., 1973.A classic on time management, Lakein's book is appropriate for everyone—working or not.

MILLER, JEAN BAKER, *Toward a New Psychology of Women.* Boston, Mass.: Beacon Press, 1976.Although it is written in a more scholarly manner than most books in this bibliography, most readers will find this book on the psychological development of both men and women very readable and interesting. The author's chapters on strengths, passivity, and needs for serving others should be especially helpful to those women returning to work after having served primarily as caretakers for their families.

REYNOLDS, HELEN, and TRAMEL, MARY E., *Executive Time Management.* Englewood Cliffs, N.J.: Prentice-Hall, 1979.This book is written not only for executives but also those who work for executives. The focus is on time management practices at work. The book is helpful both for people just starting work and for those who have worked for some time.

SCHOLZ, NELLE, et al., *How to Decide: A Workbook for Women*. New York: Avon, 1975. This is a helpful guide for becoming a more decisive, directed person. The book contains many exercises related to values, goals, and decisions.

SIMON, SIDNEY, *Meeting Yourself Halfway*. Niles, Ill.: Argus Communications, 1974. A good beginning book on values and the values clarification process, it provides many exercises and examples helpful to the reader.

TERKEL, STUDS, *Working: People Talk About What They Do All Day and How They Feel About What They Do*. New York: Pantheon Books, 1974. This marvelous book explores work in America—the nature of work and how people feel about what they do. The book uses interviews from people in a variety of occupations. It is not a "how-to-do-it" guide; this is a book about the human feelings—hope, aspirations, despair and anger—of people at work.

WINSTON, STEPHANIE, *Getting Organized*. New York: W.W. Norton & Co., Inc., 1978. This book goes beyond time management and discusses organizational techniques for practically every situation one can think of. Efficient arrangement of materials, selection of work spaces, etc. are examples of topics covered in this book.

Developing Personal Effectiveness

ADAMS, LINDA, *Effectiveness Training For Women*. New York: Wyden Books, 1979. Based upon the principles developed by Dr. Thomas Gordon for Parent Effectiveness Training, this book provides a method for developing assertiveness using a step-by-step approach, with many case examples and actual dialogues. It is particularly helpful for those who wish to develop good communications skills when faced with confrontation and conflict.

BAER, JEAN, *How to Be An Assertive (Not Aggressive) Woman In Life, In Love, and On the Job*. New York: Rawson, 1976. This is another good book on assertiveness, in which the author uses many examples and sample dialogues to help you become better at communicating effectively. The book offers a method for spotting your own assertiveness difficulties and includes a particularly enjoyable chapter using interviews with women such as television star Barbara Walters and Watergate lawyer Jill Wine Volner, who discuss their own assertiveness hangups.

HANNON, SHARON, *The Working Woman's Beauty Book.* Briarcliff Manor, New York: Stein & Day, 1979.Based on the beauty problems encountered by many working women, this book has helpful advice on many aspects of appearance. Particularly helpful are the sections about on-the-job beauty repairs and professional beauty services and consultation.

MOLLOY, JOHN, *Women's Dress for Success Book.* Warner Books, New York, 1978.A controversial but highly influential book on dressing for business, this should be read particularly by those women going to work in large, conservative business organizations. The author has a blunt, tell-it-like-it-is style and describes in detail the kinds of colors, fabrics, and styles that have proven most successful in his research on business dress.

PERKINS, GAIL, and JUDITH RHOADES, *The Women's Financial Survival Handbook*, New York: Plume, 1980.Written specifically for women, this book has some very helpful chapters on such topics as financial problems of special groups of women, such as about-to-be or already-divorced women, widows, women living with other people, women returning to school, and so on. The book also contains good advice on purchasing automobiles and homes.

QUINN, JANE BRYANT, *Everyone's Money Book.* Delacorte Press, 1979.This comprehensive guide to money management is an extremely useful resource. The book covers everything from budgeting to home ownership, investments and retirement planning. It also includes sample worksheets for many different areas of money management.

WALLACH, JANET, *Working Wardrobe.* Washington, D.C.: Acropolis Books, 1981.This book provides a formula for coordinating separate clothing components based on color, fabric, and design. It augments and expands on many of the ideas given in Chapter Six. It is one of the best recent books on putting together a career wardrobe.

Getting the Job

A Working Woman's Guide to Her Job Rights. U.S. Department of Labor, Women's Bureau, December, 1976.An extremely helpful government pamphlet which considers such subjects as employment services, apprenticeships, equal pay, occupational safety and health protection, retirement benefits, and sources of assistance.

BOLLES, RICHARD NELSON, *What Color Is Your Parachute?* Berkeley, Cal.: Ten Speed Press, 1980. A very readable and often amusing book about job hunting. The resources guide in the appendix is especially helpful.

GREENLEAF, BARBARA KAYE, *Help: A Handbook for Working Mothers.* New York: Berkeley Books, 1979. A helpful book for working mothers covering topics such as guilt about working, child care services, shared parenting, housekeeping, sick children, working during pregnancy, and single parenting.

JACKSON, TOM, *The Perfect Resume.* Garden City, N.Y.: Anchor Books, 1981. This book uses a workbook format to inventory skills and interests, target jobs, and explain resumé and cover letter preparation. It contains many examples of resumés in a variety of formats (including functional) and has up-to-date ideas on the entire job campaign.

Merchandising Your Job Talents. U.S. Department of Labor Employment and Training Administration, 1980 (revised). Topics in this government pamphlet include resumé writing, sources of job information, testing and interviewing. This is a brief but helpful guide.

MOORE, CHARLES GUY, *The Career Game.* New York: Ballantine Books, 1976. Written by an economist, this book is particularly helpful for its section on career economics (job security, supply and demand forces, wage levels, etc.). Most of the advice is directed to the young college graduate, but there is general information for men and women of all ages and educational backgrounds.

Succeeding on the Job

BURACK, ELMER H., ALBRECHT, MARYANN, and SEITLER, HELENE, *A Woman's Guide To Career Satisfaction.* Belmont, Cal.: Lifetime Learning Publications, 1980. This book covers topics such as goals and skills assessment, but then moves on to activities relating to career development, such as analysis of individual career styles, environments, and career problems. A good book for the woman who is presently working and wants to make some career changes.

CANNIE, JOAN KOOB, *The Women's Guide to Management Success: How to Win Power in the Real Organizational World.* Englewood Cliffs, N.J.: Prentice-Hall, 1979. Although this book is written primarily for the woman who wants a management position, the sections on basic human needs, communications skills, negotiating and persuading, and conflicts are helpful for working women in any position. This book has very good examples and exercises for practicing what is discussed.

CATALYST, *Making the Most of your First Job*. New York: G. P. Putnam's Sons, 1981. This book came out just before we went to press, but we decided to include it because of its practical, readable approach. The book covers topics such as visibility, time management, working with groups, business etiquette, office decoration, and money management. Like other Catalyst publications, it is excellent.

FENN, MARGARET, *Making It In Management: A Behavioral Approach For Women Executives*. Englewood Cliffs, N.J.: Prentice-Hall, 1978. An excellent "nuts and bolts" book about identifying and developing management skills with particular reference to women, this is a good introduction to the behavioral aspects of management and is jargon-free and very readable.

GREENBERG, HERBERT M., *Coping With Job Stress*. Englewood Cliffs, N.J.: Prentice-Hall, 1980. A good "how to" book for dealing with job stress, with an emphasis on personal stress management.

HENLEY, NANCY M., *Body Politics*. Englewood Cliffs, N.J.: Prentice-Hall, Inc., 1977. This is an excellent book on power and body language with some particular concerns for women's issues. As the author says in the preface, "...the book is for people who are curious about nonverbal communication, who want to know what is passing between them and others on levels they aren't aware of."

HIGGINSON, MARGARET, and QUICK, THOMAS L., *The Ambitious Woman's Guide To A Successful Career*. New York: AMACOM, 1975. An updated version of this book has just been published, but even the early version is extremely helpful for women considering management careers. This book has excellent sections on attitudes toward women in business.

JOSEFOWITZ, NATASHA, *Paths to Power*. Reading, Mass.: Addison-Wesley, 1980. This book provides practical, timely information for women seeking leadership positions. From first job, to middle management, to top executive, the author describes various job positions and gives instructions for progressing on a career path. The author is also very sensitive to returning and "late entry" career women.

KLEIMAN, CAROL, *Women's Networks*. New York: Lippincott & Crowell, 1980.This is an excellent guide for understanding the concept of "networking" and what kinds of networks have been formed for working women in the United States.

McLEAN, ALAN A., *Work Stress*. Reading, Mass.: Addison-Wesley, 1979.This book on stress, written by a physician, is not limited to just the physiological aspects of stress. There are excellent sections on stress research and the sociological aspects of stress as well as on personal stress management.

MORGAN, MARILYN A., *Managing Career Development*. New York: D. Van Nostrand, 1980.This book contains a selection of essays and articles on developing and managing careers. The book is particularly helpful for the person who has at least several years of work experience and is looking for help with career changes and directions. The articles and essays are reprinted from technical and professional journals, so the writing style is scholarly rather than conversational.

PINKSTAFF, MARLENE ARTHUR, and WILKINSON, ANNABELL, *Women at Work: Overcoming the Obstacles*. Reading, Mass.: Addison-Wesley, 1979.This book provides a methodology for examining the obstacles facing women in the workplace. Topics covered include self-image, guilt, support systems, achievement, networks, sexism, resentment and stress.

SELYE, HANS, *Stress Without Distress*. New York: J. B. Lippincott, 1974.A classic on stress, this book explains the physiological mechanisms of stress and gives specific advice for avoiding the type of stress that is harmful.

STEAD, BETTE ANN, *Women In Management*. Englewood Cliffs, N.J.: Prentice-Hall, 1978.This book contains a collection of good essays by a variety of experts discussing women and organizations. Topics covered include debunking myths and stereotypes, implementing equal opportunity, identifying language barriers and remedies, understanding organizational constraints, analyzing women's leadership styles, and developing strategies for progress. The book is excellent for women seeking careers in management but also helpful for women in other types of jobs.

INDEX

Harassment, sexual, 193-97
Health habits, 209
Help, asking for, 34-35
Hidden job market, 109-10
Hiring process, nature of, 131-32
"Honeymoon" period on job, 164-65
Household management for re-entry
    women, 153

I

Illegal questions at job interview, 139
Image, professional, 54-58
"In groups," 233
Income, budgeting for, 84-89
Income tax, 85
Indecision, 25
Informal organizational structure, 173-74
Interests, 10-11
Internal Revenue Service, 85
Interpersonal skills, 214
Instinct, decision making and, 44-45
Insurance plans, 85
Interviews, 131-45
    body language in, 140
    closing off, 141-42
    coming across positively in, 141
    dressing for, 69-70
    follow-up on, 142-43
    follow-up thank you for, 129-30
    impressing interviewer, 132-34
    listening skills in, 140
    preparing for, 131-40
    silence in, 141
Introductions, handling of, 170-71

J

Job descriptions, 144
Job market:
    characteristics of, 98-100
    matching skills to, 95-110
    nontraditional, 109-10
    traditional sources, 109

L

Labor Department, U.S., 80, 159-60
    Equal Employment Opportunity
        Commission, 197
    Women's Bureau of, 151-52
Language:
    de-sexing, 187
    powerless, 188
    sexism and, 186
Leadership:
    out of necessity, 236
    responsibilities of, 235-36

League of Women Voters, 238
Liabilities, 83-84
Life stress, 208-9
Life values, career values and, 5-10
Lifelong learning, 106
Lifestyle, job and, 95-97
Lipstick and lip gloss, 64
Listening:
    in office protocol, 168-69
    skills, 140, 176

M

Makeup:
    for Asians, 64-65
    for blacks, 65
    business and, 58-59
    common mistakes with, 59
    cost of, 60
    eyeglasses and, 65-66
    selecting and applying, 61-64
    tools and supplies for, 60-61
Male vocabularies, 186
Martyrdom, giving up, 39
Mascara, 64
Meditation techniques, 213
Men, career planning by, 13-14
Money management, basic concepts of,
    78-82

N

Nail care, 65
Names, handling of, 170-71
National Bureau of Economic Research, 216
National Foundation for Consumer Credit,
    93
Net worth, 80, 83-84
Networks, 236-37
Neutral skin tone, 59-60
No, learning to say, 38, 48-49
Nonassertiveness, 46-49
Nontraditional jobs, 232
Nonverbal communication, sexism in, 188-89

O

Occupational Outlook Handbook, 97, 139
Office protocol, 168-72
    discretion and, 170
    handling names and introductions, 8-9,
        170-71
    on smoking, 171-72
    talking and listening in, 168-69
    telephone courtesy in, 171
"Old boy" networks, 233
Organization, power and politics in, 172-74
Organizational career management, 221

250

P

Pace, slowing, 213
Paint-by-number approach to makeup, 61-62
Pay:
  discrimination in, 182
  paycheck, and deductions, 85-86
  See also Salary
Pension plans, 85-86
Perfection, giving up, 36
Personal place, work environment as, 32-34
Personal skills, 101, 102
Personal strengths, 10-11
Personal time, 31
Personalities at work, 97
Physical attending, 176-77
Planning:
  of time use, 27-29
  of wardrobe, 71-73
  See also Career Planning; Goals
Politics, 238-39
  in organization, 172-74
Power:
  direct, sexism and, 185
  in organization, 172-74
Powerless language, 188
Priorities, in time use, 28
Professional attitude, 40-53
  decision making and, 42-46
  destructive attitudes and, 52-53
  self-assertion and, 46-49
  success and, 40-42
  teamwork and, 49-51
Professional help, 214
Professional image, 54-58
  attractiveness standards in business and,
    56-57
  body language and, 57-58
Professional organizations, 234-35
Promotion, 224-27
  discrimination in, 183
Protocol, *see* Office protocol
Psychological attending, 176-77

Q

"Queen Bees," 232
Questions, asked in interview, 134-36, 138-39

R

Rational decision making, 44-45
Real estate, 83
Re-entry women, special job search
    problems of, 151-55
Reference requests, 128-29
Reflection, 177
Rehabilitation Act (1973), 160
Relaxation techniques, 213

Resumé, 111-25
  chronological format, 114-16, 121-22
  combination of application letter and, 118
  defined, 111-12
  functional format, 115-17, 122-23
  organizing and writing, 114-23
  typing of, 123
  value of, 112-14
Retirement plans, 85-86
Rewards, for self, 25
Risk taking, 45-46
Role conflict, 203
Role models, 3-4
Routine tasks, 28
Rules, company, 144
  breaking, 168
  finding out, 166-67

S

Salary, 144
Scheduling of time, 27-29
Seasonal work pressures, 97
Security, job, lack of, 205
Self-assertion, 46-49
Self-awareness, 5-8
Self-esteem, career planning and, 219-20
"Self-made" women, 232
Sexism, 179-98
  attitudes supporting, 181-82
  comparable worth and, 182-83
  conversational practices and, 188
  defined, 179-80
  direct power and, 185
  discounting capabilities by emphasizing
    appearance, 183
  discrimination in pay and, 182
  discrimination in promotion and, 183
  display of emotions and, 184-85
  language and, 186
  in nonverbal communications, 188-89
  overcoming, 189-92
  in workplace, 180-81
Sexual harassment, 193-97
  dealing with, 196-97
  defined, 193
  groups most likely to suffer, 195-96
  myths about, 193-94
  perpetrators of, 196
Shopping for clothes, 75-76
Silence in interviews, 141
Single parents, special job search problems
    of, 155-58
Skills:
  for career movement, 221-22
  functional, 101, 103-5
  goals and, 15-16
  interpersonal skills, 214
  matched to job market, 95-110
  personal, 101, 102
  putting together, 108-9

251